Conversations with Robert Coles

Literary Conversations Series

Peggy Whitman Prenshaw
General Editor

D1378259

Conversations
with Robert Coles

Edited by
Jay Woodruff and Sarah Carew Woodruff

University Press of Mississippi
Jackson and London

Copyright © 1992 by the University Press of Mississippi
All rights reserved
Manufactured in the United States of America

95 94 93 92   4 3 2 1

The paper in this book meets the guidelines for permanence and durability
of the Committee on Production Guidelines for Book Longevity of the Council
on Library Resources.

Library of Congress Cataloging-in-Publication Data

Coles, Robert.
    Conversations with Robert Coles / edited by Jay Woodruff and Sarah
Carew Woodruff.
        p. cm. — (Literary conversations series)
    Includes index.
    ISBN 0-87805-552-5 (cloth : alk. paper). — ISBN 0-87805-553-3
(paper : alk. paper)
    1. Coles, Robert—Interviews. 2. Authors, American—20th century—
Interviews. 3. Psychiatrists—United States—Interviews.
4. Educators—United States—Interviews. I. Woodruff, Jay.
II. Woodruff, Sarah Carew.   III. Title. IV. Series.
PS3553.O47456Z465   1992
808'.0092—dc20
                                                        91-36584
                                                        CIP

British Library Cataloging-in-Publication data available

Books by Robert Coles

Children of Crisis: A Study of Courage and Fear. Boston: Atlantic-Little, Brown, 1967.

Dead End School. Atlantic-Little, Brown, 1968.

Still Hungry in America. New York: World Publishing—New American Library, 1969.

The Grass Pipe. Boston: Atlantic-Little, Brown, 1969.

The Image Is You. Boston: Houghton Mifflin, 1969.

Wages of Neglect. Chicago: Quandrangle Press, 1969.

Uprooted Children: The Early Lives of Migrant Farmers. Pittsburgh: University of Pittsburgh Press, 1970.

Teachers and the Children of Poverty. Washington, D.C.: The Potomac Institute, 1970.

Drugs and Youth: Medical, Psychiatric and Legal Facts. New York: Liveright Publishing, 1970.

Erik H. Erikson: The Growth of His Work. Boston: Atlantic-Little, Brown, 1970.

The Middle Americans. Boston: Atlantic-Little, Brown, 1970.

The Geography of Faith: Conversations Between Daniel Berrigan, When Underground, and Robert Coles. Boston: Beacon Press, 1971.

Migrants, Sharecroppers and Mountaineers, Volume II of *Children of Crisis.* Boston: Atlantic-Little, Brown, 1972.

The South Goes North, Volume III of *Children of Crisis.* Boston: Atlantic-Little, Brown, 1972.

Saving Face. Boston: Atlantic-Little, Brown, 1972.

Farewell to the South. Boston: Atlantic-Little, Brown, 1972.

Twelve to Sixteen: Early Adolescence. With Jerome Kagan. New York: Norton, 1972.

A Spectacle Unto the World. New York: Viking, 1973.

Riding Free. Boston: Atlantic-Little, Brown, 1973.

The Old Ones of New Mexico. Albuquerque: University of New Mexico Press, 1973.

The Students Themselves. Cambridge: Schenkman Books, 1974.

The Darkness and the Light. New York: Aperture, 1974.

The Buses Roll. New York: Norton, 1974.

Irony in the Mind's Life: Essays on Novels by James Agee, Elizabeth Bowen, and George Eliot. Charlottesville: University of Virginia Press, 1974.

Headsparks. Boston: Atlantic-Little, Brown, 1975.

William Carlos Williams: The Knack of Survival in America. New Brunswick: Rutgers University Press, 1975.

The Mind's Fate. Boston: Atlantic-Little, Brown, 1975.

Eskimos, Chicanos, Indians, Volume IV of *Children of Crisis.* Boston: Atlantic-Little, Brown, 1978.

Privileged Ones: The Well-Off and the Rich in America, Volume V of *Children of Crisis.* Boston: Atlantic-Little, Brown, 1978.

A Festering Sweetness. Pittsburgh: University of Pittsburgh Press, 1978.

Women of Crisis: Lives of Struggle and Hope. New York: Delacorte/Seymour Lawrence. With Jane Hallowell Coles. 1978.

The Last and First Eskimos. New York: New York Graphic Society, 1978.

Walker Percy: An American Search. Boston: Atlantic-Little, Brown, 1978.

Flannery O'Connor's South. Baton Rouge: Louisiana State University Press, 1980.

Women of Crisis, Volume II: Lives of Work and Dreams. With Jane Hallowell Coles. New York: Delacorte, 1980.

I Will Always Stay Me: Writings of Migrant Children. Co-edited with Sherry Kafka. Austin: Texas Monthly Press, 1982.

Dorothea Lange: Photographs of Lifetime. New York: Aperture, 1982.

The Doctor Stories of William Carlos Williams, ed. New York: New Directions, 1984.

Agee. With Ross Spears. New York: Holt-Rinehart, 1985.

Sex and the American Teenager. New York: Harper & Row, 1985.

The Moral Life of Children. Boston: Atlantic Monthly Press, 1986.

The Political Life of Children. Boston: Atlantic Monthly Press, 1986.

In the Street, with Helen Levitt. Durham: Duke University Press, 1987.

Dorothy Day: A Radical Devotion. Reading: Addison-Wesley Press, 1987.

Simone Weil: A Modern Pilgrimage. Reading: Addison-Wesley Press, 1987.

Times of Surrender: Selected Essays. Iowa City: University of Iowa Press, 1988.

Harvard Diary. New York: Crossroads/Continuum, 1988.

That Red Wheelbarrow: Selected Literary Essays. Iowa City: University of Iowa Press, 1988.

The Call of Stories: Teaching and the Moral Imagination. Boston: Houghton Mifflin, 1989.

Rumors of Separate Worlds. Iowa City: University of Iowa Press, 1989.

The Child In Our Times: Studies in the Development of Resiliency. Co-edited with Timothy Dugan. New York: Brunner-Mazel, 1989.

The Spiritual Life of Children. Boston: Houghton Mifflin, 1990.

Anna Freud: The Dream of Psychoanalysis. Reading: Addison-Wesley, 1992.

Breaking the Cycle: Survivors of Child Abuse and Neglect. With Pamela Fong. New York: Norton, 1992.

Contents

Introduction

In January 1954, during his final year of medical school, Robert
Coles published his first article, "A Case of Failure of Generalization
of Imitation Across Drives and Across Situations," in the *Journal of
Abnormal and Social Psychology.* Now nearly forty years later, one
phrase in that cumbersome title seems prescient of the more than
one thousand articles and fifty books that have followed: "failure of
generalization." There is, of course, an obvious irony in reducing
Robert Coles's tremendously varied work to this particular phrase.
Still, the idea expressed by "failure of generalization" is germane to
his work and pervades the interviews collected here.

Again and again in the pages that follow, Coles cautions against the
hazards of generalization—a reductionism that may simply belabor
the obvious, adding no new understanding; or, in the case of his own
field of psychiatry, a reductionism that deteriorates into merely a
sophisticated form of name-calling. He continually challenges the
general assumptions underlying technical and professional jargon.
"When the heart dies," he wrote more than three decades ago in his
first essay to appear in a major magazine ("A Young Psychiatrist
Looks at His Profession," *The Atlantic Monthly,* July, 1961), "we slip
into wordy and doctrinaire caricatures of life. Our journals, our habits
of talk become cluttered with jargon or the trivial. There are negative
cathects, libido quanta, 'presymbiotic, normalautistic phases of
mother-infant unity,' and 'a hierarchically stratified, firmly cathected
organization of self-representations.' Such dross is excused as a short
cut to understanding a complicated message by those versed in the
trade; its practitioners call on the authority of symbolic communication in the sciences. But the real test is whether we best understand
by this strange proliferation of language the worries, fears, or loves in
individual people."

Coles warns us that in this century of unprecedented technological
advance, we have grown too enamored of the head and too dismis-
sive of the heart. The ever-expanding explosion of new gadgetry may

require innovative language for its explanation, but have the human character and soul undergone any truly fundamental transformation? Aren't each of us, at heart, concerned with the same basic questions that nagged our ancient ancestors, those questions included in one of Coles's favorite paintings, Gauguin's famous Tahiti masterpiece: "Where Do We Come from? What Are We? Where Are We Going?"

If Robert Coles were simply another uncertified social observer, his assaults against the moot objectivity and authority of scientific language might be more easily dismissed or ignored. Long before his writing began to appear, however, in *The Atlantic* and *The New Republic, The New Yorker* and *Daedalus, The New England Journal of Medicine* and *The New York Review of Books,* he had acquired what may be, in our psychology-obsessed, secular culture, the most daunting and coveted of all intellectual credentials—the M.D., with a specialty in psychiatry. Coles has been hailed (by *Time, U.S. News & World Report, The Atlantic,* the American Psychiatric Association) as one of the world's pre-eminent psychiatrists. Still, in this age afflicted by what Christopher Lasch has called "the culture of narcissism," a culture that at times seems dedicated chiefly to calibrating every new psychiatric assertion, Coles has refused to come forth with abstruse, hyphenated formulations, reminding us instead to stay tuned to what Faulkner called the "old verities and truths of the heart."

Although Coles has frequently challenged psychiatry, questioning the broad authority it has assumed in contemporary Western culture, he also defends this specialty and reminds us of the tremendous debt we owe to psychoanalytic pioneers—especially, in Coles's opinion, to Sigmund Freud, Erik Erikson and Anna Freud. Sigmund Freud once said, "The poets and philosophers before me discovered the unconscious; what I discovered was the scientific method by which the unconscious can be studied." Always respectful of the founder of psychoanalysis (though decidedly *not* always respectful of many of Freud's followers), Coles has nevertheless attempted to point us back to those poets and philosophers, the story-tellers and novelists, the painters and musicians. As he told Al Sanoff for a 1990 *U.S. News & World Report* profile: "My work has brought me back to human particularily, brought me back to my years as a student reading Conrad and Tolstoy—a time in my life when I had been told by English teachers, 'Beware of generalizations about human beings.'"

Since Coles has always challenged the reader's assumptions, perhaps it is appropriate that time and time again interviewers seem to have been taken aback by the appearance and manner of the man they encounter when they meet him. His reputation for accomplishment, for an almost aggressive prolificacy, surely precedes him—the dozens of books, the Pulitzer Prize, the MacArthur Fellowship,—and one would think that the resulting publicity (a *Time* cover story, profiles in *People* and on TV's *Primetime Live*) would have prepared interviewers for the casual and down-to-earth manner of Robert Coles. Yet, judging from their descriptions, one senses that many interviewers still have anticipated from Coles a somewhat tweedy aloofness.

Quite the contrary, the man who greets them is both warm and shy, quick to laugh and modest, self-deprecating and disarmingly unimposing. His attire is almost always casual—a cotton, button-down shirt and comfortable chinos, a well-worn crewneck sweater and sensible shoes for the long walks and bike rides he enjoys. One suspects the last time he bought a tie, a Democrat occupied the White House. "With his unruly black hair, bushy eyebrows and ratty green sweater," Phil McCombs writes in a 1986 profile for *The Washington Post,* "he resembles photos of his hero, James Agee." Although nearly six feet tall, Coles walks with a slope-shouldered shuffle that combines with his thinness to make him appear smaller. His embarrassment at being the center of attention has been known to make him ring his hands and tug at his thick, dark hair. "To see Robert Coles in public," Paul Wilkes writes in his 1978 *New York Times Magazine* profile, "is to realize why the people he studies find him so easy to talk with. If anything, they must take pity on him. There is a childlike innocence, a vague sort of confusion that belies the intelligence within."

Once the interview begins, however, and Coles begins to speak, any signs of awkwardness or discomfort vanish. Reading these interviews, one can sometimes sense that interviewers are as surprised by the eloquence and forcefulness of Coles's responses as they seem to have been by his modest appearance. In one conversation, a 1989 interview published in *The Door,* the initial (and one fears, at first, hopelessly irrepressible) glibness of the interviewers is simply no match for Coles's forthrightness. It should hardly come as any great surprise that Coles is a master of the interview: he has been interviewed hundreds of times and is also, after all, a psychiatrist, professionally trained in the art of conversation, who has gained an international reputation for his ability to establish rapport with a wide variety of strangers, gaining their confidence, talking with them.

A collection of interviews such as this is bound to contain repetitions, but in the case of Robert Coles the repetitions may seem amplified. His interviewers often seize on apparent contradictions—the physician without a conventional practice who teaches college literature, the psychiatrist who rejects much of the language of his field—and seem at great pains to piece together Coles's precise intellectual evolution. Here is a man, the interviewers often seem to be thinking, who has absorbed what may be the finest of educations—the Boston Latin School, Harvard, the Columbia College of Physicians and Surgeons; the often terrible lessons of the wards; the hollows of Appalachia; the migrant camps of Florida; the favelas of Brazil; the shantytowns of South Africa; one who reads classics in Latin; Simone Weil in French; is equally at home in the pages of Sören Kierkegaard and Raymond Carver—and yet who rejects what many perceive to be the most sophisticated language of his day.

To explain the development of his suspicions about abstractions and generalizations, Coles tells stories, recounting how he came to know the various people who have influenced him. He often begins by recalling his parents. "I can still remember my father's words as he tried to tell me, with patient conviction, that novels contain 'reservoirs of wisdom,' out of which he and our mother were drinking," Coles recalls in the introduction to his book *The Call of Stories.* "A visual image suddenly crossed my mind—books floating like flotsam and jetsam on Houghton's Pond, near Milton, Massachusetts, where we lived."

He frequently tells the story of how, at the urging of his undergraduate tutor, Perry Miller, he came to know William Carlos Williams and of that poet/physician's influence on him—first to pursue medicine, then to stick with it. As Coles makes clear, he was not the most enthusiastic of medical students. He found the curriculum and rote learning of the first two years so dreary that he fled to audit classes offered by Reinhold Niebuhr at Union Theological Seminary and to volunteer in the Bowery, at the Catholic Worker soup kitchen, where he met Dorothy Day. His enthusiasm for medicine was rekindled when he began seeing patients in the third and fourth years. "Each new patient became someone for me to talk with and talk with and talk with," he recalls in his essay "The End of the Affair," [*Katallagete,* Vol. 4, No. 2–3, Fall-Winter, 1972, pp. 46–58], "to the point that my laboratory work, blood tests and such which we had to do on all patients, was slow and I failed to 'work up' my 'cases' quickly enough. 'The point is to make a diagnosis as quickly as possible and know how to get sick people better,' I was told by my preceptor, as he was called. Then he added his punch-line: 'You're not here to do psychiatry.'"

Coles recalls his years of uncertainty after medical school, when he was not at all sure of the direction of his career and found himself in the Deep South, an Air Force captain stationed in Biloxi, Mississippi, commuting daily to New Orleans for the psychoanalysis he needed as part of his training, but also, perhaps, as a means of figuring out what to do with himself. It was on one of these trips to New Orleans that Coles first encountered the scene that would set the direction of his future work. Caught in a traffic jam near an elementary school, he observed a young black girl surrounded by dozens of armed federal marshals who were ushering her through a furious mob. He could hear the epithets and death threats the white adults were screaming at the calm girl, who, Coles would soon learn, was named Ruby Bridges.

Coles had, by this time, already observed children in a variety of crises: girls imprisoned for delinquency as well as children imprisoned in iron lungs after Boston's last polio epidemic before the introduction of the Salk vaccine. He was, it now seems in retrospect, ideally suited and prepared for the opportunity Ruby Bridges presented— an opportunity to combine all of his various interests and preoccupations: the social and the psychiatric, the religious and the spiritual, the literary and the political. He sensed immediately the enormous social and historical magnitude of the little girl's particular crisis. "When I saw that," Coles recalled nearly thirty years later in an interview with Alice Steinbach ["Studying Children in Stress," *The Baltimore Sun,* F1&5, November 12, 1989], "that little girl surrounded by a mob of men dealing with a mob of people—it was a real conversion. Something very, very important happened to my head."

One can hardly exaggerate the significance of Coles's friendship with Ruby Bridges. What began as a modest effort to meet and learn from her would eventually develop into *Children of Crisis,* the massive, five-volume study published between 1967 and 1978, and later extended into *The Inner Lives of Children,* the three-volume series published between 1986 and 1990 that completes Coles's study of children. In Ruby, Coles had met a child who challenged many of the assumptions he had acquired from child psychiatry. Here was an apparently normal child in a terribly abnormal situation, coping with the daily stress in a way not easily explainable by conventional psychiatric language. Ruby prayed each day for her tormentors.

"How are we to make sense of such moral behavior in psychodynamic terms?" Coles asks in *The Moral Life of Children.* "I think it fair to say that a child such as Ruby was in 1961 (aged six, black, southern, of extremely poor background) would not be a likely candidate for the usual kind of moral accolades."

As a psychiatrist and writer, Coles has always emphasized the uniqueness and particularity of the individual. "What he is saying," David Riesman pointed out to *Time* in 1972 [February 14, p. 36], "is 'People are more complicated, more varied, more interesting, have more resiliency and more survivability than you might think. I listen to them! You listen to them!'" Or, as Coles himself tells Steven Nickman, "An individual is more than the sum of 'defense mechanisms' and 'drives.'"

This emphasis appeals to that part of the American sensibility still connected to the ideals of individual rights and the romance of rugged individualism. Coles's attempt to document individual lives also places his work squarely within the broader range of a Western literary tradition that at its best has always emphasized the particular experiences of individual characters.

Coles is modest about where he fits into that tradition. He confides to Dulcy Brainard that he considers himself "a novelist manqué." Although he does admit to Steven Nickman that "I would call myself a social essayist, I suppose," Coles does not easily refer to himself as a writer—despite having written more than fifty books, including two collections of poetry, half a dozen novels for older children, biographies, collections of essays. The eight volumes that comprise Coles's hugely ambitious documentary studies of children prompted

Neil Postman to comment, "[Coles] is to the stories that children
have to tell what Homer was to the tale of the Trojan War."

"I make a distinction between many people who are called writers
and myself in the sense that I feel that my writing is based on the
work I do as a physician," Coles tells Jay Woodruff. "Maybe I'm
quibbling about language here. Maybe it's just a shyness or feeling of
inadequacy manifesting itself in this kind of quibbling, but I regard
myself as an observer of other people, as a doctor, as a field worker,
whatever, who happens to write a lot."

Robert Coles, these interviews remind us, is a psychiatrist with a
novelist's sensibility. He has combined his medical and literary
training to create a unique body of work that attests to the resiliency
of the individual, and he reminds us again and again that the infinite
number of variables that ultimately shape each particular life—the
luck and chance, the circumstance and fate—are at some point
irreducible and remain, to large extent, a great mystery. More than
once in the pages that follow, Coles paraphrases a quote from one of
his favorite writers, Flannery O'Connor. In her essay "The Teaching
of Literature" she wrote: "It is the business of fiction to embody
mystery through manners, and mystery is a great embarrassment to
the modern mind."

We chose the interviews collected here from approximately one
hundred we were able to locate. We have attempted to include the
best interviews we could find and also to create a collection that
might approximate the full range of Coles's varied interests and
accomplishments. Although Coles has been interviewed fairly regularly since the late 1960s, very few interviews exist between 1981
and 1985. During this time, he was shifting direction, having completed his exhaustive *Children of Crisis* series. He was travelling all
over the world, often with one of his three sons, to Belfast,
Jerusalem, Johannesburg—to conduct the reseach that enabled him
to write *The Moral Life of Children, The Political Life of Children* and
The Spiritual Life of Children.

Any collection imposes certain constraints on its editors, and we
regret that we could not include every interview we would have liked
to. Two interviews, which already appear in books, are particularly
instructive: *The Geography of Faith: Conversations Between Daniel*

Berrigan, When Underground, and Robert Coles (Boston: Beacon
Press, 1971), and the interview Robert and Jane Coles conducted
with one another, appearing as "The Way We Work," the final
appendix to one of the books they coauthored, *Women of Crisis II:
Lives of Work and Dreams, second edition* (Boston: Addison-Wesley,
1990). A filmed interview conducted by Bruce Baird-Middleton is
available on video-cassette from Harvard University Press.

Consistent with other volumes in the Literary Conversations series,
these inteviews are reprinted uncut and unedited. Aside from
typographical errors and factual mistakes, which have been silently
corrected, the interviews appear in their original forms. Two of the
interviews have not been previously published. The interview by
Studs Terkel was transcribed and edited from an audio tape of Mr.
Terkel's Chicago radio program. Jay Woodruff's interview was
transcribed and edited from audio tapes.

We would like to thank the writers and publishers who granted
permission to reprint their interviews. Tom Kelley and Alex Lightfoot
offered numerous suggestions and provided helpful perspective. Bill
Stull, of the University of Hartford and also an editor of another
volume in this series, encouraged us throughout the project. Carl
Orgren of the University of Iowa helped us track down several
deceased publications. Seetha Srinivasan, Susan Blumenthal, Ginger
Tucker and Phoebe Woolbright, all of the University Press of
Mississippi, were helpful and encouraging. And finally, we'd like to
thank Robert Coles himself. His work has become an important part
of our lives. This book is for our son, Joey, and other children we
hope for.

JW
SCW
August 1991

Chronology

1929   Martin Robert Coles born on 12 October, in Boston, Massachusetts, to Philip Coles, an immigrant from Leeds, England, and Sandra Young Coles, originally of Sioux City, Iowa.

1931   Coles's only sibling, a brother, William Allan, is born 15 October.

1940   Coles enters Boston Latin School, where he plays tennis, runs track and edits the school literary magazine.

1946   After graduating from Boston Latin, Coles enters Harvard, where he majors in English and helps edit the undergraduate literary magazine, *The Advocate*.

1948   In the spring of his sophomore year, Coles enrolls in "Classics of the Christian Tradition," offered by Professor Perry Miller, who soon becomes Coles's academic mentor and advisor.

1949   Coles writes his junior essay on William Carlos Williams' *Paterson,* and Miller urges him to send the final version to the poet-physician. Coles sends the thesis to Williams, who promptly replies, sending a note scribbled on a prescription form, telling Coles that if he ever happens to be in Rutherford, New Jersey, to please stop by. Within a week, Coles "happens to be in Rutherford" and goes to visit Williams. Williams takes Coles along on his rounds and urges him to pursue a career in medicine. Coles returns to Harvard and begins taking premed courses.

1950   After graduating magna cum laude and earning Phi Beta

Kappa honors at Harvard, Coles enrolls in medical school at Columbia University's College of Physicians and Surgeons.

1951   Frustrated with the hard sciences, Coles contemplates dropping out, but Williams urges him to stick with it.

1952   Coles audits Reinhold Niebuhr's seminars at Union Theological Seminary and also begins volunteer work at the Catholic Worker, where he meets and gets to know Dorothy Day. Lives for several months with a Catholic Worker community on the Lower East Side of Manhattan.

1954   Taking an M.D. from P&S, Coles serves an internship at the University of Chicago clinics, then moves on to psychiatric residencies at Massachusetts General Hospital and McLean Hospital in Belmont, Massachusetts.

1955   Encountering children stricken with polio, in the last major epidemic before the introduction of the Salk vaccine, Coles begins to take note of the profound existential questions posed by his young patients, many of whom are hopelessly ill. Coles also begins to employ crayons and paper as a means of establishing rapport with his young patients and to learn from them.

1957–58 Coles serves a child psychiatric residency at Judge Baker Guidance Center-Children's Hospital, Boston, and supervises the girls' section of the children's unit at Metropolitan State Hospital and serves on the staff of the alcoholism clinic at Massachusetts General Hospital. Teaching fellow at Harvard Medical School; audits Paul Tillich's theology seminar at Harvard.

1958   Knowing that he is to be called under the "doctors draft," Coles joins the Air Force and, assigned the rank of captain, serves as chief of neuropsychiatric services at

Keesler Hospital in Biloxi, Mississippi. Begins psychoanalysis with Dr. Kenneth H. Beach in New Orleans.

1960   Upon his discharge from the Air Force, Coles returns
            briefly to Boston. On 4 July, he marries Jane Hallowell, a
            graduate of Radcliffe College and a high school teacher of
            English and history. Finishes his child psychiatry training
            at the Children's Hospital and returns to the South, living
            in New Orleans.

1961   Publishes "A Young Psychiatrist Looks at His Profession"
            in the July issue of *The Atlantic Monthly*. Commutes from
            New Orleans to Atlanta, talking with black children who
            initiated school desegregation, and with their white
            schoolmates. One night, racing to make a flight to
            Atlanta, he and his wife arrive at the gate just as the plane
            is taxiing away. The next morning they learn that this
            plane had crashed into Lake Ponchartrain, killing all
            aboard. He and his wife often attend the Ebeneezer
            Baptist Church, in Atlanta, where they become ac-
            quainted with the Reverend Martin Luther King, Jr.

1962   Coles is actively involved with the Student Nonviolent
            Coordinating Committee.

1963   A second article, "In the South These Children Proph-
            esy," appears in *The Atlantic*. Other articles appear in
            The New Republic, Saturday Review, the *American
            Journal of Psychiatry* and *The Times* of London.
            "Serpents and Doves: Non-Violent youth in the South"
            appears as a chapter in *Youth: Change and Challenge,*
            edited by Erik H. Erikson. Takes part in the Selma march.
            Appointed Research Psychiatrist, Harvard University
            Health Services.

1964   Participates in training program for the Mississippi Sum-
            mer Project. Spends the summer in various "freedom
            houses" in the Mississippi Delta. Coles narrowly escapes

catastrophe on several occasions: he is in a "freedom
house" in McComb, Mississippi, when it is bombed.
Later, after being released from jail and while driving to
Jackson, Coles and another Summer Project co-worker
are chased and shot at by a group in a pick-up truck. A
first child, Robert Emmet, is born to Robert and Jane
Coles on 21 August.

1965   Returning to Boston, Coles begins serving as a teaching
       fellow in Erik H. Erikson's course at Harvard, "The
       Human Life Cycle."

1966   Appointed Lecturer in General Education at Harvard. By
       now more than a hundred articles have appeared in a
       wide variety of publications, though primarily in *The New
       Republic,* where Coles becomes a contributing editor.
       Begins correspondence with Anna Freud. Would later
       meet with her many times. A second son, Daniel Agee, is
       born on 15 August.

1967   Coles's first book, *Children of Crisis: A Study of Courage
       and Fear* is published to outstanding reviews and numer-
       ous awards. Coles testifies before the Senate subcommit-
       tee on hunger and poverty. Travels to Appalachia and the
       South with Robert Kennedy.

1968   Coles receives the Hofheimer Prize for Research from the
       American Psychiatric Association. His second and third
       books, *Dead End School* and *The Grass Pipe,* novels for
       children, are published.

1969   *Still Hungry in America* and *The Wages of Neglect* are
       published. Begins writing reviews and other pieces for
       The New Yorker.

1970   *Uprooted Childen: The Early Lives of Migrant Farmers*
       and *Erik H. Erikson: the Growth of His Work* are
       published. Coles invites Father Daniel Berrigan to stay

with him and his family in their Concord home while
Berrigan hides out from the FBI. Carries on an intensive,
tape-recorded discussion with the Jesuit priest. Michael
Hallowell is born on 7 July.

1971   Elected to the American Academy of Arts and Sciences.
The Middle Americans and *Geography of Faith: Conversations Between Daniel Berrigan, When Underground,
and Robert Coles* are published.

1972   *Migrants, Sharecroppers, Mountaineers* and *The South
Goes North,* volumes two and three of *Children of Crisis,*
and *Saving Face* and *Farewell to the South* are published.
Receives honorary degrees, the first of dozens, from
Temple, Notre Dame and Bates. Appears on the cover of
Time in February, and in an effort to escape the attendant
publicity, moves with family from Massachusetts to New
Mexico.

1973   Receives numerous awards and honors for volumes two
and three of *Children of Crisis,* including the Pulitzer
Prize. Visiting Professor of Public Policy at Duke University. *Riding Free* and *The Old Ones of New Mexico,* with
photographs by Alex Harris, are published.

1974   Family illness forces the Coleses back to Massachusetts,
where Coles begins teaching a seminar on the documentary work of James Agee and George Orwell to freshmen
at Harvard. *The Buses Roll* and *Irony in the Mind's Life:
Essays on Novels by James Agee, Elizabeth Bowen and
George Eliot* are published.

1975   *Headsparks,* a novel for young people, and *William
Carlos Williams: The Knack of Survival in America* and
The Mind's Fate are published.

1977   Appointed Professor of Psychiatry and Medical Humanities at Harvard Medical School. Begins teaching lecture

course at Harvard College, "The Literature of Social Reflection."

1978   *Eskimos, Chicanos, Indians* and *Privileged Ones: The Well Off and the Rich in America,* volumes four and five of *Children of Crisis,* are published. Appears on the cover of *The New York Times Magazine. A Festering Sweetness,* a collection of poems, and *Women of Crisis: Lives of Struggle and Hope,* with Jane Hallowell Coles, are published. "The Search," a two-part profile of Walker Percy, appears in *The New Yorker* and is subsequently published as *Walker Percy: An American Search. The Last and First Eskimos* is published.

1980   *Flannery O'Connor's South* and *Women of Crisis: Lives of Work and Dreams,* with Jane Hallowell Coles, are published.

1981   Becomes contributing editor to *Literature and Medicine* and to *New Oxford Review;* becomes a member of the first group of MacArthur Prize Fellows.

1982   *Dorothea Lange* is published; becomes a contributing editor to *American Poetry Review.*

1985   *Agee,* with Ross Spears, is published. Becomes member of the board of directors for the Medical Education for South African Blacks. Both of Coles's parents die, within six weeks of one another, after a sixty-year marriage.

1986   *The Moral Life of Children* and *The Political Life of Children* are published.

1987   *In the Streets,* with Helen Levitt, *Simone Weil: A Modern Pilgrimage* and *Dorothy Day: A Radical Devotion* are published.

1988   *Times of Surrender: Selected Essays, That Red Wheelbar-*

row: Selected Literary Essays, and *Harvard Diary* are published. The last receives "Best Spiritual Book of 1988" award from the Catholic Press Association. Coles's 1000th published article, "Bringing Poems to Medical Students: A Memoir," appears in *Poetry.*

1989   *The Call of Stories: Teaching and the Moral Imagination* and *Rumors of Separate Worlds,* a collection of poetry, are published. Receives the Christopher Award, given annually by the Christopher society in New York to the author whose work "affirms the highest values of the human spirit." Visiting Professor of Psychiatry, Dartmouth Medical School. Helps establish the Center for Documentary Studies at Duke University.

1990   *The Spiritual Life of Children,* the eighth and final volume in Coles's series on children, is published.

1991   *The Spiritual Life of Children* becomes Coles's first book ever to reach the *New York Times* bestseller list. Coles awarded the Oskar Pfister Award of the American Psychiatric Association, a second Christopher Award, and an alumni medal from Columbia University's College of Physicians and Surgeons for "distinguished service in medicine."

1992   *Anna Freud: The Dream of Psychoanalysis* is published.

Conversations with Robert Coles

Robert Coles on Activism

Marion E. Bodian/1968

From *The Harvard Crimson* (Cambridge, MA, May 29, 1968, pp. 1–4). Reprinted by permission of *The Harvard Crimson*.

The interview that follows deals obliquely with one of the great sources of frustration for social activists: How can you support and work for people you do not—even if you want to—genuinely know? On what terms can a Harvard intellectual learn to know a sharecropper in Mississippi, or a Roxbury mother on welfare?

More specifically, it is an interview with Robert Coles, Research Psychiatrist for University Health Services, who as a writer and psychiatrist has since 1958 gotten to know the lives of sharecropper families in the South, of mountain families in Appalachia, and of the ghetto families in Roxbury.

Coles has developed loyalties to two communities which are in many ways alienated from each other—academia and the poor. This dual loyalty puts Coles in a somewhat anomalous position. His personal and immediate contact with the poor families he studies leaves him critical of attitudes toward the poor held widely in the liberal-radical community he belongs to.

Coles cites SDS' response to riot-control in Roxbury last March as an example of activist thinking spawned in academic isolation. SDS at the time demanded that police—as enforcers of a repressive status quo—be withdrawn from Roxbury. Coles sharply criticized SDS for taking an ideological stance toward the plight of Negroes "whose houses are being gutted, whose children are being killed."

Coles: I've had reservations about what I said afterwards, not because I disagreed with anything I said, but because I know there are people who will use what I said irrelevantly to try to crush legitimate dissent on the part of students who *want* to be allied with the poor, but who I am afraid are *not* allied with them—not allied

3

with them because they have yet to understand the terrible
ambiguities that poor people face living in America today, whether
they be black or white.

I hasten to add that my camaraderie, my sense of belonging, is
with the aspirations of the students who level those charges. I'm
certainly not opposed to the kind of social analysis they have made.
But I *am* against a kind of short-circuited thinking that says because
we know that the police are trying to enforce a certain kind of status
quo, the solution is to get rid of the police—where?—in Roxbury,
where the police, God knows, are needed all the time by the very
poor people the students and I presumably want to help.

I think that students and I presumably want to help.

I think that students, *and* people like me, are terribly isolated from
the very people we claim we want to help. Students want more
money in the welfare program, they want better housing and more
jobs for these people, but they don't know the people, they don't see
life the way people do in Roxbury—people who, regardless of our
explanations of American society, have to contend with that society
rather than analyze it, who do not have the luxury of long-range
historical and social critiques.

The people in Roxbury—regardless of what the leaders of SDS or I
have to think about it—want to get into the system rather than leave
it. The families I work with want to be able to get better service at the
Boston City Hospital, they want garbage collection more frequently,
they want better heating, they want welfare workers who will help
them out. They are not going to take to the streets in order to storm
the Winter Palace—there is no Winter Palace to storm.

Many of the students in this country are ideological leaders in
search of a proletariat, any kind of proletariat. And they can't find it,
because what they're looking for doesn't exist. They've found the
proletariat in theory, they've found it in their text-books, they've
found it by observing it.

But they haven't found it in the sense of being able to work with
the proletariat, or being in a genuine emphatic and responsive
relationship to the proletariat—if there is such a thing as the
proletariat as they think of it. I have to qualify here, too, because one
of the most frustrating things in American life is that even in the

worse parts of this country, there is just enough to prevent starvation, just enough to provide for malnutrition rather than starvation.

Now whether one approves of this kind of ambiguity in American life or not, it exists. I think some of the people who make an analysis of this society in terms of who owns stock in this or that institution, are not taking into consideration just how complicated and disarming American society is—by disarming I mean anti-ideological in its frustrating complexity.

I don't think the object of criticism ought to be the policeman. The police are caught in the middle, between those who rise up, often without any purpose in mind other than the moment's rage, and on the other side the white intellectuals who often put the blame on the police rather than on more fundamental things that are responsible for the police action—action which is often, in the existential moment, absolutely necessary. I would aim criticism at people of far greater influence, people with a lot more power and social respect and status, a lot more money and—ironically—a lot more willingness to be flexible.

Question: Political leadership, in other words, is capable of working with the poor community?

Coles: I find that people like Kevin White and Bobby Kennedy can reach across and obtain the alliance of both poor Negroes and poor whites. But not that of the intellectual community. Students are ready to jump on Kevin White without comprehending the enormously complicated job this man has got. Boston is a city that voted 47 percent for Louise Day Hicks. White is trying to deal with the needs of a predominantly lower-middle-class community which has been led into the same trap the white southerner has been led into, the trap of bigotry as a means of avoiding social and economic realities.

It's curious to me that I can find support for Bobby Kennedy from the poor in Appalachia, where Harry Cardill called him the greatest man since Franklin D. Roosevelt; I can find support for him in lower-middle class, and particularly so-called back-lash regions, in Boston. But again—we have McCarthy. I don't think this is just an idle, irrelevant distinction. It ties in with the estrangement I spoke of between the white upper-middle-class intellectual liberal, and even

radical, community, and the very people whose lives they want
changed, but changed from the distance of their analysis—rather
than through any real communion, the kind of communion that
people like Agee and Simone Weil have talked about, the communion that goes with living with people and being a part of them.

*Coles's effort to adopt the point of view of the people he studies is
the effort of a man who concedes he is a "romantic" and who
perhaps has a more-than-ordinary admiration for people trying to
cope with poverty. Since he began working in the South ten years
ago, he has shaped his work around that point of view.*

*Since 1964, with a foundation grant and an appointment as a
research psychiatrist at the Health Services, Coles has been working
with the group of parents who first started bussing their children from
Roxbury to white schools—the Boardman Parents Group. He has
since extended the study to include the black and white families in
Roxbury. In the following section he evaluates his own outlook and
work:*

Coles: I am in favor—I want to emphasize this—of a large measure
of the social and economic analysis of America that the student
radicals have made. But I suppose my loyalties as a person and as a
worker are with the immediate lives of the people that I work with,
and in that sense I suppose I am not ideological. I want the police to
protect these families from fires, from sniping, and I want the children
that I know in Roxbury not to be killed by a burning building or by
bullets.

I don't recommend this as a political program, and I think this is
frankly the limitation of my kind of thinking and my kind of work. I'm
neither a political scientist nor a political leader. I'm working with
people who are terribly caught up in a country they love—and they
do love America, this is not romantic talk—a country they both love
and want more from. I want these people to have the kinds of lives
they want to have. I don't want to impose my idea of the Good Life
on them.

Question: Don't you think this view can be paralyzing if you want
to eliminate poverty?

Coles: Well, you're right. In the section I taught in Professor
Erikson's course a couple of years ago this same theme came up

again and again. The students accused me of being anti-ideological
and a romantic, and I suppose they're right. My heroes are not the
New Left heroes, and this is the problem, I guess. My heroes are
Bernanos and Agee and Orwell and Simone Weil and Flannery
O'Connor and Walker Percy—and Reinhold Niebuhr. And I would
add within my own profession Erik Erikson and Anna Freud.

Now none of these people have ever stormed a barricade, none of
them have ever formulated large-scale political programs. If you look
at some of these people politically, you can imagine what emerges.
But I don't care. And I suppose I respect the right of someone to say,
"You are a frivolous Western liberal who for all your involvement is
never fundamentally going to change this society."

Well, here we get into a very complicated issue. We've seen
enough in this century to make us suspicious of people like me, but
also to make us suspicious of people who say, "You cannot look at
particular human beings and their needs when you're out to change
society." This latter viewpoint can be used as a rationalization and
justification for the most mean and cruel and inhuman political acts
imaginable.

I suppose I'm interested in certain kinds of spiritual changes in life,
changes that may not be obtainable by any *program.*

Now, I've been involved in a number of larger social movements—
with the civil rights movement in the South, with the Appalachian
volunteers, with migrant farmers and with groups that have been
trying to effect very fundamental changes.

But I'm very worried about the dangers of a kind of political
activity that ignores the ironies and ambiguities of life, including
political life. And I am worried about the apparently inevitable things
that happen to all institutions, the legal calcifications and rigidities
that occur in even the most militantly free and flexible of groups once
they have obtained power, once they start consolidating themselves
and become self-protective. These are problems that I think
transcend even the New Left: they're human problems.

I think a lot of these doubts are shared by people in the New Left,
shared by a lot of students, but I don't think these people always act
on their doubts, and I'm afraid I want them to act on their doubts as
well as on their political principles. I want them to demonstrate some
of the tension that goes between humility and arrogance, some of the

tension that goes between idealism and pragmatism, some of the
tension that goes between pride and self-doubt and a kind of inner
agony.

I worry about my own privileged position as someone who is here
in this office, and can go back and forth between communities, and
can read [T.S. Eliot's] *Four Quartets* and get something out of them,
but who is not struggling for his next week's salary. I think that the
criticism that is leveled against people like me is a valid one: We are
privileged; if we don't know it, we are living in sin—I use the word
sin.

On the other hand, if I try to destroy myself to be like the people I
work with, if I shed myself of the privileges that I've had all my life—
well, I think that's impossible. If there's anything I've learned about
the people I've worked with, I have found that they are perhaps more
accepting of my life than I am of it. I think we live with guilt, we live
with our Puritan heritage, we live with all of the self-derogation and
self-assault that goes with complicated middle-class Western life.

Let me give you an example of the kind of agonizing I am talking
about, how unnecessary and irrelevant it is. I happen to drive a
sports car. When I first started working in the South ten years ago, I
knew that I couldn't go with that sports car into some of these
communities because I had decided that that would interfere with my
relationship with these people. Well, it took me a long time to feel
free enough to get to know some of these children well enough so
that they could visit us in our home, and now, of course, I have found
that these children *love* my sports car, and that these children don't
begrudge me it, and that these children don't begrudge me a lot of
the thinks I begrudge myself.

*Coles, dissatisfied with children's books that "abusively romanticize"
real experience, wrote a children's book this year—*Dead End
School*—depicting the difficulties faced by two ghetto boys when
they are thrust into a desegregation effort. The boys, Larry and Jim,
are modeled after two boys Coles got to know in Roxbury. The story
gives Jim's view of his own experience in the bussing crisis. Larry
peripherally presents a black militant reaction to that same experience.*

Coles comments on the difficulty of communicating social complexity to children:

Coles: The book was described by one critic as "well-scrubbed." It was meant to be a compliment, but it's a terribly accurate and I think just criticism of the book. Those children emerge as well-scrubbed because I couldn't use some of the swear words I would have liked to.

As it is, the book is not the usual children's book, and I'm afraid it isn't going to be overwhelmingly received by a lot of conventionally-minded guardians of children's literature.

I meant this book to reach middle-class white children. I wasn't really trying to describe Negro children or their view of the world. I wanted to describe through the activities of children how some of these confusing social and political events occur, what gets them going, how ambiguous and tentative and accidental a lot of them are.

The real challenge that I failed to make in writing that book was the challenge of writing it from the point of view of Larry rather than Jim, of conveying Larry's life to middle-class children—Larry being the boy who came from a much more disorganized home, really a black militant. But it's difficult anyway to communicate these lives to other lives that are so different, and so I chose the easier way out, I chose the black boy who is more like white middle-class boys.

Question: Do you think middle-class children are receptive to social themes, or to lives so far outside their experience?

Coles: I know that this book will not be the easiest book for a lot of children to read, but I think it will get things going in their minds, even if they don't really totally comprehend everything that I had in mind when I was writing it—that is at least a beginning.

I've written another children's book—on another complicated subject, marijuana; and this is directed at junior high children. I think after this I'm going to stop for a while, because these are such complicated subjects to write about for young people. They require more sweat from me than anything else I've done.

Question: When I read *Dead End School* I got the feeling that if I were ten years old I might feel preached to.

Coles: What that clearly says—and I think correctly—is that I'm not a really accomplished writer of children's books. I admire writers like Faulkner and Tolstoy, who take important human problems and give them a dimension that transcends preachiness, transcends the political novel, the social novel. I don't see how I can escape the burden of that when I look at my own minor effort in *Dead End School.*

One problem, of course, is that the poor are constantly being preached at, and they become preachers themselves, to one another. I don't think Richard Nixon and his cohorts have any idea how ironically loyal thousands and thousands of poor people are to Max Weber's *Protestant Ethic and the Spirit of Capitalism.*

Coles' main effort to unite a psychiatrist's view and an artist's "whole" view of lives is Children of Crisis. *The book deals with a number of children and families Coles observed while they were involved in desegregation efforts in the South. Coles comments on what he wanted to convey:*

Coles: What I tried to do in *Children of Crisis* was to give some sense of particular lives that were caught up in a social and historical crisis. I wrote not as a psychiatrist nor as a social scientist nor as a "participant-observer," nor as a writer for that matter, but as some of all of these.

I'm writing a second volume which deals with migrant farmers, sharecroppers, and what I call mountaineers, the Appalachian families that I first got to know in western North Carolina, and later in West Virginia and eastern Kentucky.

I try to describe how they live, what they do with time, what they do with themselves. I try to keep in mind as I'm with them and as I write things like daytime, nighttime, physical activities, psychological activities.

I try to pose for myself relatively simple-minded questions, like, what does it mean for this young man here in this hollow to watch television, and in contrast what does it mean for my son to watch the same program? What kind of food does this family like, how would they feel if they were eating what I eat, how would they feel if they lived in my home?

I keep in mind thinks like where do they sleep, what is on their walls, what do they do with their hands, how do they like to dress, what are the changes in clothing they choose to make for themselves in the course of a week? Thinks like that.

Now the model for this, if there is a model, is Agee's *Let Us Now Praise Famous Men*. Agee was a disciplined and canny observer, he was an observer who refused to allow himself to be straight-jacketed by his political and social views. He was an observer who dared face ambiguities that he himself wished were not around to plague him. And I think he would be willing to call himself most of all a human being who remembers what the *Book of Common Prayer* has to say, namely that in all of us there are mixtures of arrogance and humility, and intelligence and near-sightedness if not blindness, and of compassion and cruelty, and that no one is beyond those kinds of terrible limitations—I say no one. I have seen among some of the cruelest segregationists in this country, members of the Klan that I got to know in the South, evidence of compassion and decency.

Psychiatry and Belief

George Abbott White/1972

From *Commonweal* (New York, October 27, 1972, pp. 78–82).
Reprinted by permission of the Commonweal Foundation.

What began earlier this year as a discussion about the
"political" content of Robert Coles' latest two books—
Migrants, Sharecroppers, Mountaineers, and *The South
Goes North, Volumes II and III* of *Children of Crisis* (Atlantic-Little, Brown)—rapidly grew into a series of conversations that ranged, geographically, from Coles' white
frame home in pastoral Concord to his crowded office in
the basement Annex of the Harvard University Health
Services, where he is a research psychiatrist. While the
"Middle Americans," Daniel Berrigan, the Movement, the
war in Vietnam, moved in and out of focus, questions of
faith and belief seemed not only at the center of both
minds, but the very thread that tied all the other people
and concerns together.

White: Last October writing of William James' *Varieties of Religious
Experience* in *The New Republic,* you noted James' personal and
professional indecision about faith and yet his willingness to portray
with sympathy, even generosity, the entire range of "religious"
experience. You also recalled your own "snide, unbelieving remarks
. . . clever psychological interpretations . . . quick dismissals of this or
that . . ." in the book's margins. How is it that you came to read that
book, at Harvard, in the late Forties, with Perry Miller?

    Coles: It was a course called "Classics of the Christian Tradition"
and I was only 18 years old and Miller opened it to 50 people and
interviewed every single one of them before he let them in. "Will you
be able to stand this?" he asked me. "Most of your colleagues will be
veterans, will have fought four or five years. I'm afraid you're going
to be all alone."

    White: The Veterans had asked him to do the course and

apparently they evoked something in him. But I thought Miller was
without religious belief?

Coles: That may well be true . . . Although you know a person
like that can be the instrument of another's belief. He helped a lot of
confused veterans by introducing Pascal and Kierkegaard very
thoughtfully, and then, of course, the Puritan divines. He made them
real, their ethical struggles and religious doubts alive. I was struggling
and shy and he was generous and kind, to all of us. He treated us like
kings and took our own predicaments seriously.

White: Those "predicaments" reoccur in *The Geography of Faith*
(1971) in an ironic way. A friend, after reading the first few sections of
the book, saw the opposition between you and Dan as one of
pastoral and prophetic modes of being: on the one hand the minister
or priest who needs to stay close to his flock and feels that if he goes
too far ahead he won't have any touch at all, and on the other the
minister or priest who feels that he must be prophetic to draw them
out of where they are to a new reality. When I finished the book I had
an image of you as an older now-gently, now-sternly cautioning
priest, and Dan as some kind of idealistic young psychiatrist.

Coles: I think that's an interesting way of putting that. Maybe
there's a lot to that. Of course, I'm not a priest. Nor—and this should
be emphasized—nor has my role been or have I ever conceived
myself as one who could ultimately supply for them, offer them, the
kinds of coherence and consolation a priest offers them. I'm not
being coy or modest about this. I know the limits of a social observer
like me and I'm not an organizer either. But I think I have become a
friend of the people I've worked with, and so far as you mention the
pastoral obligation to stay close to people, I knew that unless I had at
least discussed involvement with Dan and Phil—if they would see my
name in the paper or learn that I was actively involved—I felt that
this would have jeopardized what was anyway a difficult relationship.
(It took me seven years to get into a situation which I think now is
reasonably one of trust and confidence on both sides.)

And as far as the prophetic, remember that psychoanalysis was
one more 20th century messianic sect. I say this, by the way, not to
criticize the legitimate value and worth of psychiatric thinking. It's
what happens when thinking and ideas become in the minds of one
particular group of people more than that, become a *redemptive*

experience for them and then a *perspective* experience which they
demand of others. They demand that others go through it and they
isolate those others if they haven't gone through it and tell them that
until they go through it they're not the saved ones.

White: Of course in our secular age—a world "come of age," in
Bonhoeffer's phrase—religious salvation is no longer a "realistic"
option. It's always thrown into the face of the faithful that Freud
dispensed with "illusion" . . .

Coles: Oh, that's nonsense; really. Psychoanalysts have illusions
just like others. One of Freud's illusions was that somehow more and
more people would become psychoanalyzed and that way the world
would become a better place. Well, maybe so—but frankly I doubt it.
What I'm pointing out is that there was a utopian thread in his
thinking. I don't criticize it. But I think Freud did *not* understand the
nature of religious faith. He didn't feel it, yet he presumed to write
about it in others with authority. That was a mistake—he became too
theoretical; his genius, the most valuable part of his thinking, was that
which emerged from his contact with patients. Those were the years
of discovery. Towards the end of his life he became too preoccupied
with social theory in such a way that rather than going out and talking
with a lot of people whose religious faith was of some value to them,
that he might have learned about, he came up with conclusions very
much like Marx's: religion in some way an opiate. There he was
detached from concrete experience with people of faith.

White: That is certainly not the case with your work.

Coles: Yes, I guess religious concerns keep on coming up in my
writing, as they have in my life. When I was in college and medical
school I would slip off to churches, usually Catholic churches,
because one could be left alone there, left to be with oneself, left to
pray or sit and day-dream. The churches I went to as a boy, with my
mother, were suburban churches, usually Episcopalian. Most of the
people knew one another, or felt constrained to meet and talk
afterwards. I know, it all had something to do with being part of a
"community." And more and more Catholic churches resemble the
Protestant churches I know so well—people link arms, turn around
and address one another, feel responsive to each other. I have no
right to criticize that development. Who am I, not a Catholic, to yearn
for the church's past, a good deal of it, politically, rather unfortunate,

though no less so than much of the history of our Protestant sects? Still, there should be room for"privacy" as well as "community" in a church, and why shouldn't our eyes be directed toward the altar, toward God, or be directed inward, in contemplation of God (within the mind's limited capacity to do so) rather than toward one's neighbors.

For just one hour on Sunday I should think we might have allowance to forget one another, forget the Rotary and the Lion's Club and the President and the Model Cities Act and yes, our need for "community," even our need for "community mental health." I'm not so sure, while I'm being so cranky, that I shouldn't add our theologians to that list; sometimes they, too, can keep us from Christ, even as they push and pull the church, and maybe upon occasion become (for priests and bishops as well as "ordinary" believers) confused with the Lord Himself. In that sense secular prophets aren't the only danger to the "man of faith"; the holy church itself is subject to its own temptations, and not all of them come from pagans or messianic secular cults.

White: What you write indicates something deeper than a vague *ethical* concern. There is a sense of formality, a structure . . .

Coles: Well, that's right, I have studied theology—not in any full-time way, but at different points in my life, and sometimes, I might add, with some desperation. In medical school, during the '50's, I audited a course Reinhold Niebuhr gave, the last one before a stroke incapacitated him. I found it helpful to leave the Columbia-Presbyterian Medical Center and sit and listen to Niebuhr and his students at Union Theological Seminary. I didn't always understand what they were saying, but they would mention books, and I would go and hunt them down. It was Dr. Niebuhr who introduced me to Simone Weil, and that was a large gift to receive. In my last year of medical school I belonged to a Bible study group; there were five of us medical students, and we read and discussed sections from the New Testament. Two of those five are now medical missionaries. I was the agnostic or "devil's disciple," and I now realize how much I needed them, and perhaps how much they needed me, as we argued back and forth. I recall that the five of us, sitting there way up on top of Bard Hall, the student dormitory, holding on to our Bibles, surrounded by modern bustling Gotham, struck many of our classmates as an odd bunch indeed—and since we weren't a "group" then and we weren't out to "sensitize" each other, it wasn't all that bad in the Eisenhower era.

We just read and tried to make sense of what we read. After arguing skeptically for a couple of hours, I would retreat to my room and go over a passage from St. Paul, or especially, the Revelation of St. John the Divine, and find myself strangely moved, for which I had to apologize to myself. I'm sorry if this sounds childish or foolish. All I know is that during those years I was begining to get interested in psychiatry, was in analysis, and so I had a very simple-minded if fashionable view of what religion was all about. Obsessions, illusions, rationalizations, neurotic guilt, masochistic "surrender"—those are the words that still summon so much of our interest, and correctly so, because there is a lot that goes on in the mind that such words (and the train of ideas that they are meant to summarize) manage to explain. Nevertheless, the world is larger than a psychiatrist's consulting room, something both he and his patients are all too likely to forget, and I suppose that the psychiatrist is especially obligated to remember that, because, after all, the patient has a right to be obsessed with himself, to be obsessed with his obsessions, so to speak—he comes to the doctor and declares himself a patient, hence to some degree more on the wrong track than he or she feels to be "right," or maybe than others think "appropriate." (Oh, these words, and all that they imply, and how treacherous they can be, not just abstractly, but to so many particular men and women—and as a child psychiatrist I would have to add children, too, because so often I have heard children, like the rest of us, wonder who is to be believed, who is "right" and who is "wrong," which standards are correct, and why.)

Anyway, in analysis the first time around, I heard my religious "concerns" (as you call them) called other things, given a series of psychological names. And I could only agree, or maybe "give in" is the expression. Later, in New Orleans, another psychoanalyst had a different way of looking at those "urges" I had—to go into St. Louis Cathedral there in Jackson Square and sit for a while. I think the doctor I was seeing—God bless him—used to try it himself, without finding it necessary to confess his sin to his colleagues, and submit himself to further analysis!

White: In your conversations with Dan one more than sensed his appreciation or admiration for Bonhoeffer. That stands in marked contrast with the "realistic" Augustinian-Christian view of dependence and limitation, even sin, one finds in Niebuhr and Tillich.

Coles: I think Dan is more hopeful about the "nature" of man than Niebuhr and Tillich were. I studied with Tillich when I was a resident in psychiatry at the Massachusetts General Hospital, and Tillich had a seminar in "systematic theology." I went to see him and asked him if I could join up; I asked him if he'd mind if I sat and listened. He said no, but he'd mind if I didn't speak up. That was quite a year, learning to be "systematic" about some of my religious concerns from a man who, I believe, used the word "systematic" a little wryly. I loved his mixture of religious and political sensibility. He could combine hopefulness and skepticism almost uncannily. In that sense he was like Simone Weil—and Georges Bernanos.

White: That is both a powerful and subtle linkage. The single item that connects the two for me is the letter she wrote to him during the Spanish Civil War, she condemning the atrocities of the Left while in solidarity with his condemnation of those of the Right. What does Bernanos call up for you?

Coles: I can't put into words what Bernanos means to me. I keep *The Diary of a Country Priest* near me, and go back to it often. Also, *Joy* and *Mouchette*. His political essays are sometimes way off kilter, but every once in a while right on the mark, rather like Orwell's. Bernanos was a passionate pilgrim; though utterly faithful to the church, he was plagued by doubts and even more, plagued by moments, many of them, in which he lost all charity and gave in to despair, and its not uncommon mask, or equivalent, scorn or sarcasm. I think he knew the Devil rather intimately. It's a pity that he is not better known in this country. I say this not to detract from the stature of Camus, but I really do think that Bernanos was a greater writer, and it does mean something, that in this country there is such a small audience for one like him and such a large and responsive audience for Camus or Sartre—and I would also contrast the attention Sartre gets with, say the response Emmanuel Mounier or Gabriel Marcel get from America's intellectuals.

White: You've stressed how your "method" differs from, say Oscar Lewis'. I know there must be miles of tape and mountains of notes, yet each of the three volumes of *Children of Crisis* has an evocative quality one associates with a well-wrought novel; the concreteness, the vivid particularity, the profound unity. Which novelists do you admire?

Coles: Among living writers, Walker Percy is my favorite. I find myself going to his three novels over and over again; *The Last Gentleman,* especially, moved me—and very much unsettled me. I'd read five or ten pages, and have to stop. I've read Dr. Percy's philosophical articles, too; he comes across as a remarkable person, a wise man, a kind of decent man as well as a gifted man—and such qualities, naturally, don't always go together. For years, in the course of my work in New Orleans, I've wanted to try to go see him, but so far I've not had the courage to make the attempt. Another writer from the South I keep reading is Flannery O'Connor. We lived not far from her in Georgia, and I heard her speak once. The sentences were not unlike some she writes, and her painfully shy manner could not for long conceal the force and passion in her, and the spiritual life-and-death struggles she knew she was waging, not to mention the battle with a disease whose name (I hope I'm not being presumptuous) I think she might have smiled at—lupus erythematosus.

White: Others?

Coles: Two, and that's it: James Agee and George Orwell. Some of my students tell me they were fussy and hopelessly "unrealistic," so far as politics go, but there has to be room in this world for people who say "yes—but." Maybe I am *too* suspicious of ideologies, all of them; but I distrust those who turn any century's secular preoccupations, however valuable, into a faith—and I fear that not a few psychiatrists and political organizers and physicists are tempted to do so (in the name of the exploration of the unconscious, the improvement of the lot of the poor, or the struggle for mastery over "matter").

Orwell means so much *now* because he struggled so hard with these ambiguities: He struggled hard to know working class people as well as poor people; he struggled with the complexities of social life as it affects individuals and institutions and parties and movements; and he was a very *concrete* person. He may have been a poor novelist but he had a sense of the real.

White: The achievement of the last two volumes is massive; they struck me as important and as rich and as moving as anything I'd read in the last two or three years. The praise seemed substantial though there was something missing.

Coles: I have been struck at the way those last chapters in each book ("Rural Religion" and "The Lord in Our Cities") have been so thoroughly ignored, even by critics who have had only kind words to say about the books. I deliberately chose to end the books with those chapters, and in a way struggled harder with them than any others—even as the people I have worked with have to fight hard to make sense of this world, and find some "meaning" in it. I have been urged to come up with more "conclusions," more "formulations" about what it is like for poor people, how they think, What goes on in their heads. We hunger after tidy abstractions—and so often they are used to *do in* people, thoroughly do them in. Meanwhile, the sharecroppers or hill people of West Virginia I have spent time with, or the people in our Northern ghettos I have visited, have their own ideas about life and its purposes—yet some of us who say we are "for" them, or working on their "behalf," or trying to "organize" them, are not always that anxious to listen to them and hear what they happen to believe in and want out of life—apart from more money and power.

When a ghetto mother says *that,* says she wants to take up arms against the injustices of this society, political activists and intellectuals are likely to pay attention and (hopefully) be responsive; but when that same mother talks of her faith in God someone like me becomes embarrassed, dismisses her passionate convictions as superstitions or evidence of ignorance or "brainwashing" or "passivity." I do not deny that a certain kind of religious faith can be *palliative,* in the various senses of the word. But if we are condescending to the poor with respect to their "culture," their qualities as human beings and citizens (and in that regard many of us concerned with this nation's social problems are always examining and re-examining ourselves, aware that we may have blindspots) we can also be condescending so far as the religious faith of a Mississippi tenant farmer or Appalachian mountaineer or Harlem welfare mother goes. Frankly, most of us, people like me, tend to understand "unconscious dynamics" or political antagonisms or economic disparities, and well we should; yet, when we look at religious and philosophical viewpoints that are

not ours, we tend to put them down in one way or another. Among
many of the families I have worked with, religious faith is not
"adaptive" (a sort of psychological accolade these days) or a
contribution to political inertia or apathy, but an effort to understand
the world, and find Something (Someone) believable, and also, a
means of voicing all kinds of revolutionary passions—which, of
course, might otherwise go unexpressed or get crushed.

During the Mississippi Summer Project [1964] a black field hand
told me this: "The college students, they say that the churches dull
you and make you feel satisfied with the way things are. But I don't
think they've ever read their Bible. They killed our Lord Jesus for
fighting against the big people. He didn't say give in; He said fight
them where they're wrong. What keeps us dull is the sheriff's guns
and the Mississippi Highway Patrol's guns. What keeps our hopes
going, what inspires us, what we believe in—that's what church is all
about." Well, maybe at times I *do* overlook some of his lapses in
reasoning, some of his flaws. Maybe I do romanticize him as I think
about him and try to write about him. But I find in him an impressive
mixture of religious devotion and political activism. Nor is he as
unusual as some of us who think about "the poor" or from a distance
advocate their "cause."

White: Every denomination seems to have its caucus of "charismatic worship," and the latest media spectacle seems to be the
"Jesus Freaks." I say "seems to be" because in spite of my ideological blinders—my need to see students in retreat from political
action or social change, appropriating the vitality of the poor and the
dispossessed just as another generation of consuming Americans
appropriated the vitality of the Jews and very nearly appropriated the
vitality of blacks—there is a quality about this movement, these
actions, that is real; pathetic to me, but real nevertheless.

Coles: That is right, children of the upper-middle-class, including
the academic and professional cadres, have their religious hunger,
too. I say "hunger" because I believe we are driven to know the
world and find our place in it. Maybe I should say we are driven to
find God and find our place in His world. When that utterly human
"need" is frustrated, denied, ridiculed, all sorts of "substitutes"
arise—hence the sectarianism of the proudly godless, and hence the
"answers," the "final explanations" so many of us in the liberal and

radical intellectual world manage to find, only to discard and replace
with new and more "definitive" replacements. No wonder some of
our young people today throw their hands up in confusion and
annoyance and return, in various ways, to the Bible, to churches,
maybe churches different from ours, but still places of worship. How
long can we be expected (can we expect our children) to believe in
the atomic table, a three-car garage, as filled up as the house to
which it's attached, and the revelations of yet another year of
psychotherapy? I agree, no one in his right mind wants this world to
turn its back on man's successes as a rational being who is able to fly
to the moon and probe the unconscious and build assembly lines.
And most of the world wants, *needs* more of that—food, housing,
medical care, much of it tied to "technology." Still (excuse me for
going back and forth all the time) there are things we can lose when
we go ahead, things we have to go back and find again, or suffer if
we do without them, or seek after in strange places and surprising
ways.

White: The wandering of a Bernanos or Agee or the young, the
anguished search for something decent (Orwell's word), is your
search too. Could you characterize your path, or what you've found?

Coles: Oh, I'm afraid I can't be very precise or respond satis-
factorily. I've tried to get to know some people these recent years,
some people I may not have been destined, by the social and
economic "facts of life" of my particular life, to get to know. I've also
tried to work alongside them, as a doctor, as someone who struggled
with SNCC and CORE and the Appalachian Volunteers and a
number of political organizing efforts in cities like Boston and
Cleveland. I've tried to write about what I've seen and heard, and
also, tried to say what I believe. But often I'm not sure what I believe,
so maybe I come across as uncertain or mixed-up or hesitant or
whatever. I don't like preaching at others, and I don't ike to be
preached at—not outside of church. Inside is another story.

But if I were to say whom I admire politically and spiritually, I think
I could pull myself together and come forth with an answer that
combines the directions of the mind and heart—Dorothy Day and
the Catholic Worker Movement, and Simone Weil's religious and
political struggle, as it comes across in *The Need for Roots* and
Gravity and Grace. Often I wish I could be more sure of myself, be

less doubtful religiously and politically. Often I wish I could spend my lifetime working in one of the Catholic Worker "hospitality houses," or perhaps trying to challenge the "powers and principalities" of this world more unreservedly, with more total political commitment—that is, a commitment unqualified by my interest in observing, taking note of contradictions or ironies, writing such things down, treating individual patients, some of them from "privileged" backgrounds, but nonetheless entitled to acknowledge pain and confusion and find out some things about themselves with the help of another person who has had a certain kind of "training."

But I am grateful to Daniel Berrigan for something he told me in the summer of 1970, when we talked while he was "underground." We agreed to disagree at times, as he put it, but we also agreed to assume certain shared values, and not go after one another abusively, question each other's right to travel in certain respects along our own particular roads.

Lord, I hope this *world's,* not just this country's, social and economic order one day sees an end to man's economic and political exploitation of man; but far off though even *that* day be, I fear there will be still other hazards and evils to contend with. One wants various things for all mankind, but more concretely, one prays for something kind and honorable to go on between oneself and one's next-door neighbor, however "like" or "unlike" me or you or so-and-so he or she happens to be.

Coles: Tightrope Between Literary Sensibility and Social Consciousness

Christopher Agee and James Rice/1974

From *The Phillipian* (Phillips Andover Academy, Andover, MA. February 28, 1974, pp. 5 and 17). Reprinted by permission of *The Phillipian*.

Phillipian Editor Christopher Agee and Upper James Rice recently interviewed Harvard psychiatrist Robert Coles, the 1974 Sterns Lecturer. Dr. Coles has written 14 books and over 350 articles, including the nationally renowned series, *Children of Crisis*. His most recently published work is *The Old Ones of New Mexico*, describing the aged in northern New Mexico. The following are Dr. Coles' comments about his work, and about sociology in general.

Agee: What do you see yourself accomplishing as a psychiatrist? What is your value to the people being helped apart from your friendship?

Coles: I don't think the momentum for my work is primarily furnished by the profession of psychiatry. I think perhaps the years I spent in medical school were more important than those spent in psychiatry and psychoanalysis, because in medicine one learns to pay attention to particular individuals.

And that's important for me because before I went into medicine my interests were primarily literary. If one is going to use writing to relate to particular individuals and try to get to know them and do justice to their lives rather than to one's imaginary life—you are dealing in the difference between fiction and nonfiction. To do this one needs some kind of discipline. And so I think psychoanalysis and psychiatry, in so far as they teach one person to listen to another, are enormously helpful. But the dangers are that one learns jargon, one learns distance from people through wordiness and the distance social science provides. Social science can be helpful but it can also

23

be an enemy. It can be a political enemy. There are social scientists
who abuse social science in a variety of ways: to further causes,
determine inheritance of acquired characteristics, determine genetic
factors of intelligence in Negro families. All these things have been
furnished to us through various so-called social scientists.

In so far as one learns to understand people, it is perhaps a little
better through the psychiatric discipline, but I repeat, it can be a
danger. It can help in that process of abstraction that removes people
from actuality, human actuality. So what I'm trying to do is not do
psychiatric studies of blacks or Appalachians or Chicanos or the
working class in Massachusetts. Whatever, I'm trying to understand as
best I can the manner of different kinds of people that live in this
country, drawing upon my particular way of doing it which would be
some mixture of writing and thus the problem of words as a means of
evoking what one sees and hears—and also as a doctor who is
interested in the ways people come to terms with life: adjust, survive,
and endure. As a psychiatrist, too—because I am interested in the
mind. I'm also interested in children, and how they grow up. But I
don't want to get into any particular category because I do believe
this kind of work requires a sense of caution about who he or she is,
about what one is trying to do. Some are inclined to categorize, to
stereotype, to come up with conclusions which the country desperately wants and which the readers desperately seek. In that sense, the
people that mean most to me are not the psychiatrists, who have
done work in social psychiatry, or the social scientist who has studied
the black family, but the people who mean most to me are the
people like George Orwell, James Agee and Simone Weil—writers
who have gone out and tried to understand others different from
themselves.

We have walked on that tightrope between literary sensibility and
social consciousness, between middle class life and an interest in
social change. There is constant tension in this, and there are
perplexing issues that are never going to be solved in this kind of
work. There is a constant challenge. I don't mean a challenge in the
sense that you're doing any great thing. For instance, people have
said to me, "Why don't you live in a ghetto?" I don't know how to
answer that dilemma.

Agee: But aren't Agee, Orwell and yourself acting as human beings from the heart? So it's not so much your position or your role as your feelings?

Coles: Well, you're right. I just don't like social science talk and I don't like its pernicious influence on a lot of American thought, particularly in the universities and perhaps in the secondary schools. I don't know if you're learning sociology and psychology here at Andover, but I do worry about the influence of these disciplines on the thinking and feeling of people.

Agee: You mentioned the terms "redemptive" and "prescriptive" in one article as the roles of psychiatrists in particular.

Coles: Well, it would be nice if psychiatrists were more re-demptive. At times it's a faddish indulgence, at times it's a desperate response to a dilemma, but this is a profession which I think in its distortions and grandiosities and its relationship to American life, is a very revealing one—because it's a prominent reflection of a highly secular culture. With a loss of faith in God and a general uncertainty, people have— psychiatrists have—inherited a certain role which they're not well trained for. They do go into the field, though and sometimes do make fools of themselves.

Agee: Your work seems to have a religious thread running through it—a concern for the individual and his personal attitudes toward life.

The story you told about the black sharecropper who felt very close to the church and resented what the white man in the university thought—does this reflect that idea?

Coles: Yes, this also has been a source of constant tension created by those who come from outside the community for idealistic reasons, those who want to help, save, get voting rights—we have our own values—and it's very hard for us to appreciate how other people feel about things that don't mean much to us. The Catholic Church in New Mexico, for instance, is different from the one here, but it too has a significance to the people. I don't think the people who are thinking about the "oppressed Chicanos" appreciate that. Once you think about a person in a village in New Mexico as an "oppressed Chicano" you've already cut off all kinds of possibilities of interaction between human beings. I'm not denying the importance of political activism in the lives of poor people, but I think that a political reformer can also be blind to things—and, in their own way, be prejudiced.

I remember in Mississippi in 1964 white students came from all over the country who wanted to change the situation down there, and they did. But there were large parts of the lives of people whom they visited that were very hard for them to understand and appreciate. I too am at fault for that. Our tone was political, liberal agnosticism and the beginning of the counter culture was getting under way. Meanwhile the poor people were very conservative in many ways, they had deep religious feelings, their whole mode of looking at the world is different from those who wanted to "save" them and who also, by the way, romanticized them. It was an incredible experience being a part of a situation where you want to save people. Then you learn about strengths they had that you never realized before. They are teaching you things rather than you only saving them. A lot is going on there that is not accounted for when you pick an anthropology or sociology book. Some of these books, for instance, say the Appalachians are mistrustful and isolated, then you go out into their community, not as a particularly skilled interviewer, but simply as a human being and just talk to them, and you discover differently. You'll find that they are friendly and hospitable.

We could have had a two-year seminar saying how we were going to go and what we were going to do, but it wouldn't have accomplished anything. There is no way about this at all, maybe no way of writing about the experience, except to say "go, do it," and to relate the friendships cemented. There is a contrast between the actual · experience and what you read in these books about how the Navajos have certain characteristics and the Appalachians have others, etc. I can only say without getting any nastier than I already have, that there is an air of unreality in those books. People say to me, "You're going up to Alaska, you must be doing reading." I don't read anything about it at all. I don't want to read anything about the people.

I hope all these books are meant to be ironic, just as when I write a chaper and give it the title "Method," that's an irony. Because the real method is to look, to live, to see, to get to know, and to write down on paper. That's a methodological process, and I use this tongue in cheek. I mean if one keeps going on with all these words, "methodological," "techniques," "field work," and pretty soon there aren't many people left in your life that you actually keep with you, and try to call upon as a witness for other people through the printed word.

Rice: Would you say that because the social sciences have become generally secluded to the world outside of academia that they have lost much of their virility, and become a sterile field of work?

Coles: I wouldn't say that social sciences are so secluded. The thing is that social sciences really are interested with the world. If you pick up some sociological/anthropological magazines, there they are. They all deal with the world, they're on cities, concerned with the race problems, and with classes and casts, and have been for a long time. In this sense then, particularly in the 60's and 70's, they have had a great deal of influence among students in school and colleges. Because students say, "I'm tired, I don't want to read Alfred Lord Tennyson and *The Iliad,* I want to be part of this world, I want to know about it. There is something desicated in the old classical tradition." Now I'm stating this as something one would be tempted to say. Personally, I felt quite the opposite.

Another problem you meet is that the humanities in a way have become the property of a lot of pedants, who take Faulkner or Dos Passos and dry them up, shrivel them up with these endless analyses that take the life out of these novels, plays, and poems. So the student says, "I can't stand this, I can't stand what they do to the writers, I can't stand this endless glorification of the past. I want to go out into the world, the world's changing." So they turn to sociologists and anthropologists, and why shouldn't they? What worries me is that again, these critics of Faulkner and Dos Passos take the living reality of something and get involved in a technical language, and this highly abstract process, but that's right for them, but not for me. I don't have the mental or emotional make-up to do the things they do, and I think I share this feeling with a lot of students who also can't get what they really want out of sociology and anthropology. What they want is similar to what they want out of a good novelist or artist interested in the world. What I'm saying is that it really bothers me when people who respond to my work, and give it credit because I'm a social scientist. It's not because I'm a social scientist that the work has any value. There is an element of social science in it, but the

work is not part of the social science tradition, but there is a tradition
for it. If I could only write the way Dickens or Dos Passos wrote about
the poor, in a non-fictional way, if I could evoke the complexities of
characters and do justice to the subtleties of the mind and of social
actions the way these and other writers did, then I would be more
successful at being the kind of person I want to become. It's that
tradition I call upon. But if my work is given credit because I am a
child psychiatrist, and I'm another American expert, then that's just
sad, both for me and for the people who do it. There must be a sense
of sadness in all this. A sense of humor and sadness. Look at the
people who are our secular priests and heros. There's Ann Landers
and Dr. Spock, who told millions of parents how to bring up their
children, and then 20 years later repented, saying, "No, I made a
mistake." The worship and faith and the idolatry that goes into this, I
think, are remarkable phenomena and also deserve some study.

Rice: Do you think, politically speaking, your books which are
written "close to the heart" would have more impact on political
leaders than someone who wrote a more academic exercise?

Coles: One of the books I wrote, *Still Hungry in America,* came
out of a long association I had with Robert Kennedy. The book is
dedicated to him and there is no question that he helped us with the
issue of hunger in the South. Yes, there are political leaders, he being
the most important of them, who have responded to some of these
things, who were interested in what we saw, and wrote, but he died in
1968 and *we* have been living ever since in a state of purgatory,
limbo, hell—choose one of the three.

Agee: You said the task that's facing us in government is to bring
the people into the mainstream of life. How do you envision doing
this without destroying, for example, what is good in the Appalachian
mountaineer life? How is this done?

Coles: Well, I don't believe it ever really can be done, but I think
one of the important things is that there has to be reverence for
variation and more respect for the digniy of the many different ways
of getting on in this world than there has been in this country. We
have demanded rather ruthlessly that one accommodate oneself to
the middle-class world. There's no question that there are large
islands of resistance to those who have held off, paying the price, and
it could be that if we educate ourselves enough to respect and hold

dear the values of the people in the mountains of New Mexico or
Appalachia while not making them pay an economic price. If
Americans could accept the fact that every American is entitled to an
honorable standard of living, and then to live with that, that would be
the beginning.

Agee: So it goes to the heart of the technological society?

Coles: Yes. I think it should be possible for people in Appalachia,
for instance, to continue their life of subsistence farming along with
their handicrafts, etc., and also have a guaranteed annual income
from the government. This should be possible without turning them
all into cheap labor for northern industry. The Yankee plants in
Lawrence, for instance, are going to go down to the South to build
factories and pay lower wages. That's going to bring benefits to the
South, but I think a lot was lost by those people in rural towns. I
wonder if there aren't ways of helping people through the cycle, ways
of helping people leave poverty while at the same time keeping their
heritage and strengths.

Agee: But how are such decisions made? How is this done?

Coles: That's what I loved about Robert Kennedy. He went out,
into the Mississippi and Appalachia and had these one-man hearings,
he went out into these hollows and talked to the families. But he was
the exception—the problem in this area of the social sciences
remains. What do people who go to Harvard and major in political
science do? They don't learn about the things that Kennedy
employed. They learn about the Constitution and sectionalism. O.K.,
that's fine—but I don't think there has been enough of an effort on
the part of political scientists and psychiatrists, to try to get out and
learn from the people of different parts of this country. They don't
necessarily have to talk of the evils of capitalists. I'm not urging a
Blakian vision, I don't think the 150 million working people would
accept anything which would leave them jobless, but they should be
able to maintain their heritage. We must realize how many little
nations there are within this one nation. On the one hand, we don't
want to fragment it, but on the other hand one must learn to respect
the variation.

Agee: In the same interviews above, Daniel Berrigan said "that the
institutions that exist now, because they are unfounded in morality,
are not capable of instituting change, and that America's greatness

lies virtually within itself, while it is not able to give any good to the world." Do you agree with this?

Coles: I think that this is too sweeping a statement. I do not believe that this country has come to that. Although this may sound like a statement from the moderate, liberal, middle-class American, I guess that's what I am. I think there are possibilities for changing this country. I don't think the American people want a Richard Nixon as president, but I think the American people would have responded to, say, Robert Kennedy. I believe that the war sidetracked the whole decade of liberal and social change. I truly think that there are people in the government who through the basic democratic insights could make this society more just and equitable. But I think it's a horrible thing to take the cause of the poor, and the needs of the poor and use that to bludgeon political democracy today as some are doing. The poor have enough problems without becoming like the Soviet automatons to be controlled by a corrupt government. I believe we live in a democracy with institutions of enormous value, we must struggle to make them viable. To throw all that out and say the country is hopelessly corrupt as some have done, is wrong. Therefore these unqualified exhortations, whether they be political or educational, I think deserve study. It is the elite who say, "Down with schools, down with the government." It happens on campuses, not among the poor.

Agee: Do you worry sometimes that in destroying certain stereotypes, you may create new ones?

Coles: Well, my words are both an opportunity, a challenge and also they are treachery, there's no question about it. I don't know how you can beat the categorical game. But I think there is an educational problem here. Too often we learn "either, or" instead of "both, and" or "yes, but." That begins very early in life. It's hard for us to accept paradox, ambiguity, and inconsistency. We are taught that consistency is a virtue, while inconsistency is ridiculous. It's not reality. Life is inconsistent.

A Talk with Robert Coles

Steven L. Nickman/1975

From *Bulletin* (Boston, The New England Council of Child Psychiatry, May 1975, pp. 9–12). Reprinted by permission of Dr. Steven Nickman and the New England Council of Child Psychiatry.

Robert Coles is in his mid-forties, about 5 feet 10, slim and rangy, with thick black hair closely cropped at the sides. He speaks at a variable rate, often with low-pitched intensity. He works in a large, neat, book-lined room in his house in Concord, in which Mrs. Coles and his three sons also live. He offered me his comfortable chair, seated himself in a rocker, and we had the conversation of which the following are highlights.

Nickman: I wanted to talk to you because a number of us are interested in what is going on in Boston, and there is a feeling that you have a lot of ideas about it. Your piece in the *Globe* last fall, for example.* Your name has come up in discussions, particularly with regard to what's been happening in South Boston and what those of us in psychiatry can do about it.

Coles: I have tried not to say anything about what's going on in Boston, because I feel that in my books, in *Children of Crisis,* I've said all I had to say about the South and the North. I've just returned from Albuquerque, where I've been talking to Chicanos and Indians. That's the largest part of the work. The *Globe* editors approached me last fall, and wanted to know if I had anything to say about the situation, because I had told them some of my thoughts several years before. I thought it was important to point out that both sides had to be listened to. After the article appeared, I was criticized by many

*In which, at the height of the busing crisis, Dr. Coles pointed out that both Roxbury blacks and South Boston whites felt powerless and victimized by forces beyond their control, and that what was going on could be seen as a manipulation of both populations by other people of a higher socioeconomic class.

liberals. Maybe they were right. Maybe I over-stated the case I was trying to make. I think of something George Wallace said not long ago—"We have the South in South Boston, and in parts of other large Northern cities, in the form of people who have small incomes and are afraid of change . . . the South in which poor whites and poor blacks fight each other instead of the powers that be."

Nickman: Having read *Children of Crisis* and the Berrigan book and some other things, I found myself wondering what in your background made you such a good listener. What prepared you for this work?

Coles: Well, I never particularly started out to become a psychiatrist or even a doctor. I was a literature major in college, and became interested in William Carlos Williams—

Nickman: —a doctor—

Coles: —and got to know him, and wrote my thesis on him. The people who have influenced me most are Walker Percy, James Agee (one of my sons has Agee as a middle name), Flannery O'Connor, Georges Bernanos, Dorothy Day. I think O'Connor especially has a marvelous sense of the South, and was a very fine writer and moral essayist.

Nickman: You often refer to Bonhoeffer and Weil.

Coles: I've long been interested in Simone Weil. When this present work is over, I would like to write about her. Another influence was Anna Freud. She took her father's ideas and used them, but she stressed in *Normality and Pathology in Childhood* the importance of direct observation, that has to come *before* theory and ought to help determine the nature of theory. I've been trying to record what people say and how they live, without trying to force the complexities, ironies and ambiguities of their lives into the confines of a theory. I'm certainly not alone in this work; there is Oscar Lewis, Studs Terkel, and many others. What I do, I guess, is social documentation; I would call myself a social essayist, I suppose.

Nickman: Now that we've gotten into the book, I wanted to ask you about the people you interviewed. They seem so articulate, one wonders if these people were specially selected, or whether anyone can be articulate given the right circumstances, and it's a prejudice to think otherwise.

Coles: There's a great deal of eloquence in ordinary life. (I think of the things I heard from an 80 year old woman in New Mexico, amazing things; it was published as a profile in *The New Yorker* under the title "Una Anciana," and they were deluged with letters— many of them speaking of her eloquence.) But you should remember that her words didn't all come out that way in one sitting. The books are my creation, for better or worse—woven out of numerous encounters with individuals over several years. There's a novelistic quality to them. It's true, though, that one is attracted to the more articulate people. Of course, on the other hand, a lot of my work has been with children; they draw, and I draw, and there's not quite so much talking.

And actually, when I was a resident, I often liked the quiet, less articulate ones. I still remember my first patient at the Judge Baker, a black boy from Roxbury. He was troubled, but there was a lot to him. He was deep. In those days (I don't know how it is now) certain residency programs were sometimes rigid and theoretical. I had some trouble in my residency; I used to take my patients over to the Art Museum and Mrs. Gardner's house, and afterwards buy them a Coke. We would enjoy it. I think I felt better outside of my office.

Nickman: I heard that about you when I was there.

Coles: My young, black patient said to me at one point: "Why don't you come and see me in Roxbury, so you can see what it's like where I live?" and I wanted to do it, but I was sure there would be five conferences about how I was "acting out," so I didn't. It was the 1950's, then! People don't stress enough the importance of the larger social context on the development of an individual; the classical analytic approach has focused so much on the "intrafamilial" events, which are important, of course, but never unaffected by the "outside," as Erikson has shown us so well.

Nickman: You are worried about the way a body of ideas gets crystallized and rigid.

Coles: Yes. I've been reading Roazen's book, *Freud and His Followers,* and it's clear that in addition to being a brilliant clinician and theorist, Freud was a political leader. He built up a political "structure," and that "structure" is what, to a degree, still exists all over the world. It was, arguably, a necessary development. But there were hazards.

Nickman: Somewhere you speak of having a "berth" at the

Health Services, and when you bring up political matters it reminds me that, for many of us, if we want a "berth" we have to adapt ourselves to the current political realities that departments of psychiatry operate under. It puts constraints—

Coles: I hadn't realized it was that way in child psychiatry. Incidentally, I guess you and I and most of us psychiatrists in the Northeast think of ourselves as "liberals," but if you go to the South or the Southwest, you find a different situation. Many psychiatrists there are quite "conservative." That difference could make an evening of discussion! Anyway, the question of the larger context that a family lives in leads one to ask: what do a child's parents encourage him to believe about his future, what will the world be like for him?

Nickman: You discussed that in your article, "Political Children," in the *New York Review of Books.*

Coles: Yes; how a South Boston father, or a Midwestern father, talks to his kids, tells them about the government and their relationship to it, has a great deal to do with the way the child grows up in relation to the society.

Nickman: You asked Father Berrigan if he would venture to prescribe for others, tell them what they should do. Would you want to tell people in the mental health field what you think they might be able to do in the current situation, what those of us who have contractual relationships with the schools can do to help them in their difficulty? Or have you said as much as you can about Boston?

Coles: (pause) That's so hard. The best I can say is that it's so important to keep in mind the feelings of all the different groups that are concerned.

I keep coming back to what it must be like for the kids who are being bused to the different schools: the white kids from South Boston to the overcrowded schools in Roxbury, and the black kids— for them to be going to South Boston High is a pyrrhic victory, considering the quality of the school.

Nickman: I read your children's book, *Dead End School,* about the first busing in Boston.

Coles: I've tried to write *for* as well as *about* children. I've written

five children's books. The latest, called *Headsparks,* is about a
teenage girl who feels on the verge of a breakdown.

Nickman: You've been exposed to people with a very narrow
world view (I think of the black hooker in the section called "My
Room") and people who inhabit a much wider world. What is it that
makes for narrowness or breadth of human feeling and relatedness?

Coles: You may not like my terminology, but I would want to use
the word "grace" here. Psychiatric ideology will carry you only so far,
and then one is surprised by what one finds in a person one might
have thought completely impoverished in spirit. An individual is more
than the sum of "defense mechanisms" and "drives." For a more or
less "psychiatric" book coming out this summer, a collection of
papers, I've used the title *The Mind's Fate;* "fate" because of the
"unknowns" that you find in the lives of individuals.

Nickman: Is this what you would call a Christian world view?

Coles: Well, Judeo-Christian. What I would stress is the importance of looking at a life on its own terms. If you try to fit it rigidly
into a theory you lose 80 to 90 per cent of what you hear. Remember
that the people I talked to weren't patients, they were ordinary
people living their lives. In the beginning, alas, I didn't think that
way—

Nickman: —you approached them with the notion of helping
them?

Coles: Yes, thinking they were under a terrible strain, that they
would crack. But usually they didn't. And that led to a change of
emphasis on my part, toward their wholeness and strengths. What I
drew most from was medicine, with its emphasis on a broad clinical
view, rather than the more dogmatic side of psychiatry, to which I fear
many of us have been exposed.

Nickman: With regard to psychiatry, I found in reading the book
a certain ambivalence about using psychiatric terms. They had
quotes around them, and it seemed you weren't quite willing to do
without them, but still did not feel that they belonged to you. As
though using technical terms were allied to an illegitimate kind of
control over others.

Coles: That's a good way to put it—a way to control, and also
something to hide behind. It's important for us as psychiatrists to

have our theory and our professional standards, but you also have to have your own ideals and beliefs and be willing to communicate them and take a stand. Using technical words can be a way of avoiding involvement, and also of avoiding certain important *psychological* issues, by calling them someone else's business. And then, there is the relationship between psychiatry and upper middle class American life, or at least a segment of it . . . that is, I think, a religious issue!

Investigative Reporter of People in Crisis and How They Survive

Neil Ashby/1975

From *Modern Medicine* (Cleveland, OH, June 15, 1975, pp. 77–92). Reprinted by permission of *Modern Medicine.*

One of the most remarkable practices in America is conducted by a child psychiatrist who maintains no office but instead roams the United States working out of a briefcase with a tape recorder, notepad, pencils, and crayons.

He talks to Americans who are living, as he terms it, "in crisis"— blacks and whites embroiled in school desegregation, the poor straining to survive on the rocky soil of Appalachia or the hot sands of New Mexico, migrant crop pickers with only the next field of carrots for a home, or the seemingly secure middle class in their well-kept, mortgaged homes.

Harvard child psychiatrist Robert Coles chats mostly with children but he also talks with parents, teachers, and other adults, seeking to learn how they view their lives, how they cope with crisis, from where they draw their strength to persevere.

Later, perhaps sitting in his car or a coffee shop or aboard an airplane, he jots down lengthy summaries of these conversations.

Finally, he returns home to Concord, Massachusetts, to shape these firsthand accounts into articles and books through which the people themselves describe their lives and difficulties—an output of 500 articles, published in both technical and popular magazines, and some 24 books in the past 10 years.

This "definitive work on America's poor and powerless in the twentieth century," as Harry Caudill has called it in the *New York Review of Books,* has brought Dr. Coles many personal rewards:

As an author, he has gained best-sellerdom, and his three-going-on-five volume *Children of Crisis* series, particularly, has attracted thousands of readers and critical acclaim.

He has won numerous prizes, including the 1973 Pulitzer prize for nonfiction.

He lives an idyllic life—when he's home—surrounded by animals, children, and his devoted wife in the history-rich Concord woods.

How does Dr. Coles view his own career? Where does it fit in the diverse profession of medicine? What is he trying to contribute? At the outset, he believes that his investigations are medical, in its broadest sense, and add to medical knowledge in a new way. He is gripped by the importance of studying and trying to understand the hard circumstances in which some persons find themselves and the strengths and mechanisms that enable them to survive. He also is interested in a continuing examination of how severe stress causes some humans to falter and become ill (but only ill to a degree, he emphasizes, rarely to total collapse).

Dr. Coles' stories tell how individuals cope, rationalize, and hold on. He terms them studies of the "inner lives" of his subjects, made in faithful clinical fashion but with methods necessarily self-developed.

"As a doctor, my mind focuses on the vulnerabilities and the physical and mental problems of people, of course," Dr. Coles says. "But having done *that,* it focuses on the *competencies* they've developed to meet whatever difficulties they face. I think doctors and psychiatrists need to understand the situations in which their patients live and also how people *make do,* survive, get through life, not just how they develop complaints. We need to know the sources of human character, human will.

"I think a doctor would better understand a particular physical symptom if he knew more about what the patient must deal with in life.

"Instead of saying, 'Here are more tranquilizers or antacids or aspirin, and cut down on the alcohol,' we've got to ask, 'What's this life like? Is it unduly difficult and stressful in some way?' When you closely examine some people's lives, you begin to wonder how they're alive at all!

"And if more physicians would concentrate on the islands and reservoirs of strength in a 'disturbed' patient, perhaps those reservoirs could be made larger, those islands become a whole mainland.

"Now obviously, doctors today don't have time to be reporters.

They're already overburdened by the enormous demands made on them.

"So there may be room for a few doctors like me who go out and do this documentary work. That's why I've poured out all these books—in the hope that doctors, and indeed the general public, will gain a little more insight into the lives of struggling Americans."

Dr. Coles recently talked about his life and work early one morning in the study of his large, old colonial home that is concealed by trees far back from a narrow road at the edge of Concord. The house has been modernized, notably to install wide, single-pane windows to expose the tranquil groves and meadows outside. The Coleses' three sons, Bobby, age 10; Daniel, 8; and Michael, 4, have left for school. The psychiatrist's wife, Jane Hallowell Coles, slim and youthful in jeans, is off in the station wagon to buy feed for the chickens, geese, and horses ambling about in the pens out back.

The study is light and cheery. On the broad, white table-desk lie papers, folders, one of the yellow legal pads on which Dr. Coles sets down his accounts in a cramped, irregular hand, with a ballpoint pen. Wearing a gray sweater with worn elbows, he is sitting in a rocker. Dark, intense eyes are hooded by heavy black eyebrows. His hair is short, black, and tousled and he is friendly and unassuming from the start.

Dr. Coles was born in Boston on October 12, 1929, son of an engineer. He attended Boston schools and went through Harvard, majoring in English literature. By then he had decided to pursue medicine and moved on to Columbia University College of Physicians and Surgeons. He interned in pediatrics at the University of Chicago.

"But I found it difficult for me to work with children surgically," Dr. Coles relates. "I had several of my own crises with them, which I think a lot of young interns go through. I wondered if I would ever be a competent pediatrician, with all that goes with it, and my interest began to shift toward child psychiatry. I had been reading Freud and moved on to his daughter Anna and her work with children who went through the Nazi blitz in England in the early 1940s."

Dr. Coles returned to Boston for a four-year residency in adult and child psychiatry at Massachusetts General, McLean, and Children's hospitals. And during this period he had his first personal experience

with "children of crisis": It was during his first year, 1955, at
Massachusetts General, and the adults and children were victims of
the last serious polio epidemic in the nation.

"I talked with these youngsters on a long-term basis," Dr. Coles
recalls, his speech tinged with a New England accent. "Paralysis is a
long-term problem. I became terribly involved with them—their
efforts to accept what had happened to them—to the point where
my supervisors thought it was a distraction from what *they* wanted
me to be doing in residency training."

In 1958, at age 29, Dr. Coles entered the Air Force to fulfill his
military obligation and was given charge of a neuropsychiatric unit at
Keesler Air Force Base in Biloxi, Mississippi. As one accustomed to a
life of comfort and civility, he found he slipped easily into southern
white middle-class society. *Black* society didn't particularly concern
him.

And then about one year later an experience jarred Dr. Coles onto
the roadless course he has since followed. Bicycling along the sand
on the Mississippi Gulf Coast, he came upon a "vicious" fight
between blacks who were asserting their right to use the beach and
whites who were trying to keep them off.

The injustice of the scene seared him. There were no blacks, he
realized, anywhere he routinely went. Yet newspapers were reporting
blacks' battles for equality in many other places.

There has always been something mystical, something of a not
fully understood "calling" to Dr. Coles' unique work. But there in
Mississippi, the skills that he has brought to his mission began to
come together: the psychiatrist's urge to probe the mind and the
environment that influences it, the physician's hope to heal, a
particular concern for children; the journalist's ability to go among
strangers and get them to tell what they know and feel; and the
writer's skill at setting down his material in a compelling way.

Dr. Coles soon found himself in New Orleans trying to gain the
confidence of little black children who were in the process of
integrating elementary schools, the parents who sent them forth, and
the red-neck whites who screamed insults and threats at the
youngsters as they marched into the buildings. Dr. Coles wanted
them to tell why they were doing what they were and how they felt
about it.

He had his problems. The people had not sent for him. The blacks were deeply fearful—no white had ever come to them "except to take something away." The whites thought he was a "nigger lover."

But, by making contacts through organizations, pleading that he was just a doctor who wanted to learn about their lives, being polite and respectful to black and white, and projecting an inherent innocence, the Boston psychiatrist induced his subjects to bare their souls.

Six-year-old Tessie told him one way she was coping: "It's scary sometimes, going to school. But not as scary as what I can dream up. So I told Granny that as bad as they make it for us, the stronger I'll get, because I'll beat them to the punch by imagining it even worse than it is."

A Louisiana segregationist who admitted participating in physical attacks on blacks told Dr. Coles he believed blacks are "just like animals. You wouldn't let a wild animal go free in your home or in school with your kids, would you? They rape and kill our women and dirty the whole city up."

But this man with typically barbaric thoughts also told the psychiatrist in long conversations that he was never favored by his parents, that the excitement had left his marriage, and that his son was a great disappointment.

After years of listening to the people of the South talk about the conflicts in desegregation, Dr. Coles went back to Massachusetts and wrote the first volume of *Children of Crisis: A Study of Courage and Fear* (Boston, Atlantic-Little, Brown and Company, 1967). It won awards from Phi Beta Kappa, the Child Study Association, B'nai B'rith, and the American Psychiatric Association, and is now in its sixth printing.

Since then, aided by his wife who often accompanies him, Dr. Coles has produced studies of people who don't get enough to eat, "middle Americans," and neglected children, among others. And two more volumes of the *Crisis* series have been published.

In volume 2, *Migrants, Sharecroppers, Mountaineers,* Dr. Coles describes migrants' children who sleep in the backseats of cars, have no toilets or showers, possess nothing of their own except memories. One boy told Dr. Coles how he rationalizes a nomadic existence in which one is never sure what his welcome will be.

"I like to be moving along. If you keep moving you're safer than if you just stop in a field, and someone comes by, and they can ask you what you're doing, and they can tell you to get back in the car and go away as fast as the motor will go."

In volume 3, *The South Goes North,* Dr. Coles follows poor southerners, pickers, and mountain folk who survive by giving up their homes and clawing a new start in the slums of northern cities. Here, for many, a fifth-floor apartment is a frightening height. Numbers on houses and the need to lock up possessions are puzzling realities.

The author records how 10-year-old Sally, originally from Kentucky and now in Chicago, finds support in her father's perseverance: "My daddy has a bad arm, but he goes out every day and uses it, and uses his good one, too; he shovels and rakes and lifts things and pushes things and moves things, and then he comes home dead tired but glad to have the dollar bills."

The Pulitzer Prize was awarded for volumes 2 and 3.

Dr. Coles at this writing is completing volume 4, *Chicanos, Indians, and Eskimos,* for which he has done several years of research in appropriate locales. He's also begun work on volume 5, devoted to middleclass citizens in all parts of the nation who are weathering social or economic conflict. He insists that volume 5 will be the last in the series.

On the interview trail, Dr. Coles distributes no questionnaires. Instead, he simply emphasizes that he's a doctor who's interested in studying the lives of certain people. "And the people respond with enthusiasm," he says, "as if, why, of course, why *wouldn't* a doctor be interested in how people live their lives?"

He visits schools and places of work, as well as homes, listening to all sides—black and white; child, parent, and teacher; boss, worker, and worker's child; Klansman and activist. Dr. Coles finds each person eager to describe his plight, once he trusts the listener.

In a home, Dr. Coles may plop down and join the family in watching TV, perhaps saying little at first but observing how the family lives and interacts.

Or, he'll begin with a vague, small-talk question like, "How's it going today?" Or, "How's your daughter doing in school?" Or, "How's your husband's job going?"

"But," Dr. Coles stresses, "I never ask them any standard psychologic questions like, 'How are you sleeping?' Or, 'What are your dreams about?' Because after all, they never asked a psychiatrist to come to their home. Who am I to come in there and start analyzing them? If I did I'd be thrown out and told not to come back!"

He takes paper and crayons along and often asks the children to draw a picture. A deprived child often depicts himself without arms and gives the bossman an ogre's ugly teeth.

At first Dr. Coles wore a conventional white shirt, tie, and jacket but since has learned that a sport shirt or sweater is less formidable.

Back home in Concord, he is at his desk by 8:30 A.M., writes until noon. He receives stenographic assistance from Harvard's University Health Services, to which he is attached and through which his grants are channeled.

He writes steadily, having mentally plotted out in advance the ground he's going to cover. Unlike many writers, he is not distracted if his children come in and out or play in the same room.

Probably the most unlikely aspect of Dr. Coles' work is his writing, for which he's had no training other than the study of literature.

"It's almost an accident," he says. "I began by writing up reports on my interviews. Then magazine and book editors turned out to be interested in what I was doing. The editors really taught me to write. Now I find myself writing articles and reviewing books that have nothing to do with my own work and writings."

Afternoons are for correspondence, reading, and other details. By 9:30 or 10 P.M., he has retired.

Yet he is not entirely removed from the physician's world. He is on the staff of Cambridge City Hospital, where he provides some supervision for psychiatric residents and conducts seminars, and he occasionally lectures at Harvard Medical School.

"With the combination of the foundation support and the writing, well, I'm not making a fortune, but I'm not by any means starving either. So I don't charge the few patients I see. And I also try to plow back a percentage of the royalties I get into the causes I get involved with—Martin Luther King's group and Cesar Chavez's, for example."

Still, there are those who do not view everything about Dr. Coles with admiration.

Writers and journalists have complained that some of the quotes that he admittedly recreates after interviews don't sound like authentic speech. Some doctors have called Dr. Coles' efforts "mere journalism." He doesn't mind: "I'm delighted to hear that; out-and-out investigative journalism *is* one of the dimensions of this work!"

Radical activists have told him that if he truly is devoted to helping the downtrodden, he ought to live in the ghetto, give away all his money, and be poor. Dr. Coles replies:

"That's one of the tensions I have to contend with. I spend a lot of time with the poor, yet I don't live in poverty myself. I tell them where I live, and I've brought some of the children out here. It's difficult in many ways. It's embarrassing, and I feel both fortunate and guilty. But we're never going to abolish guilt—it's what one does with it.

"I've tried to do the best I could within the hours of the day. I have responsibilities to my family. No one *wants* to be poor. And, finally, if I were to take a vow of extreme poverty, it wouldn't improve the fate of the migrant workers, the sharecroppers, or the black people in the ghettos one bit."

Perhaps the most incisive criticism of Dr. Coles' contributions is that for all his research he gives little more than generalized conclusions that people show a lot of grit and that we need to make a better world. What *are* the secret strengths that enable some of the unfortunate to hang on? Can these attributes be taught or nurtured? What can we *do* to eliminate the inequities and the suffering in our society?

In a critical essay in the magazine *Commentary,* Joseph Epstein, author of *Divorced in America,* says Dr. Coles has produced "a gigantic body of raw data (about two-thirds of the material is quotation) which in the end proves self-defeating. In the general din of talk . . . no single voice can really be heard. . . . The two-sidedness of every subject Coles touches upon is perceived so incessantly that it becomes a kind of tic in the prose." Epstein concludes that this "good and decent man" spent "10 years trying to 'understand' his subject and confesses himself at the end no less bewildered and incompetent and helpless at the complexity of it all than he was at the beginning."

Dr. Coles replies that what he is doing is basically "naturalistic observation, with no great pretensions to theory." Indeed, he says he feels no need to "take this human experience and fit it into the rigid categories that social scientists are so comfortable with."

His work cuts across many disciplines—social anthropology, social and psychologic geography, journalism, and, most important to him, medicine and psychiatry.

"I'm looking at the resonances between personal lives and social, political, economic, and historical circumstances—which sounds vague, but which *excludes* an *emphasis* on psychopathologic inquiry. I'm getting to know these people so others will get to know them. I'm trying to illuminate—that's all I can do."

For American Youth: Demands No Other Generation Has Had to Face

U. S. News & World Report/1976

From *U. S. News & World Report* (Washington, D.C., September 6, 1976, pp. 59–61). Reprinted by permission of U.S. News and World Report, Inc., copyright, 1976.

Q: Dr. Coles, what changes do you see taking place in America's young people today?

A: Well, I think there's a tendency among social scientists to flatter ourselves by saying that the problems American children face today are distinct and extraordinary compared to earlier generations. Therefore, I would exercise caution in interpreting many of the dire pronouncements made recently about American family life and the ways that young people are growing up.

I do believe that children are maturing at an earlier age and becoming more worldly-wise than earlier generations. The increased presence of radio and television and the accumulation of knowledge that is more instantly available in the schools certainly contribute to the sensibility of youth about themselves and their world. Thirty or 40 years ago, young people could be much more insulated from society. Now they are more in touch with the predominant social and cultural changes.

They also retain a marked awareness that certain aspects of American culture have their own dignity, strength and stability. I detect in youth a tempering of the attitudes about race and sex and class that were held 10 or 15 years ago. This is very noticeable.

It is a growing and very healthy trend. Young persons are acting on their belief that people should not have to put up with certain indignities and obstacles because of prejudices against certain groups.

Q: Do you find that adult attitudes toward youth have changed?

A: Society in general is adjusting more responsibly to children. Our youngsters are increasingly likely to have been carefully chosen—in the sense that contraceptive devices and pills, along with legalized

46

abortion, have separated sex from the inevitability of childbearing. Families are smaller. Childhood has been extended well into the end of the second decade of life.

Children are by no means hurried into adult responsibilities as they were, say, in the early days of the nation.

Q: What other accommodations have adults made?

A: The so-called life-style issues are an obvious example. Dress styles, music, sexual experimentation, milder drugs like marijuana—the older generations in America have accepted some of these in a relatively short period of time. In the late '60s, I saw a lot of tension between working-class families and upper-middle-class families on these life-style issues. That has certainly blurred, not only among different social classes but across generations.

Young people themselves begin to make accommodations. There is a capacity in American culture to absorb new ideas and trends that even the most militant youths find hard to struggle against endlessly.

Q: Do you believe this process writes the epitaph to the so-called youth revolt of the 1960s?

A: Yes. The civil-rights and antiwar protest movements were a part of the tension that has always existed in this republic between the elements of change and the elements of stability—tension that often pits young against old.

The '60s tipped that balance slightly toward the forces of radical change, but many of the activists have joined the mainstream. As people get older, get married, become breadwinners and have children, I think some of the more radical kind of questioning goes away. People begin to think of their generational responsibilities. The activist youth of the '60s own homes now, and have to worry about getting and keeping a job and paying the bills.

Also we should remember this: Even at the height of the protests, the activist youth were a distinct minority. Over three quarters of the universities and colleges were calm—a much neglected statistic.

Q: Are today's young people more cynical and apathetic than those of 10 years ago?

A: Let me tell you about some people I know:

At Vanderbilt University, there is a student-health coalition that has been working for five years in rural Tennessee to provide medical care to poor and working-class people.

These are young, idealistic, mostly white undergraduates who are conservative in many ways.

Another group—15 students at Duke University—is working with mostly black migrant workers in North Carolina. They help these migrants deal with the bureaucracy in getting proper housing, schooling for their children, health care, food stamps and the adequate working conditions.

For six years, students at the University of New Mexico have staffed a health clinic in northern New Mexico to deliver medical care to poor, mostly Spanish-speaking people.

These are ordinary young people—not "crazies" or political radicals—who are continuing a stream of idealism that runs very broadly throughout this nation's history.

Q: How will that idealism be transmitted to children now growing up in an atmosphere of rising divorce, constant television and more working mothers?

A: True, the divorce rate is higher today than it has ever been. In my work with families over the past 25 years, however, I have seen marriages in which there were enormous tensions—no divorces but constant fights, squabbles, and an artificial version of love and devotion. I would argue that these relationships placed enormous burdens on the children, perhaps more harmful than those of children of divorced parents. I'm not for more divorces, of course, but I think the increase in broken marriages is due to the wider availability of divorce than in the past, when the tensions in homes were just as great.

Television is a great transforming element in the lives of children, as radio was in the '20s and '30s. If you observe these children, you find they do get brainwashed to a degree—mesmerized by the "tube"—to the point where they even parrot commercials. But there comes a point when that begins to stop. After "Batman" and "Superman" and, yes, "The Electric Company," the natural process of growing up takes over. There is just so much the children can take. They become bored, they don't listen, they go outside and play and fight, just like kids have always done. It is childhood asserting itself over a technological instrument.

Q: What about the high level of violence on TV?

A: One has to be careful here, but I think some common sense should prevail. Children who are already troubled and who see violent things can be hurt by it, just as some normal children who see constant violence on TV can find a sanction for violent acts of their own. But I part company with people who underestimate the capacity of children to maintain a perspective. In general, I think children can play with toy guns, they can see violence on television, and still grow up to be normal children—and, indeed, not really be all that affected by what they have seen.

Q: Will increasing numbers of working mothers affect the way American children are reared?

A: Frankly, this increase is being seen primarily among educated, well-to-do families—women who a generation ago would not have worked but would have devoted much time outside the home to volunteer causes and charities. So now we have middle-class women going to work for the first time because it has practically become a social obligation. If these are responsible women, they will find ways to care for their children, or they won't have them at all.

Let's not forget that women have been working in factories since the beginning of the free-enterprise system. These were women from the lower economic brackets who had to work because they needed the income, and their condition hasn't changed that much. In fact, "women's liberation" hasn't encouraged these working-class mothers to get jobs. A lot of them are bitter about having to work, and would be only too happy to stay at home with their kids.

Q: Is mobility a problem for today's children?

A: Yes, for both the rich and poor. Constant moving of families from one place to another definitely has harmed the "rootedness" that I think family life requires.

I'll tell you about one family I've been working with. The father has a high-paying job as vice president of a corporation. The family has lived in 10 different cities in the past 20 years. As a result, the children have known seven or eight different school systems, and it's very hard for them to know exactly where they really "come from."

This aspect of our lives has its psychological consequences. It makes for a certain fragility in establishing friendships. It also makes for a certain guardedness and tentativeness among young people about life in general.

Q: Recent legislation designed to aid families with day care and

health maintenance was vetoed by Mr. Ford after opposition was
expressed that such a law might bring Government intrusion into
family life. Are such fears justified?

A: Yes, I think this is a legitimate concern. Although I was not
specifically opposed to this legislation, the opposition that developed
should not be brushed aside by liberals who want more federal
programs "to strengthen family life." There are justified doubts about
the bureaucratic manipulation of American families. The right of
parents to rear their children is vested by our legal and cultural
systems, by our moral code and by our social history. We don't have
kibbutzim, nor do we have communal rearing of children sanctioned
by the state, as in China or Russia.

In our system, the family is the means by which moral values are
inculcated. This built-in authority that we give to families is an integral
part of the American social and economic system, and it separates us
from much of the rest of the world. That is why some of the radical
critics of American society want to undercut the authority of the
family and move toward communes, or toward a statist social control
of family life.

Now, the same thing goes for the family legislation. Are we going
to have Government social workers with the power to intrude upon
family life? In many poor families—who are the most seriously
shackled by bureaucratic intrusions—the welfare workers sometimes
want to take away the children. They have decided that some families
are unsuited to have children. I would be in favor of removing the
power of these bureaucrats—get them off the backs of the poor. I
certainly wouldn't want to extend their power into the middle class.

Q: How would you remove this power?

A: One way is through a family-income maintenance program that
gives families a right to a minimum standard income and also
removes a bureaucracy of sorts.

In addition, I think programs that provide job training and
employment are a needed alternative. More and more Americans
take for granted that a large pool of unemployed youth—approach-
ing 50 per cent among ghetto youth—is a disruptive and unstable
force in the life of the country, and that it should be ameliorated.

Q: Some critics have suggested that schools have failed in their
responsibilities to children. Do you agree?

A: Many of the complaints made by parents stem from their profound feeling that the school systems have gotten into the hands of an educational bureaucracy that is rigid and insensitive and unenlightened. There is indeed resentment by both liberal and conservative parents toward this kind of school administration, and I think it is often well founded. In too many school systems, these administrators are hampering the spontaneity and flexibility and ingenuity of schoolteachers—intimidating them, in fact. They have an arbitrary kind of power that is divorced from the wishes of the community.

Q: Yet haven't many parents asked for this by demanding all kinds of "fringes" from the schools—hot lunches, health care, guidance and job placement, and so on?

A: Yes, they certainly have demanded everything from the schools, from the nursery level up. This includes loving attention, learning that competes successfully with that offered anywhere else, character building, athletic excellence, and, of course, psychological health— whatever that is. In asking for these things as well as hot lunches and all the rest, however, parents didn't expect or deserve to get the kind of educational bureaucracy that they have now. They don't like it— and worse, they don't know how to express their dissatisfaction. When we see these sporadic protest movements—about textbooks and prayer in the classroom and saluting the flag—parents are objecting as much to the loss of control over their schools as they are to any particular issue.

In a broader sense, I do think that parents may have turned over to other people—such as doctors, psychologists, teachers, counselors— too much of the responsibility for nurturing their children.

Q: Do teachers share the blame with administrators for the loss of confidence in schools?

A: Emphatically not. Teachers should not be made the scapegoat. Teaching is tough, wearing work that requires dedication and loyalty to children. Some social critics who lambaste teachers should be put in a classroom day in and day out, week after week. I doubt if most of them could do it.

Q: Has the increasing secularization of our society affected children?

A: Yes. This is one of the sadder developments, particularly for upper-middle-class families. I'm talking about the loss of faith in anything that goes outside of their own particular experience. The theology of many such parents today is concretely symbolized in their offspring: "I believe in my children. I don't believe in an afterlife. I don't believe in God. What I really believe in is my children. I'm going to give them the best of everything." That kind of faith generates demands on these children such as no other generation has ever had to face.

Q: What kinds of demands?

A: One is simply how to make sense of an avalanche of possessions, opportunities and possibilities that are given to middle-class children. That is a debilitating task for many kids in highly motivated families.

Another is simply learning to deal with the high expectations placed on these young people. They are supposed to be stronger, sounder, more ambitious, more effective, more competent, better able to get ahead and, very important, able to "cut the mustard"— meaning to surmount the obstacles presented to people in a highly advanced and still quite competitive society.

I know one mother who is confident that her children will find worthwhile jobs or professions when they are older.

Nevertheless, she tells me she wants more from them—high competence, excellence and repeated demonstrations of academic and social success—because, of all things, such achievements would "prove" that the children have been brought up wisely and are, as a consequence, quite "happy."

Q: Does this extreme faith in children result in parents' treating them too permissively?

A: I wouldn't want to generalize, but I believe this does constitute a strong element in upper-middle-class life—in both liberal and conservative families, I might add. It seems to me that such over-permissiveness begins around ages 8, 9 and 10, when the stage is being set for adolescence, and parents begin to ask: "What can we do for these children?" The result in a number of affluent homes has been the "spoiled brat," the self-indulgent youth, the child who lacks tenacity.

Q: What can parents do to avoid this?

A: There are a number of ways open to them. The first thing, I think, is to place less reliance on every new child-rearing fad and psychological philosophy.

Broadly, parents should not only give their children love, but place limits on them. Children need control, and I would go so far as to say that I see nothing wrong with swatting a kid occasionally. Even Dr. [Benjamin] Spock has acknowledged that perhaps he ought to have advised more firmness toward children at certain points in their lives.

An increasing number of parents are learning that children need to be asked of as well as given to. They are realizing the importance of obedience, restraint, the denial of certain goods and gifts, and the willingness to contribute to a family's life as well as to take from a family's affluence. Parents are entitled to assume the right, even an obligation, to hold on to certain ethical propositions, beliefs and standards. For some, this would include a strong religious feeling in the family.

Q: Are parents beginning to realize this?

A: Yes. And I believe that many of the ominous predictions that get momentum from both journalists and social scientists are undercut by the larger elements of life: birth, living and death, and the instinctive desire of people to grow up, have children and grandchildren. The chances are that parents will continue to worry about children, and try to do well by them.

Let me add this: People living 25 years from now, who survived the impact of more television, higher divorce rates, working mothers—and who knows what else—may look back and say:

"You know, in the '70s and '60s, that was a pretty good and solid kind of life we had then."

Rich Kids
Ted Morgan/1977

From *Across the Board* (New York, February 1977, pp. 5–10).
Reprinted by permission of The Conference Board [New York].

To paraphrase the celebration exchange between F. Scott Fitzgerald and Ernest Hemingway:
—*The children of the rich are different from our children.*
—*Yes, their parents have more money.*
After dealing with the children of the poor in the first four volumes of his *Children of Crisis* series, Robert Coles has examined the children of the rich in the final volume, called *Privileged Ones: The Children of the Well-Off and the Rich,* to be published this fall. Coles is a child psychiatrist by training, but his work is at the crossroads of psychology and anthropology. He has spent time with ordinary people rather than sick people. He has left the office to do field work among rural and urban poor, migrant farmers, mountaineers, sharecroppers, Eskimos, Chicanos, and Indians. And he has focused on the attitudes of children. He believes that their responses tell us a great deal about our society.

Coles found his lifework almost by accident. He grew up in Boston, the son of a Yorkshire Jew who came to America as an immigrant and became an engineer, and who married the daughter of an Episcopalian minister from Iowa. Coles went to Boston Latin High School and to Harvard, then decided to become a doctor. Uncomfortable with most medical specialties, he decided on psychiatry and became a pupil of Erik Erikson, who formulated the theory of "identity" as a central psychological concept in such books as *Childhood and Society* and *Young Man Luther.*

Coles went south in the late 1950's to perform his military service in an Air Force psychiatric hospital in Mississippi. One day he saw some blacks being beaten as they tried to integrate a beach. He became interested in the sit-in movement, and in the way the various groups involved reacted under stress. He decided to study the people who were caught up in the desegregation crisis of the 1960's.

In New Orleans in 1960 there was an attempt at token desegregation. Four little black girls volunteered to attend two all-white elementary schools in the eastern section of town. Each morning, Federal marshals escorted the black girls through mobs of angry whites shouting insults. The school was at first boycotted by white pupils, and the black girls were alone with their teachers.

These were the first children Coles studied, the black girls and the white pupils whose parents eventually braved the boycott. It took him weeks to arrange to see the black children. The families were suspicious at first. They had never had a white man come to their door except to take something away from them.

Coles's technique was to talk to the children after school and to ask them to make drawings. He carried crayons everywhere. He became known to children as the Crayon Man. With drawings, Coles felt, children tell you something about their world view, they tell you whether they see themselves as worthwhile or expendable. Six-year-old Ruby, one of the four black girls who were integrating the New Orleans public school system, drew whites larger and more lifelike, and blacks smaller and less intact. A white girl her own size she drew several times taller. Her own face was missing an eye or an ear.

Incredible pressures were being brought to bear on this child of six. Each day she faced the mob, trying to look straight ahead, trying not to hear the shouts, flanked by armed marshals twice her size. One woman yelled the same thing every morning: We're going to poison you until you choke to death. Every day, Ruby was told that she would die from something she ate. As a result, she stopped eating. Her parents wondered why she had lost her appetite. Ruby's story gives some indication of what Coles means by children of crisis.

From this initial experience, Coles went on to interview many more children in many parts of the country, in their homes, in their schools, at basketball games, in parks, in stores, in restaurants. He once rode a school bus across Boston from black Roxbury to a white neighborhood for a year. He did not come up with any statistics, graphs, charts, questionnaires, percentages, or representative samples. What he did have was hundreds of hours of interviews, and experience based on direct observation. He strove to avoid stereotypes. He showed that despite their misery, the poor were often healthy in body and undaunted in spirit. He made his own the central conviction of the writer James Agee that every experience is unique. Agee wrote: "All that each person is, and experiences, and shall ever experience, in body and mind, all these things are differing expressions of himself and of one root, and are identical: and not one of these things nor one of these persons is ever quite to be duplicated, nor replaced, nor has it ever quite had precedent: but each is a new and incommunicably tender life, wounded in every breath and almost as hardly killed as easily wounded: sustaining, for a while, without defense, the enormous assaults of the universe." This was the model Coles had in mind when he wrote *Children of Crisis*.

When the second and third volumes were published, he won the Pulitzer Prize for nonfiction. On February 14, 1972, he was on the cover of *Time* magazine. *Time* said that he was considered "the most influential living psychiatrist in the country." Certainly, more than any other person, he had taken psychiatry off the couch and brought it out of doors to bear on social problems. At 46, Coles has a major body of work behind him with the completion of *Children of Crisis*. In all, he has written 16 books and more than 350 articles. Apparently, he has only two interests, his work and his family (his wife and collaborator Jane and their three sons). Currently, he is on the staff of the Harvard University Health Services and teaches a freshman seminar on some of his favorite writers, among them Orwell, Agee, and Walker Percy.

When Coles was visiting Ruby and her family in New Orleans in 1960, Ruby's nine-year-old sister Vivian asked him: "Why are you studying us? Over here we are only the poor. Not only us but even those white people who are hurting us, they are poor too. If you want to know what's happening in New Orleans, you better go to the Garden District." Coles thought she was teasing, or being provocative. Find out about the poor by studying the rich? But the more he thought about it, the more sense it made. He talked to the Federal judge who was handling the desegregation case, and the judge said, yes, that would be a good idea. And that is how he began to work with provident children, in the earliest stages of his research. All the children he counts as well off had parents who were making $40,000 and up in 1960. He found them in Atlanta, Boston, Princeton; in Connecticut, New York, Illinois, New Mexico, Florida, Texas, and Alaska.

Morgan: *Did you have any problems of access to the rich?*

Coles: That's one of the reasons not enough research has been done on them, they're used to keeping people away. Fortunately they thought I was trustworthy. I wasn't poking or prying. I was a doctor on the staff at Harvard and I had been on the cover of *Time.* I was able to meet the children of the landed gentry, the exurbanites, people with estates and stables and many acres of land. Mine, of course, is not a statistical sample. It's naturalistic observation tied to Agee's early study of sharecroppers, *Let Us Now Praise Famous Men,* or Orwell's *The Road to Wigan Pier.*

Did you believe in the classless society when you started out?

The issue of class is another neglected issue. To be well-to-do in this country I'd say you have to have capital of $500,000 at least. Capital is the definition of wealth. If you have to depend on a salary, you're not rich. Having an annual income of $35,000 or $40,000 from capital gives you a different sense of what the world is like. I don't believe that someone who is making $15,000 a year is middle class. I call them working class. They can be wiped out in a minute. The term middle class connotes stability. Today people making $20,000 or $25,000 are more frightened than ever of their working situation. They have a terrible time keeping up with bills. They have a high standard of living, but without some of the supports and benefits that other societies offer families. They have no health benefits. They are ambitious for their children and put them in private schools. By my father's criteria that's working-class. To be middle class means to have a small degree of protection from the insecurities of economic change.

How did you make your first contacts?

When I was in New Orleans I went to see a prominent lawyer and a stockbroker who had mildly liberal sentiments, mainly because he was afraid the city of New Orleans would be torn apart. I also got to know the children of a New Orleans judge. After that I developed a contrapuntal technique. When I interviewed the children of miners I also interviewed the children of mine owners, children of maids, children of employers, poor urban blacks, and a family that had a tradition of doing philanthropic work in Harlem. In 1966 when I was

working in Roxbury (a black ghetto of Boston), I got to know a
slumlord.

What was your modus operandi with these rich kids?
I talked to them after school and I made contact with the school
people. They were all between 10 and 14, young enough not to be
teenagers and young enough to draw, but old enough to have
formed views of themselves and of what this country is about. I asked
them to make drawings. Drawings are the way children tell you
things.

What did the drawings of the rich tell you?
One thing was what I call the sense of entitlement. One of the
children, when I asked her how she felt about having so much more
than other people, said: "We're entitled to it, my daddy worked
harder to get it." So I turned that into a noun and called it a sense of
entitlement. From this sense they derive the conviction that their
future will be of a certain kind, that they will continue to have the
things they had as children, a good home and a bright future. They
know that they will travel a lot. They take for granted a second home,
skiing in the winter, sailing in the summer. They have a sense of their
position in the world and a sense of real self-assurance about the
future.

They take their material wealth for granted?
Yes, they are surrounded by toys, gadgets, hobbies. They can
indulge in idiosyncratic pursuits. One boy had an enormous
collection of rocks, which he displayed with elaborate fluorescent
lighting. Rich kids draw large toys, in scale with the grandeur of their
lives. They ask for more paper. Ghetto kids don't. One child drew a
hippo. I had never seen a child draw a hippo before. It was an
inflatable pool toy as big as a baby hippo.

*Don't poor children have hobbies too, even it it's only collecting
baseball cards?*
A poor child might clutch at one thing. The nine-year-old daughter
of migrant farm workers drew the suitcase she wanted but did not
have to keep her pitiful belongings together. "I have a few things that
are mine," she said. "The comb, the rabbit's tail my daddy gave me
before he died, the lipstick and the fan, and like that—and I don't

want to go and lose them, and I've already lost a lot of things. I had a luck bracelet and I left it someplace, and I had a scarf, a real pretty one, and it got lost, and a mirror, too." The affluence of the rich child leads him to form a different self-image. One kid drew himself on top of Mount Everest. "What makes you think you'll get up there?" I asked him. "It's been climbed before," he said, "and I really want to do it." Now an Indian child living on a reservation at the foot of the Rockies doesn't draw himself on top of the mountain.

Isn't there a reverse side to the sense of entitlement?

Yes, there's a sense of real concern and worry. There are children who worry how long the country will put up with it. They sense that something is wrong. They've picked up enough concern to express it. They hear their father say that it's getting harder and harder to hang on to what he's got. Watergate affected them. They saw corruption at the highest level. They ask themselves: Will this be the prelude to a fundamental change where the rich and powerful will also be subject to scrutiny, as the President was? Will there be changes in tax laws that are increasingly described as unfair? When Carter refers to big shots, is he talking about us?

Do rich kids generally have more confidence because of the security that wealth brings?

Not necessarily, because here too there's a reverse side which shows these children suffering from insecurities, anxieties, and a sense of jeopardy. Perhaps their mothers have not given them the kind of passionate attention that poor mothers can give. Often they have been moved around for corporate reasons and lived in seven or eight or ten cities. You get a lot of corporate migrants. The children have trouble figuring out what community they belong to. You ask them where they're from and they say they don't know. There is that real problem of upper-class rootlessness. There is a feeling of transience that will affect their own future as parents. In this sense, they begin to resemble migrant farm children who long for a sedentary life even if it means loss of money.

These farm children have no possessions, no room of their own, no place to sleep, no toys. They draw fields that don't belong to them, and roads that go nowhere. Rich children can also be affected by constant mobility. They can feel great anger at being wrenched

from the friends they've made. They can feel great resentment
against the corporate life.

What about the ones who stay put?
Wealthy parents often entrust their children to servants and
governesses. You see examples that seem to come out of Victorian
novels. I'm not talking so much about the cruelty of particular
individuals as about the transience of these people. They are
replaced, or they go away. The children are involved in a tug-of-war
of sorts, either between servants or between servants and parents.
They are caught in the middle.

*My father was raised by an English governess. When my grand-
father fired her, my father was so grief-stricken that he threw himself
out a second-story window. Fortunately he landed in a hedge.*
Yes, and on the other hand poor children can have a very firm
relationship with their parents. Of course everything I come up with
novelists have known beforehand. There are rich children who are
impoverished in their families.

*Would you say, then, that your work confirms the stereotype of the
poor little rich kid?*
I want to avoid generalizations. What I've tried to show is the range
of possibilities. There are strong and intact rich families, with mothers
and fathers who are deeply concerned about their children and who
are able to exact from them cultured behavior and achievements
based on love and caring. And there are children who know how to
best make use of what has been given in such abundance. At the
other limit you get disappointed, embattled, sad families loaded with
money and also with self-destructiveness.

Do rich kids ever develop a social conscience?
Yes, they hear things talked about at home. Or they may have an
older brother who comes home from college with radical ideas. Or
they form some sort of ethical view. They go to church, they pick up
notions of social justice. Or their private school may have been
infiltrated by liberal teachers. You get a snowball effect. If the parent
takes the kid on, you get social questions reduced to family conflict,
with the child asking: Why are we so rich when others are so poor?
The son of a Florida grower heard a minister's sermon and asked his

father why the children of the migrant workers were living in such wretched poverty. "Where'd you get that crazy idea?" the father asked. "If it weren't for me they wouldn't have jobs." The boy wasn't satisfied. He kept asking, he kept inquiring. Finally the father sent him out for counseling.

Ah, here we come to the secret weapon that the rich have to control their children.

Yes, that is the solution for the rich—they can send children who do not share their assumptions to a child psychiatrist. Our profession serves to maintain the status quo. I've seen enough of this to be prompted to reflect about the nature of my profession and to wonder about the parent who comes to me and asks: Don't you think that a child talking like this should get some professional help? They may have been told by the school psychologist that it's better to nip those ideas in the bud. They never address themselves to the substance or the justice of the child's observations. If you don't like what someone is saying, you can call them antisocial or pre-delinquent and point to a family conflict to condemn the child's behavior. One rich child watching a television program about Robin Hood concluded that stealing from the rich to give to the poor was a fine idea. When he confided his views to his family, he was sent out for counseling. This is using psychology as an instrument of repression: If you don't like what a kid is saying you call him disturbed. I am not in favor of the use of psychologists in education. The privilege of private schools of calling on psychologists amounts to the introduction of a gratuitous outside system. You get a guy who becomes an agent of the political authority of the school. It's better to have that authority open and aboveboard than to have it disguised under the term mental health. This is a problem that is essentially limited to the children of the rich. Who else can pay $50, $75 or $100 an hour to the 500 or so child psychiatrists in this country?

What about poor children who don't share the assumptions of their parents?

The poor are struggling with the external forces of repression. Although, in the rural South black parents still punish children who try to be independent and talk back to whites. "Either you better understand how to deal with white folks," I heard a black mother tell

her son, "or I'm going to take a strap to your backside." They teach
their kids to sit there and bite their tongues.

*So some of the problems of growing up are common to children of
every economic level.*
Yes, and another interesting feature is that rich children will adopt
the wariness and suspicion that is usually associated with lower-class
kids. The question is: Who can you trust if you're rich? Whose
statements do you trust? What are people's motives? They may be
trying to ingratiate themselves. A poor kid will say of school: "I think
a lot of teachers decide about you by the first week. Then you're
lucky or unlucky." But a rich kid will suspect flattery from a teacher
and say, as a 10-year old said: "When daddy sends a check, he gets a
nice letter back. He's shown it to me—because the principal says nice
things, when he's getting hundreds of dollars—thousands, I think."
You see a great deal of money consciousness, which is ironic since
they have so much of it. A 12-year-old boy in Boston worried that
someday he might have to live off capital, which would make him a
failure in the eyes of his father. A six-year old girl in New Orleans
knew that someday she was going to inherit $500,000. These kids
are aware of what money can do, and how it affects the judgment
that others have of them. They can use money to become little
plotters with manipulative schemes. In other cases, where the parents
know how to handle it, they transmit the beneficent aspects of money
rather than the paranoid, exploitative, arrogant aspects.

So it can go either way.
That's it, wealth can be either an opportunity or a hazard for a
child. It can be yet another psychological pitfall or it can be a part of
healthy growth.

*Does wealth sometimes lead to a lack of drive or ambition, since
they already have as a birthright what it takes others a lifetime to
earn?*
Yes, in many homes you see a diffusion of goals that comes from
too many possibilities. But that can become a stereotype. Other
families are able to transmit ambition to their children in the form of
the Puritan ethic or a pride in the family name. They derive strength
from their heritage. Here again you get the two sides, those families

who don't know how to handle wealth and transmit their mistakes
to their children, and those families who are able to transmit a sense
of purpose and motivation.

Doesn't great wealth insulate you from the real world?
Yes, estate living removes you from reality. Some of these kids
never see another house. They come to the city to go to the
symphony or the theater. No wonder they draw themselves in the
middle of a lot of land which is obviously theirs, or on a horse. Poor
kids don't portray themselves as landowners or on horseback. If you
show me 100 drawings and 25 come from rich kids I will be able to
tell you which ones they are, and I don't mean to sound self-serving.

But fragments of reality do reach these kids, through newspapers,
television, teachers, or older brothers. Despite the protection, a
curious kid will find out. They can create their own vision of the
world despite the Maginot Line of wealth.

Does it last?
It becomes tougher as the child gets older and is admitted to the
largely unobserved rituals of the rich. We know the rituals of the
poor. The ghetto kid is taken by his parents to the welfare office. This
is part of his education. He is learning the dependency of his family,
and how rudely and condescendingly he can expect to be treated as
an adult. The rich kid, meanwhile, is taken to have lunch with the
trust officer at the bank. That is part of his education. He is learning
that he will always be financially self-sufficient, and that as a result he
will always be treated with respect.

Robert Coles: Doctor of Crisis

Paul Wilkes/1978

From *The New York Times Magazine* (cover story, March 26, 1978, pp. 14–66). Reprinted by permission of Paul Wilkes and *The New York Times.*

In the late 1950's, dozens of idealistic young men and women went to Kenneth Clark for direction. He was an academic, black, articulate, and already a veteran in the movement—civil rights—they wanted, fervently, to join. He remembers one of them well: "Bob Coles didn't smile, didn't have any rhetoric; there was a curious kind of solidness, seriousness about him. He said that everybody up at Harvard thought he was crazy because he didn't want to practice as the child psychiatrist he'd been trained to be, but he wanted to study what would happen to these black kids who were integrating Southern schools. He asked if his being white would prevent that. Hell, I'm a paranoid black and I felt at home with him; I knew that anybody could trust him."

While many once-passionate "movement" voices are silent, and faces once highly visible are now unseen, Dr. Robert Coles has continued to study and write about the people who remain oppressed. With a doctor's black bag, a notebook, tape recorder and the paper and crayons with which children draw the landscapes of their lives, he has crisscrossed the country, pointing up the strength and dignity of the shadowy poor, while showing how ubiquitous "socioeconomic forces" rule their lives. There has been a prodigious outpouring of words—30 books and more than 550 articles—a Pulitzer and numerous other prizes, honorary degrees, reams of testimony before Congress and the courts.

However, Dr. Clark sees Coles's importance in other terms: "He's one of those people you can always look to and know that hope is alive. I don't know if he's one of the 10 just men required to keep this world spinning around but . . . you can't judge him by normal standards any more than you could Martin Luther King; they are men possessed."

The 48-year-old man under discussion looks out on a bleak
Massachusetts day from his home in Concord, runs his hand through
coarse dark hair which looks as if it had been playfully blunt cut by
one of his three children. Of medium height, he is slightly stooped
and wears an oxford-cloth shirt with a frayed collar. His mannerisms,
his high-pitched nasal voice, are more like those of a tortured
adolescent than of an influential writer and thinker.

"Listen, anyone who publishes as much as I do has a towering
ego," he says. "I must feel I have something important to say. Pride,
arrogance. God, do I have a good dose of both! It all frightens me,
but I don't know what to do. I leave a migrant's home and go back to
a comfortable motel and I'm positively haunted. And then I'm
tempted: Write a sex book, how to do it a million ways, get a six-
figure paperback sale. The hell with all this business. What am I
fighting? It's hopeless. Then I think about that coal miner who has to
go into a dark hole to survive and realize that I have to go in there
with him—and write about him—for my survival."

With the completion of Coles's five-volume, million-word series
called *Children of Crisis* and the publication this June of *Women of
Crisis: Lives of Struggle and Hope,* it's a good time to take a close
look at both the body and the impact of his work, and at the public
and private man some so unabashedly praise. In the *Children of
Crisis* series, Coles has taken a sprawling look at America, through its
children, during these two tumultuous decades of social change. And
in the process he has virtually invented "social psychiatry"—a
combination of anthropological and journalistic reporting, oral history
and psychological analysis. He started with school desegregation
and moved to the plight of the sons and daughters of migrants,
sharecroppers and mountaineers; then to Southerners who moved
North supposedly to better their lives. Just issued by his publishers,
Atlantic-Little, Brown, are *Eskimos, Chicanos, Indians,* and *Privileged
Ones: The Well Off and the Rich in America,* a book inspired by a
poor child who told him: "The rich folks are the ones who decide
how poor folks live."

In *Women of Crisis,* Coles (who collaborated with his wife, Jane)
presents portraits of five poor women, who, far from wallowing in
apathetic resignation, rise up from the pages in towering strength and
simple dignity. These, the doubly oppressed, by being both poor and

female, show an uncanny ability to survive in a hostile world
and to understand how it works. Ruth James, a migrant worker, has
insights into her crew leader and minister that rival, if not surpass,
those of Coles, the trained observer. In studying children, Coles
looked into their unconscious minds by interpreting their drawings.
Here, with adults, he includes their dreams, thus rounding out the
characterizations by probing out the darker corners of their
psyches.

The seed for the book was planted in 1960 by the simple but
weighty words of Ruby Bridges, a 6-year-old black girl whom Coles
was studying as, all by herself after three other black children
dropped out, she integrated a New Orleans grade school. Ruby was
being encouraged by an older black woman to be strong, to cry to
herself but greet the world with a confident smile. The child thought
for a moment, then said, "If you're a man, you can be nice to your
enemy and get away with it. If you're a woman, you probably *have*
to be nice to your enemy and you may not get away with it." Years
passed, and Coles continued his relationship with Ruby, who,
without being a proponent of the new women's consciousness, knew
that poor women faced unique problems and, as Ruby said, were
people "who aren't mentioned in a lot of the books we've been
reading in our high-school social-studies course." Then, when Ruby
entered college, she virtually forced Coles to do this book by saying,
"There comes a time when some 'children of crisis' become 'women
of crisis.' That's important—what happens to us then?" Some time
later, Matina Horner, the president of Radcliffe, and Seymour
Lawrence, the publisher, jointly asked Coles to write about the
women he found in his travels for a series that would show "how it
has gone and still goes for women quite different in important
respects" from the students or other women who buy books in an
attempt to "come to terms with themselves and their world as
women."

It was a logical spinoff for Coles, who has probably come in
contact with more and more varied women from different poor
cultures than anyone else in the field. Now that the book is about to
be published by Delacorte Press/Seymour Lawrence, however, he
will go back to studying children, this time outside America—in strife-
ridden Ireland, politically tumultuous Italy and racially volatile South

Africa. His methodology has been and will be the same: a decep-
tively simple approach of getting to know families and talking to them
over a period of years, asking few questions and allowing them to
lead him to the issues that lie deep in their lives.

In his writing, he has concentrated not on pathology, but on
possibility. For instance, he finds that both youngsters born in
poverty in Appalachian hollows and in silk-stocking families have
inherent reserves; that newly integrated Southern schools caused less
anxiety than the racially imbalanced schools in the North; that a
strong family life is a bulwark against any traumatic change. Because
he talked to blacks and segregationists, mine workers and owners,
policemen and suspects, maid and lady of the house, and their
children, Coles has "contributed antistereotypes," according to David
Riesman, the sociologist and co-author of *The Lonely Crowd.*
"Policemen are not pigs," says Riesman, "white Southerners are not
rednecks and blacks are not all suffering in exotic misery. The child
who had to be escorted by Federal marshals into an all-white school
can gather strength and courage to face other crises in life."

Although Coles's work has generally been received well, there is a
consistent theme among his critics: The books are too long,
predictable, and they lack focus. In *The New York Times* review of
the second and third volumes, which later won the Pulitzer,
Christopher Lehmann-Haupt said, ". . . the two present volumes
reveal so many things, pursue so many routes, imply so many
possible responses and suggest so many different conclusions that
altogether they add up to nothing at all and leave the reader numbed
and bewildered."

Joseph Epstein, in *Commentary,* called Coles "the prototypical
liberal who, by virtue of understanding everything, finally disqualifies
himself from taking a position on anything." In an interview, Epstein
goes further. "What bothers me most is that Coles is an ideologue
with a left program, masquerading as a high priest of our culture and
a pseudo-scientist. This so-called documentary method: What is left
out? Everything that doesn't jibe with his thinking? He has 'soft
authority' and he doesn't say anything dangerous, the good doctor.
No bite to him, just nibbles."

"He's criticized," Kenneth Clark responds, "for not being 'scientific,' which means he doesn't treat people like objects, as we were

trained to do as so-called professionals. Listen, anybody who can make me understand—and like—some white racist, as Coles did in *The Middle Americans,* is doing something very right. Who cares if he's not classifiable; like any original thinker, he's broken down the artificial academic barriers." Father Andrew Greeley, whose work at the National Opinion Research Center relies heavily on sophisticated polls, says, "I'm terribly skeptical of any study without numbers and hard facts but when Coles writes, you are inside the culture. What's better, to look at a computer printout on Eskimos or to be able to live inside one of them as I did—through Coles?"

"It scares me to death," Coles says, "that someone might get a formula out of one of these books. Like Oscar Lewis had this 'culture of poverty' concept—I just didn't believe it. In the book on the rich kids, I used a term—'entitlement'—to describe how kids feel about their lives, their prerogatives. And I got 20 letters thanking me for this great insight. I'm embarrassed; I didn't put enough quote marks around that word."

Now that the series is complete, Coles is careful not to link the suffering that hunger might cause a poor child with the emotional deprivation a child in a wealthy home might feel, but his message is clear. Children are resilient, courageous and healthy in mind—up to a point. That is the promise. The problem is that, as they grow older, inadequately educated, lacking in opportunities and shunned by society, poor children are more likely to give in. And the rich ones will grow more protective of their prerogatives.

To see Robert Coles in public is to realize why the people he studies find him so easy to talk with. If anything, they must take pity on him. There is a childlike innocence, a vague sort of confusion that belies the intelligence within. When he was in Washington to give a talk, he was reduced to a boyish giggle and a helpless shrug when a balky turnstile in the subway would not accept his 30-cent fare card. Even more subtle is the inner confusion, the struggle to lead a forthright life. His fame drives him inward. He cannot comfortably bask in the limelight.

He had accepted the offer of Joseph Duffey, the new chairman of the National Endowment for the Humanities, to speak at his swearing-in. It was an opportunity to stand before Washington's elite—before Vice President and Mrs. Mondale, before Rosalynn

Carter—as a hero of the humanities. Coles was one of four speakers (but, incidentally, Duffey's first choice) and he bluntly stated his position. "The humanities," Coles said, "in the hands of some, can come down to precious, bloated and murky prose. But the humanities at their best give testimony to man's continuing effort to make moral, philosophical and spiritual sense of this world." Then he quickly turned not to some well-known sources, but to a factory worker's concept of the humanities: "I tell my children to stop themselves every few days and look up at the sky, and listen to their conscience, and remember what they should believe in: Give out as good as you want to get."

At the reception following, as guests sought out the man whose talk they had responded to with the loudest applause, they found that Coles was off in a corner, alone. The half-hour until he would leave for the airport to return home was a study in a white-knuckled hand clenching a frosted beer mug. Like Groucho Marx and Woody Allen, he is a man ill at ease with any club that would have him. A well-tailored man and an elegant woman expressed appreciation for the talk and Coles's work in general. He mumbled some thank-yous and as the couple walked away his mind turned, oddly enough, to Kierkegaard. "Cheap grace. So tempting. So easy. So comfortable." The crest of white at the tips of his knuckles spread. Suddenly he broke into a smile. "Let's get out of here or I'll be toadying like the rest of them."

At Harvard, Coles's Spartan basement office is a crossroads of conscience. He is attached to the Harvard University Health Services staff, which sounds impressive but translates into no staff or salary but the paper clips, photocopying machine and academic affiliation he needs to continue his work. Students he has taught, young doctors, others looking for ways to channel their own lives into some meaningful work, come to seek his advice.

Says Gay Seidman, a former editor of The Crimson, who took Coles's course, Social Sciences 33: Moral and Social Inquiry: "The typical Harvard point of view is, 'If you were a policy maker, what would you do if. . . .' Coles has been out there studying and writing, but he doesn't hide behind his books; he's that rare kind of teacher who puts his life up for appraisal. He's struggling right alongside us."

Recently, Coles delivered a lecture in his course—which was

quickly oversubscribed at registration and subsequently renamed by students "Guilt 33"—about William Carlos Williams, the doctor-poet whose dual careers influenced him profoundly. "He had his biases, his hates; people he treated were suspicious of him," Coles told the packed lecture hall. "Yet he had this painful, overwhelming desire to help them. He was torn by the lure of the good life. . . . Don't try for an exegesis of his poetry; get inside this doctor's head as he looks at society. We all can take courses and quote from his poetry and then spend two months working the ghetto, thinking we've done our share. Then we go on about our lives and say, 'Well, I have my children to worry about now. . . .' We all have to ask, 'Have we done enough?' "

After class, a young woman lashed out at Coles: "I just feel like you're taking my freedom away. Like you expect me to act the way you would."

To an audience, Coles can be indignant; to a single, threatened Radcliffe undergraduate, he cannot. "It's my goddamn arrogance, my training, my education," he blurted out, the voice even more nasal, more plaintive.

"The way you talk, I have to feel that the ultimate goal is to apply it to my life," she returned.

"I'm sorry. I just try to give you some experiences that have touched my life, moved me. It's such a tightrope. I'm sorry."

His small seminar and this lecture course are anomalies at Harvard—as is his very presence. Few faculty members are aware that he teaches, although he is well-known to students. A tutor laughed out loud when one of his students said she was taking the course; he pronounced it "not exactly rigorous." And even the students have given Coles a mixed review. "Everybody loves Coles and respects him," says Gay Seidman, "but then there are some lectures that are just ordinary and mundane, or 'famous or well-meaning people I've known or read.' He's been too busy to prepare them well. When Coles talks about himself, he's the best, but the bind is that if he really means what he says, what's he doing talking to preppies with Gucci loafers; what is he doing at Harvard?"

"It's home to me in a way," Coles says, "I was an undergraduate here, met Erik Erikson, David Riesman, great men. Maybe I should be teaching working-class kids over at Northeastern or U. Mass., but I

love it here; the brightest kids from all over the country, a sharecropper's son and a President's daughter sitting next to each other.
I'm more establishment than I want to admit. I criticize the arrogance,
the narrowness, of Harvard, and, look, I'm part of it."

As a child psychiatrist, at least by training, Coles is aware that the
roots of his own personal conflicts (to name just two, middle-class
values versus lower-class affinity; the desire for fame and the fear of
its possible corrupting effect) go back to his own childhood. It was
not one of "crisis," as he has written of it, but one with certain
conflicts. His father was politically conservative, a cool, rational
M.I.T.-trained engineer who took his sons, Robert and William (now
a University of Michigan English professor), on long walks, during
which he pointed out where neighborhoods changed, what group
lived there and what they did. He did it, Coles recalls, "without
sentiment or compassion but with a great eye for facts." His mother
was warmer, a religious woman, almost mystical, who knew the Bible
well. When young Bob brought home a good report card, her paise
was always leavened with admonishments about the sin of pride and
the dangers of worldliness. It was implied that the Coles boys were to
do something significant—but neither commercial nor showy—with
their lives.

From the start, Coles was a loner and a seeker. He went to the
prestigious Boston Latin School, then Harvard (Phi Beta Kappa in
English), where with the late Perry Miller he studied the classics of the
Christian tradition from St. Augustine through Kierkegaard. He
found resonant voices that spoke to him down through the centuries,
but he had no response for them.

While doing a paper on William Carlos Williams, Coles was
encouraged to see him. Williams not only welcomed the awkward
Harvard undergraduate, but took him along as he visited working-
class homes in Paterson, N.J. After each visit, Coles saw this warm,
outgoing family doctor return quickly to his car. Before he would
speak to Coles, he'd pull out a pad from the glove compartment and
write down "what he had learned from the people," Coles recalls.
"He was genuinely a doctor but he was positively driven—I mean
driven—to put down on paper what he had seen."

At Columbia University College of Physicians and Surgeons, Coles
found himself repelled by the competition, by classmates who would

laugh when someone broke a flask in the laboratory. He almost
flunked out. To make his life bearable, he took courses from
Reinhold Niebuhr at Union Theological Seminary and read the Bible
with a couple of fellow students. By his own admission, he was a
"priggish snob."

After spending two "genuinely happy days" in pediatrics during his
rotation, Coles decided on that as his specialty. "Somehow," he says,
"I had found an age group I could relate to." He continued his
studies at the University of Chicago and in Boston hospitals, but
found his life continually bombarded with stimuli he didn't know how
to assimilate. He heard Anna Freud lecture about studies of English
children during German air attacks and the necessity of "direct
observation" of children. In Paul Tillich's course in systematic
theology, the concept of "the courage to be" thudded against the
turmoil in his brain. Tillich didn't talk about "life's work" or "occu-
pation;" he talked about "personal commitment as a religious act."

Coles had already discovered it was wrenching for him to draw
blood and cause a baby to cry. He desperately decided to go further
in his schooling and become a child psychiatrist, thus putting off his
confrontation with the workaday world. However, the studies, the
techniques, the terms still seemed inhuman. Instead of giving tests or
talking to his young patients in hospital-green clinic rooms, he took
them to the Boston Museum of Fine Arts and had them draw for
him. His unconventional methods were viewed with humor by his
classmates, with scorn by some of his professors. A doctor, sprawled
on a museum floor, laughing with a child!

In 1958, having used up every device to delay launching himself
into life, he was drafted into the Air Force. He applied for San
Francisco and Tokyo. He got Biloxi, Miss., and arrived in the South
more confused than ever, driving a white Porsche with red leather
seats that he bought in memory of James Dean, the "Rebel Without
a Cause" actor who was killed in a similar car. His life had become
unbearable, Coles concluded, so he began five-times-a-week analysis
in New Orleans. He would race from Biloxi after work, have a
session, spend the night, have another session in the morning, and
speed back to work. Capt. Robert Coles was chief of neuropsychiatric services at Keesler Hospital, quite the ladies' man, con-

stantly depressed and chronically fatigued. The only real pleasure he recalls from those days was driving the Porsche. Fast.

In his analysis with Dr. Kenneth Beach, he learned the obvious: He had finally unified his parents—against him—by choosing the airy field of psychiatry as a specialty. And he found himself hating the South, overinvolved with his own patients, unhappy, aimless. "Doing" therapy was too passive, yet he didn't know what else to do, especially after all his years of study.

But, also in analysis, he found a place where he could express those unspecified desires he had to help people. Where once he had tried to keep his idealistic and bewildered self hidden from other doctors, he now gave his hopes and dreams full reign. The thoughts of Kierkegaard, Tillich, Anna Freud, of writers such as George Orwell and James Agee, began to jell. "I knew there were people out there just like me," he concluded, "and they found something to do."

One Sunday morning, Coles was riding his bicycle back from church and the angry shouts at a shallow-water beach on the Gulf stopped him. Four blacks were trying to integrate the beach, which was on Federal land. That night, Coles was on duty at the hospital when the policemen who had arrested the blacks came in to cool off in the air-conditioned emergency room. "Goddamn niggers. We'll kill 'em next time."

Coles was overwhelmed. He knew these policemen, knew them to be decent men. As a psychiatrist he could sense their fear; as a man, he could see their rage. How must the objects of that rage feel?

For Coles, the pieces fell into place; he would later call the incident a "religious experience." The social idealism of his childhood, his training, this obviously historical time in the nation's life when blacks were beginning their long march for equality—all added up to something. Not only did he embark on a work that would involve him for the next two decades, but perhaps for the rest of his life. At his next session, his analyst's interpretation (that the conflict triggered by the incident wasn't necessarily rooted in "childhood neurosis," but could be a clarifying insight into what Coles wanted for his adult life) not only comforted him, but made him a believer in analysis, a field he had studied, had never quite trusted, and would later criticize. (When Coles has lashed out, it has been against the dogmatic forms of therapy and "pagan, idolatrous, insulting and vulgar self-help books that promise salvation this afternoon.")

His tour of duty over, Coles settled in Vinings, Ga., near Atlanta, with his new bride, Jane Hallowell, whom he had met and married in Boston. He began visiting in the homes of black children, embarrassedly, clumsily "sitting there with a dumb look on my face, asking all the wrong questions," he recalls. "They were silent, withdrawn. What was this white doctor doing in their houses, worried about their problems?"

Then he visited the black children at school, rode the bus with them. He talked to white students and their parents who opposed integration. He applied for foundation grants, and got form rejection slips. "What will be your results?" they asked. He didn't know. His parents and Jane's grandmother provided the young couple with about $4,500 a year, on which they lived until the first grant came through from the New World Foundation. His tenacity, his entrée to the families as a doctor who treated their illnesses at no charge, eventually won their trust. After eight years of observation, thought and writing, Coles published the first volume of *Children of Crisis,* about school desegregation, in 1967.

One of the children Coles writes about in that book is Ruby Bridges, the lone black to integrate the first grade of a New Orleans school in 1960—and the child who subsequently spurred Coles and his wife to produce *Women of Crisis.* Her father lost his job, she was threatened daily on her way to class, was told her lunch was poisoned and was alone in a classroom, except for her teacher, for more than a year. She is now 22, a travel-agent trainee in New Orleans, and her most vivid memories of those days are not of the horrors or indignities, but of a Boston doctor who "was like a father to me," she says. "I would draw for him and we'd talk and he'd take me up to the corner for Cokes and come back and set to table with my mother and father. We didn't mix much with white folks then, but it just seemed natural to have him around. Don't know why but I just remember him as good. People always ask me how I can even look a white person in the eye after going through what I did. But it didn't work that way. I don't have bad memories about it; never had a bad dream. We just elected a black mayor in New Orleans; I can go into any restaurant I want. I guess I helped get that started."

Paralleling Coles's field work in the South was his involvement in the civil-rights movement. "He was S.N.C.C.'s resident shrink, and when people got to the cracking point he was there for them," says author Pat Watters, who was an Atlanta journalist during those years. "He wasn't a day-tripper either; he was there month after month." Coles had guns put to his head, was in a home that was dynamited, and was investigated by the F.B.I. But he found himself more sure of what he was doing. While S.N.C.C.'s student activists were often derided as mentally ill, Coles felt comfortable with them. He was, in fact, exhilarated by the likes of Andrew Young, now the American Ambassador to the United Nations, and Julian Bond, now a Georgia legislator. "He was a model for grace under the pressure of those days," Bond recalls. "We had one fellow demonstrating against us who'd been accused and acquitted of bombing a synagogue; a real hater, this guy. Coles just patiently drew him out and the guy burst out in tears one day and sobbed to Bob that his mother always hated him and somehow he was getting back at her. I know it sounds theatrical, but he had this special way with people."

Although his *Children of Crisis* series showed a restrained, hopeful and accepting observer, Coles almost from the start wrote more pointed articles and books—muckraking journalism—exposing social ills, such as unhealthy mining conditions, pesticide dangers, malnutrition and poor health services. His book *Still Hungry in America* helped launch the food-stamp program and his testimony before Senate committees "forced people to have an attitude toward the poor because he made them so human and believable," says Michael Harrington, who wrote *The Other America.*

Field work, an awesome amount of writing and testifying—all the product of a man with no staff, who works only with his wife and who writes in longhand on yellow legal pads, hoping to fill four pages a day, about 1,600 words. His other books have ranged from *Erik H. Erikson, The Growth of His Work* to *The Geography of Faith,* conversations with Father Daniel Berrigan while he was underground; also children's books on such subjects as drugs, school desegregation and runaways.

Children of Crisis —and its author—have undergone an interesting transition since the first volume, as Coles readily acknowledges. "I had looked for representative types of children all along," Coles says, "those who would bring out what was stressful, instructional, significant. Now I'm trying to make it more artful and readable by selecting statements and then using whatever writing ability I've acquired in the past 10 years to shape it into an interesting story." Paul Starr, in *The New York Times Book Review,* in a generally complimentary review, noted that only Volume 1 was "tightly written" and that Coles had become "self-consciously poetic" in the later works. But in *Newsweek,* Peter S. Prescott, while praising Coles, charged him with "fixing the deck" by combining the words of children with more lyrical writing, but Prescott added, "Surprising myself, I don't mind."

"We have to consider another point in evaluating this man," says Kenneth Clark. "Here is a doctor, a psychiatrist with Boston accent, Harvard degree, who tells about scurvy and low hemoglobin counts, and all the folks in Washington have to listen and question: What manner of man is this? If he sacrificed a fat practice and an easy life, maybe he's saying something that might be true." Father Greeley, not known for showering praise, comments, "He's a man set apart from the rest of us. I used to think of him as a secular saint, but I have to change that. I'd remove the word 'secular.'"

Erik Erikson, who through his teaching, writing (especially *Childhood and Society*) and long walks he took with Coles, showed him that to understand children one must view them in a social and anthropological setting, broke his customary silence with the press to comment on his younger colleague: "He was never one to be caught in formulas, to accept simple answers. He appealed to me as a man in a field who kept on asking questions while so many others had ready answers. His way is deceptive; hardly forceful; I'd call it almost apologetic, but somehow I knew he would be great. To compare him to anyone would be an injustice; he has done fundamental work that others will be building upon for years. And he's a man of deep religious convictions, which, in these times, makes some people only smile."

As Erikson influenced Coles, now Coles is beginning to set a tone and style for younger observer-writers. One of them, Thomas Cottle, a clinical psychologist who has backed away from setting up a practice, says Coles's greatest contribution to him was to "lead me down a path of unemployment. I used to yawn when I wrote and I'm sure people yawned when they read me, a prototypical academic. Coles showed me that it's possible to walk a risky path outside the disciplines that box you in and outside the institutions that will eat you up like a cancer you don't even know is growing. I admire the man and I'm jealous; it's like he's the elephant in the field and I'm one of the fleas. Usually the elephants are so insecure that they have to stamp out the fleas. Instead, he puts me up on his shoulders; he's always encouraging. He's not negative enough, so he's not considered an intellectual, but nobody has influenced me more in my life."

You might call it *"Angst* central," the office in his home where Coles does most of his writing. He may be the friendly visitor with his subject in the field, but here he has chosen to be scrutinized by pictures of people who, by their life and work, openly challenge him. Among them, Simone Weil, a tortured, frail French writer who literally starved herself to death when the Resistance wouldn't send her on a dangerous mission; George Orwell ("People think of *1984* and forget his exposés of capitalism, of the coal mines"); The Catholic Worker's Dorothy Day; Walker Percy ("Ten pages of *The Moviegoer* are worth all the words I've written"), and George S. Bernanos, whose *The Diary of a Country Priest* is Coles's favorite book. ("He fought the temptation to ignore life's uncertainties and ambiguities.")

His children at school, his wife resting from a touch of pneumonia she has just contracted, his blind and deaf dog, Grady, curled in a chair, Robert Coles paces in front of the window. In this room, the demands are implicit: He must test himself against the courage, the literary ability of these people. It is a constant self-analysis for the analyst, and as he talks now he cannot stand still. When Robert Coles is unsure about how to handle a section of a book, he paces; when he faces the dark side of his own nature, he must do the same:

"Pride, pride. Of course, I wonder whether I'll be an important person and whether I have the 'unreflecting egoism' that George Eliot talks about. I wrestle with my greed and my self-centeredness all the time. I love the Ritz and the Plaza, I get sick to my stomach when I see lice on children or flies buzzing around food. I couldn't take migrant work after a single day; my body ached; I wanted a shower and someplace clean to sleep." He turns around. "Then I look up at them and realize they struggled with faith and belief and fought not to succumb to the secular culture. And I just go on. As St. Augustine said, 'I know I have sinned, yet I keep on sinning.' So I keep on writing.

"Like anybody, I have my passions, I have my hates. Hitler, Stalin, Exxon, Gulf, the rich, the insensitive, the powerful. A man like Russell Long who blocks tax reform and national health insurance. And here's a man whose father, Huey, had genuine concern for poor people." He smiled. "Maybe we should study Russell's Oedipal conflict."

With the day becoming darker, Coles's mood shifts. He knows how brooding and introspective he can be and how ultimately, again, he can come up with no easy solutions. "After all, I could be guilty all the time," he says, now seated at his desk, with his hands behind his head, "and what have I done for Botswana today? And what about Volume XIII of *Children of Crisis?* I think there's a plane leaving for Botswana at 9 o'clock tonight. I've got to be on it. I haven't done enough today." He is grinning.

His life is hardly strewn with the privation he has written about, and Coles admits a certain uneasiness about his spacious but modest house, set on three secluded acres. He derives his income from a yearly grant from the Ford Foundation, from teaching, a bit from lecturing and articles, and the rest from the sales of his books (royalties from three books go to the Southern Regional Council and The Catholic Worker), none of which has ever been a book-club selection nor sold more than 25,000 hard-cover copies. "It's a common dilemma: I work with the poor, but I am a middle-class doctor, a writer. If I would give away everything and live with the poor, would it help relieve poverty in this country?" He quickly answers: "Of course not." Then he looks up at the wall.

For a man who has traveled so much, Cole is very much the family man, making sure that he sees his three sons, Bobby, Daniel (whose middle name is Agee) and Michael, off to school in the morning before starting his work or leaving for Cambridge. He is often home before they return and keeps his office door open, hoping for interruptions. He and Jane have moved their family with them as the work has taken them to various parts of the country. Theirs is a quiet life, wrapped up with their children and the work.

In his dealings with his own children, he tries to forget that he is a psychiatrist and has exhaustively studied the strains that children endure. "We psychiatrists learn about character disorder, but in raising children, what does that have to say about character? Kids need affection and discipline, not analyzing." Coles finds the way he and Jane raise their children is no different from their own upbringing. No pat theories, but a special emphasis on social concerns. When coal miners went on strike, the family talked about the impact and the two older boys had a series of pertinent questions, ranging from what had the miners done for Christmas to would they be eligible for welfare payments?

Often, wives of famous men are patted on the head for "standing behind me," but Coles speaks of his Jane in different terms. "Not many Radcliffe girls of her generation would have put furniture in storage and moved to a little house in Georgia on such an ill-defined mission. I'm sure if I had married someone else, my life wouldn't have turned out the same. A lot of those families only talked to me because they liked Jane. I had these impossible questions and she would ask them for a recipe. And when it was going rough and I didn't know what I was doing and I'd get down, she was always ready to push on. She'd tell me if I didn't go out to do the interviews, she would. She's from that sturdy New England Abolitionist stock. And she's the one, when I was drinking a lot of bourbon and was trying to imitate Agee's style, who just told me to stop it and write like a doctor."

Jane and Bob Coles are affectionate with each other; not only do they lightly kiss hello and goodbye, but there is always a warm hug, like that for a good friend. Jane usually answers the phone at home (sometimes they simply shut it off to spend a quiet evening), thus deflecting some of the calls. Otherwise, she is housewife and mother, good-naturedly oblivious to the call that women must have a career of their own.

In a cabinet off to the side of Coles's desk are huge files on what will be his next series of works. He is going abroad soon to study how children are taught nationalism, political loyalty, an ideological system. "How can a child in Belfast throw a grenade? When do the children in Soweto say, 'Enough,' and strike back? Simone Weil said that tyranny is handed down from family to family; I want to look into that." For this work Coles will seek more substantial financial help and will, for the first time, use co-researchers.

"One thing," he says late one evening as he looks up again at the pictures on his wall, "I know that these people aren't demanding that I go anyplace or write anything. That wasn't their style. You see, I speak and write with so much altruism, but I'm so weak. I remember when Dan Berrigan was underground and we hid him here at the house, I was terribly nervous. I saw him part of the way to his next stop, Block Island, and then I caught a train from Westport that was going into New York. All those Wall Street guys, all those Brooks Brothers suits. They all could have been Secret Service. And I was so happy to be safe, to be with them. Courage to be, indeed, Dr. Coles."

The Doctor-as-Patient

George Abbott White/1980

From *Harvard Medical Alumni Bulletin* (Boston, MA, April 1980, pp. 18–21). Reprinted by permission of the Harvard Medical Alumni Association.

What do you mean by the doctor-as-patient?

First of all, the doctor as one who *is* patient; patient in the Latin sense of *patior:* able to respond to suffering, feeling the suffering within oneself, long-suffering in the old-fashioned sense of being willing to ride out the ups and downs of illness with patients and, inevitably, becoming part of that process. I believe that is what Christ meant, when He said, 'Physician heal thyself.' After all, long before the concept of counter-transference, Socrates in his way (with his stress upon our knowing ourselves) and Christ in a more affective way (insisting that we tend to ourselves, hear ourselves) had become part of Western culture, long before a Viennese physician in the late nineteenth century started paying attention to his dreams.

Freud is a good example of the doctor-as-patient; I know of no better one since St. Augustine. Freud had the gall to feel that if he paid enough attention to the tempest and turmoil and anguish of his own mind, he could learn from it and through that learning, be healed himself, and through that healing, reach out to others in need. St. Augustine and then Sören Kierkegaard are the high points in a tradition of subjectivity in Western intellectual life, and also in Western medicine. This tradition reaches back to the Greeks and to the Hebrew prophets.

When we speak about the subjective dimension, we are speaking about symptoms, yet modern medicine stresses signs.

If I may use a psychiatric term, ironically, the life of the mind is always in danger of "splitting." Not only patients split—separating affect from object—but intellectuals as well. Why we would want to place on a scale pain that is measured by our instruments as against pain that is felt by another human being is an example. Making this a matter of good or bad, better or worse, something that deserves our attention and something that does not, is our kind of split, our kind of judgment, and one connected to certain intellectual and class notions of value. It may well be that we, as upper-middle class scientists who have a vested interest in the measurable, will only allow for the measurable in our working lives. People come to us with all kinds of symptoms which we do not care to dignify with one of our labels or call just. Why? Because their symptoms are not measurable. This tells us as much about our education and our training as about our patients.

It has been said that doctors, as a rule, are poor patients.
I can't agree; it would depend upon the particular doctor. One who taught me medicine when I was in school was an extraordinary person and, ultimately, an extraordinary patient. He was a kind and thoughtful person whose humanity persisted to his dying day. I would not want to generalize by vocational or intellectual interests. I can imagine a future medical student taking a great many English courses, art courses and music courses, and being as arrogant and cold and mean-spirited—and as unaware about himself or herself— as the student who studies what, these days, are regarded as the unfeeling and aloof disciplines, say, engineering or statistics. This is because the humanities also generate highly-abstract responses in those who study them. The issue is not the courses, the issue is how the individual puts them together in his or her education, and then how all of it is put together in his or her life.

How do you feel as a patient?
Vulnerable . . . as we, who are patients, all do. Vulnerable and wishing that we weren't. I do not feel I have any special defenses against this because I have been trained in medicine, however. I think that goes out the window very quickly. Once in that office, one is just hoping against hope that everything is going to come out well.

A physician with cardiovascular illness once wrote, "The patient needs more than treatment and reassurance, he wants his physician to take the responsibility upon himself."
Well, I think the responsibility or weight ought to be a shared weight. It should never be solely on the patient or the physician. It's a hard job to be a doctor, to assume these matters of life and death as

day-to-day obligations. The wear is great, and to be cast as the antagonist of an inevitably victorious Death is to assume a Promethean burden. For those who believe death can be "beaten," that's one thing, but for most of us it has simply been pushed back. The struggle remains. We want that struggle to take place, and we all hope that the outcome will be as victorious as possible, giving as much time as can be had on this earth. That sounds sinful—if you want to use religious imagery—but it is also terribly human to want that time.

In this shared experience, doctors and patients have duties towards one another. That is what the French philosopher Simone Weil meant with her discussions of *affliction* and what one learns through affliction—both while experiencing it, and while understanding the affliction of others, say, physicians. After all, doctors are afflicted in bearing these serious burdens occupationally. Engaged with the hurts of the world, they are in a unique position, however, to learn from themselves and from their patients. Whether they take advantage of that, whether they are trained to take advantage of that, is another matter.

Isn't the doctor's role to prevent suffering?

Prevent, yes; avoid, no. Simone Weil said that while one does not want to search suffering out and embrace it, on the other hand, one doesn't in the course of one's life try to pretend it doesn't exist by avoidance or denial. In the ancient languages this was known; that is why *patiens* (suffering) is connected with *sapientia* (wisdom)—so that patience is one of the prime attributes of wisdom. Suffering enables vision; it enables perspective and detachment in the most useful sense of those words. It is peace and thoughtfulness, and a kind of quiet reflection. This is what we can learn from our patients, and from our own patienthood.

The doctors of doctors, don't they assume that their patients already know what is to be done?

I doubt that it matters because the doctor-as-patient is always a human being who, through language, is asking the peculiar questions that human beings have asked throughout history, namely, what am I about and what is this sickness about? Where am I going, how long will I be here, and under what circumstances? These are the questions that our friend and physician, the novelist Walker Percy, reminds us are the ultimate questions that human beings—and only human beings—know how to ask.

I know there are a number of doctors in his novels.

Oh yes. In *The Moviegoer* there is Binx Bolling, the future medical student who is also the son of a surgeon, the grandson of a surgeon. Dr. Vaught is in *The Last Gentleman,* and a number of scenes there, too, take place in a hospital. We meet Dr. Moore in *Love in the Ruins,* and in *Lancelot,* you may remember, the entire novel takes place in a psychiatric hospital. Percy has worked all manner of illness and medicine into all four of his novels. He has drawn upon certain prior characterizations of the doctor, most notably those in Albert Camus's novels, where physical illness comes to stand for kinds of ethical and spiritual illnesses. Like Camus, Percy sees the doctor as inevitably in an existential situation, that insofar as he is dealing with one of the most fundamental aspects of human existence—sickness and suffering—and the questions connected to both of them, the doctor is in a special position in terms of his own life as well as in terms of the lives of others.

Percy is a physician—a pathologist—who has become a metaphysician. The connections between the two are just as direct and as continuous as those two words imply. Metaphysics pushed medicine just a bit further. Anyone who becomes a physician ought to understand that connection and become aware of the metaphysicians, whether they are the Greek philosophers, whether they are the novelists-philosophers such as Doestoevsky, Tolstoy, George Eliot, Charles Dickens, or whether they are the philosophical writers of our century, Bernanos, Percy, William Carlos Williams or Simone Weil (who knew what it was to suffer personally, and to make of that suffering a philosophical quest). She had a father who was a physician, she knew how the physician has been buried in the material world, how people have denied to him and to themselves the dialectic between the material world and speculations about it: that connection between the specifics of illness and the mind's efforts to come to terms with what that illness *means.* She took seriously the fact that all of us will die—that is, she saw how that fact bears down upon our daily lives, no matter how "healthy" we are.

The writers you have mentioned criticize the doctor, but also seem always to find something to praise.

Certainly, because that mix exists in the world. I have come into contact with a great many doctors and in situations that are not conventional, because I do most of my work in homes. I have been visiting homes for the past twenty years, and some of them have been physicians' homes where you do see both sides of the coin, and often without apology. Look, physicians are trained to have a sense of importance and authority that opens them up to criticism, they experience this all the time at the hands of their patients. That the self-importance gets out of hand is an occupational hazard, the result of being treated like gods and of allowing ourselves to be treated like gods.

There needs to be some systematic way, in the course of our education and in our continuing education, to deal with that issue—both in our own lives and in the lives of our patients. This temptation is daily (the religious call it a terrible sin), and we do assume god-like prerogatives, but it isn't only our fault. It is obviously also the fault of those who are vesting us with it, and of a culture that supports both the giving and the taking. As Freud cautioned, there ought to be a self-critical process at work to deal with this kind of illusion of control and power, an illusion that becomes, for us, a dangerous delusion at times: a usurpation of reality. It needs undercutting. In analysis, of course, one continually undercuts by interpretation and self-interpretation. How analysis might deal with another aspect of this problem, I wonder—namely the social and cultural forces that elevate doctors so high. I mean, doctors are reasonably well-to-do people who have a privileged position within a particular economic system and a secular world. (This is insofar as money brings privilege.) We have a moral authority amongst the general public that seems to grow from that privilege, and from a widespread agnosticism. But being on that kind of a pedestal doesn't help our self-awareness and our self-critical faculties.

Have you encountered physicians who have this kind of self-awareness, perhaps as a result of their patienthood?

Yes, but more in rural parts of this country. I think of several I have met, one in eastern Kentucky, and one in the northern part of New

Mexico. They were astonishing, though we might easily dismiss them as old-fashioned country doctors. They were themselves badly ailing, old, obviously dying men, but each worked very hard, and was of enormous significance to the people and the patients they attended. I know they did lack for some contemporary medical information, but I will tell you that under those circumstances, when it was either those doctors or nothing, it was better to have them. And I also know, having gone with them on their rounds, those doctors were doing, day-to-day, not only the Lord's work, or Hippocrates's work, but they were doing good medicine in home after home. Thinking about them now, it is clear to me that in certain cases, limitation forces us back upon earlier parts of our medical training we slighted or forgot. I remember a blind pediatrician in West Virginia, blinded by an accident in mid-career, who still continued his practice in a wonderful way, but by going back: he was listening as he never listened before, he was always listening. His histories were particularly detailed, his examinations extremely thorough. But this was only what Anna Freud pointed out years ago as what the blind do: they learn other ways of coming to terms with the world so that very little is lost.

You once said the same of Dr. William Carlos Williams, that he had a passion for all experience, that his poetry was so packed with the particularity of his experience that there was no room for abstraction.

Dr. Williams's expression was, "No ideas but in things." And he is very important for us on just these issues, primary care physician that he was. If you read his *Autobiography* and the last volume of that epic poem of his, *Paterson,* you will see the doctor-as-patient, and all that he learned from being that, most vividly. The last volume, incidentally, was written after he had had a heart attack and several serious strokes. He knew he was dying, and had gone through a severe depression.

I knew Dr. Williams from 1949 on. I wrote my undergraduate thesis at Harvard on him, and visited him repeatedly when I was in medical school at Columbia Physicians and Surgeons. I went on rounds with Dr. Williams and saw that he was a doctor while he was a patient, while he was ailing. He was born in 1883 and died in 1963, but for the last fifteen of his eighty years he was in serious trouble. Nevertheless, the tie to his patients remained strong. He once said to me, "I feed off my patients." Those who have written about him "stealing" time for medicine from the poetry or the fiction have gotten it wrong. It was entirely the other way: the medicine "fed" the poetry, and Williams said it himself in print many times—in his poetry, his *Autobiography,* his short stories. Literary critics make this error because they are preoccupied with the poet as a full-time writer, which is what many of them have been. Williams was not, could not be that kind of person.

He loved those visits to the home. And by the way, the physician-as-writer in Williams merges with the physician-as-patient, because if you look at those doctor stories in *Life Along the Passaic* you immediately notice that he is writing, not only about the patients that he was treating, but he is also writing about the doctor: the doctor who is ailing, angry, impatient, confused, tired. The doctor who hurts and who wonders why, at times, he ever became a doctor—partly because of the patients he is treating, partly because of all those other interests, like the writing of poetry, the love of art, the concern with politics. The tension here is between the doctor-as-sufferer who is *also* the doctor-as-healer. Emotions, we see, are used to the good rather than used self-destructively. Williams in these doctor stories, in *Paterson,* in the novel *White Mule* is thus the self-aware doctor who can go on to worry about how people struggle when they give birth to children, when they later bring them up.

Yet there is the other side. We see the doctor who is distrusted and even feared.

Yes, and why not? He brings the "bad news" and he knows more than one wants him to know. And yet he knows what one has to know. This is a paradox we all struggle with and it is never going to be resolved. We are simply going to have to learn how to live with it. There is a kind of blasphemy in wanting to know too much and yet it is also in our nature to want someone to know too much. And as good doctors, nothing less than everything is enough in order to do our job well. So we do want to know everything, and yet have to learn how to use what we know with discretion—which means filing some of what we know, not mentioning some of what we know, using our knowledge indirectly, tactfully, sensitively. And at the proper time, and for the proper amount of time. There is a great deal of the

subjective here that must he handled with discipline and discretion.
Discretion is essential for physicians because lives are at stake,
sensibilities in jeopardy.

How would you say Dr. Williams used what he learned?
I would go with him from home to home in Paterson, New Jersey,
where he was well known in what we would now call the "ethnic
enclaves." He was known to the Greeks, the Poles, the Blacks, the
Jews and to the last remnant of working class Protestant whites of
New Jersey who hadn't escaped north to New York, or south to the
suburban or more rural parts of that state. They were all people hard
pressed or stuck and they were all his. They worked in factories and
in the shops and the stores. They were blue collar and poor white
collar who had an entire range of occupational illnesses, daily
injuries, colds, flu and alcohol problems. He went up and down the
stairs in tenements constantly, and I will tell you what he did: he had
a pad of paper in his car. He'd leave the pad there, he would go into
the homes, do his doctoring, come back to the car, and he'd write
the lines down. At least I think that is what he usually did, because
when I was with him he'd come back and say, *Did you hear that?
Did you hear what she said?* And he'd be writing it down, whether I
had heard it or not.

For whom? For some future audience and for himself, first,
because he was the audience, after all, listening. And then for the
others who would listen through him, because he was their
intermediary. This was the poetry, this was the fiction which he went
out the door with—as he once put it, "I stole those lines from all my
patients." And then he would give those lines a structure which, of
course, one has to acknowledge. (It wasn't as if the lines just fell into
place, you know. The worst of oral history, just like the worst of case
history, is taking all this *stuff* and not knowing how to edit it so that it
makes sense to a reader. Much of what passes for an "accurate
account" is not only entirely ignorant of context, but utterly lacking in
effective organization, the kind of honest, simple elegance that
Williams gave to his published work.) Then the poet—Williams—
added to it. In his writing we see the lines that he heard, but also the
lines that he created.

People make mistakes by drawing distinctions too arbitrarily. There is Williams-the-doctor who hears lines and then puts them into poetry, and here is Williams-the-poet sitting in his study listening to himself, and then making a poem out of that. Selves merge, and never more so than in Dr. Williams' case. But then I suspect they merge in every writer's life—every person's life. If you were to talk with a novelist like Walker Percy or Robert Penn Warren, a poet like Williams or Muriel Rukeyser, you would find out that what they were doing was—to use a phrase that Simone Weil favored—*paying attention.* (She once said that attention is the rarest and purest form of generosity.) They were listening to the world, in the world: listening in shops and grocery stores, in department stores and while teaching, during a visit with a friend or a neighbor or overhearing a chance conversation on the street. All those impressions, all the language that washes over, they then through the genius of the creative personality, filter into stories or poems. They filter the outside world through their inside world, but there is not this sharp distinction between the two, as though they are up there in an attic disconnected from the world. The world filters through the lives they live just as it filters through ours.

How would you relate your work with the medical humanities program to what you have just said?

Through the novels and the poetry and the short stories, I try to bring alive situations I believe doctors are going to experience. With Williams or George Eliot, one is up against the problem of the healer who, himself or herself, is desperately ailing. (What recurs in Williams is the doctor who finds himself annoyed with the very people he wants so to help, and who often feels badly that he is annoyed.) The beauty of this fiction is that it brings the reader almost unbearably close to the heart of the matter and yet, keeps a distance from it. The doctor-reader can draw upon fictional situations as though they were life, but, of course, the imagination has transformed them so that, in the act of reading, we get not the thing itself, but the *experience* of the thing. I know of no other medium that will enable us to have it both ways, so close to reality and yet at an edifying distance. One comes away with particularity rather than abstractions, with the memory of particular characters—in all their complexity—rather than the overwrought generalities that all too often pass for social science.

I have a feeling that doctors are the least cared for, least cared about.

I have not seen that studied, although I have to agree it certainly should be. We do know that doctors are subject to a fairly high rate of serious psychiatric illness, perhaps because they are under enormous pressures. Some would say that of those who go into medicine, a significant number are those who have known hurt and pain, who are trying to find a place where that past experience will be meaningful. I don't know. One has to be careful about such sweeping statements, especially since so much unfairness is directed towards physicians. Medicine is likely the most studied profession of all, overstudied perhaps, and yet so little attention is paid to the doctor's needs.

By comparison, what do we know about the people who go into business or law? Very little, I'm sure. We tend to know more about doctors, and considering the gap in our knowledge of the doctor-as-patient, perhaps far too much is made of what is known. The nature of their work encourages doctors to open themselves to the interests of others, to become vulnerable as an occasion for self-awareness, learning and growth. In my own work I have seen how much easier it is to observe the staff of a teaching hospital throughout a day, those in an emergency ward or clinic, than it is to walk into the offices of a major law firm, or the conference rooms of one or another leader in a major industry. These research limitations have their parallels, I should add, in the fact that it is all too easy to study the poor and the dispossessed rather than the wealthy and the powerful. Aren't these latter much better defended against the inquiry—if not the inquisitions—of social scientists? And aren't social scientists oddly reluctant to press forward in those cases? The point is, in spite of all the apparatus of modern social science inquiry, we know less about doctor's illnesses than about the illnesses of the countless special interest groups to which doctors minister. A change here, however, would require doctors to take themselves seriously in the ways we have been discussing—stand up for themselves, remind themselves of their special vulnerabilities, but also their social responsibilities and yes, the wonderful opportunities they have.

On Medicine & Literature
David Hellerstein/1980

From *The North American Review* (University of Northern Iowa, Cedar Falls, IA, June 1980, pp. 6–14). Reprinted by permission of Dr. David Hellerstein.

Robert Coles' five volume study, *Children of Crisis,* forms a monumental portrait of the children of America over the past two decades. Coles' work began in the late 1950s in New Orleans, where he studied several black children who were being placed in all-white schools in that city's first attempts at school integration. The first volume, published in 1967, explored the lives of these children in their own words and the words of their teachers, parents, neighbors and fellow students—and showed the strengths and weaknesses of our country at a critical point in its history. The four subsequent volumes have focussed on the crises faced by poor black and white children in Northern cities, on the children of other "disadvantaged" groups including Eskimos, Chicanos, Indians, migrant workers, Appalachian mountaineers; and, most recently, on the very different problems of children in upper class families. Currently under way is volume VI, work with children in Northern Ireland and South Africa.

Though *Children of Crisis* deals with social conflict, the series is not precisely sociology, and though Robert Coles is a child psychiatrist, it is not psychiatric or medical—or anthropological or literary, for that matter. The techniques of all these disciplines are used—cautiously, one might add—for the purpose of exploring the crises faced by various groups of children, of showing the world as it is— an aim now largely abandoned by novelists in favor of subjective fictions, and by social scientists in favor of theory. Yet Coles' fearsomely energetic impulse in *Children of Crisis* is to show the children's lives in all their complexity, to explore, to awaken. Robert Coles is a doctor who has seen everything, a writer who has read, it seems, everything, and now for two decades has been compelled to tell the world what he has seen. He is insistently, gratingly *there*. And while at times one feels his writing goes on over-long and would be better off with closer organization, at its best it forms a portrait of childhood that is *sui generis*—beyond categorization. By refusing to subjugate his writing to a particular school of thought, one or another set of sociological or psychiatric theories, Coles speaks to the public at large. And in all it is the eye of the doctor that informs his work and gives it coherence. Coles' words about William Carlos Williams apply to his own works: "The reader is confronted with a blunt, at times abrasive if wise physician who clearly knows his way around, but who seems, at times, ready to throw in the towel: all those demands from all those people." Like the Williams of the *Life along the Passaic* stories, Coles writes about "plain, ordinary people . . . whose knack of survival he [cannot] help regarding with a mixture of admiration, sadness and bitterness."

In addition to the volumes of *Children of Crisis,* Robert Coles has published twenty-five other books in the past dozen years. These have included: *Erik Erikson: The Growth of his Work,* a biography nominated for the National Book Award; *Walker Percy: An American Search,* a literary and philosophical biography of that Southern doctor novelist; *The Knack of Survival in America,* a critical work on the fiction of William Carlos Williams; *Irony in the Mind's Life,* criticism on works by Elizabeth Bowen, James Agee and George Eliot; several books done in conjunction with photographers, including *Still Hungry in America;* a half dozen children's books; a collection of poetry; and two volumes of *Women of Crisis,* co-authored by his wife, Jane Hallowell Coles. This spring a critical biography of Flannery O'Connor is due.

Robert Coles was born and raised in Boston. He graduated from Harvard College in 1950 with a major in History and Literature, then attended Columbia College of Physicians & Surgeons. He interned at U. of Chicago Clinics, and did residency training in psychiatry at the Massachusetts General and McLean Hospitals, and in child psychiatry at Children's Hospital in Boston. He subsequently served as chief of an Air Force neuropsychiatric unit in Mississippi for two years, and it was at that time that his work with black children involved in school desegregation began. Dr. Coles is Professor of Psychiatry and Medical Humanities at Harvard Medical School and teaches courses at both undergraduate and medical school levels.

The interview took place in Cambridge, Massachusetts,

at 10 a.m. of a windy March morning. Dr. Coles' office is in the basement of a brick house, a former Harvard club, across the street from Harvard University Health Services and close by Elsie's, a lunch counter popular with Harvard students for its turkey and roast beef sandwiches. At the interviewer's knock, Dr. Coles came to the door to let him in. Coles is of medium height, slightly build, with short-cropped black hair. His head is large, his face mobile and expressive, giving one the impression of great intensity, and at the same time, fatigue. His left hand is congenitally smaller than the right, so it is almost a child's hand. He wore battered high workman's boots, worn corduroy pants and an open-necked shirt.

He ushered the interviewer into his office and went through the morning's mail as the tape recorder was being set up. The basement room is windowless, containing a nappy blue couch with a pillow at one end, which occasionally serves a psychoanalytic purpose, a wooden desk and several chairs. The walls are covered by political posters from South Africa, New Mexico and Alaska—vivid images in bright reds and yellows and blacks—by large photographs of James Agee and Erik Erikson, by the framed frontispiece of Coles' *New Yorker* article on Walker Percy, a framed cover of the *New Republic*. Some yellowed newspaper clippings are taped to the side of a filing cabinet, one with a small photograph of Flannery O'Connor. The wooden bookshelf is crowded with the works of George Eliot, Anna Freud, Georges Bernanos, William Carlos Williams, Flannery O'Connor, Walker Percy, various philosophers including Kierkegaard, Hegel, Marcel and Heidegger; several of Coles' own books in paperback are interspersed among them and stacked on the floor.

When the interviewer was ready Coles moved his chair closer to the blue couch, on which rested the tape recorder—which in fact formed the subject for the first part of the interview. Coles' voice was hoarse, reinforcing the gauntness of his physical appearance. He formed his sentences with great care, often stopping in the middle of a sentence to amend or elaborate an idea, or to insist on the complexity of the situations of which he was speaking and of the need for caution in making generalizations about the children with whom he has worked—whether white, black, Indian, Mexican or Eskimo. Though one had the impression he had given innumerable interviews in the

past, he was not glib or rehearsed, or particularly self-
protective. At times he could be severely critical of his own
preconceptions as an observer and of his own work.

Interviewer: Much of the *Children of Crisis* volumes is made up of
interviews. Do you generally use a tape recorder?

Coles: When I was in college, I got to know William Carlos
Williams, and I used to follow him around and tape record his
medical rounds in northern New Jersey. He was an old-fashioned,
what we'd now call Family Practice doctor—he was a pediatrician
and an obstetrician, and basically a General Practitioner. I'd visit him
and he'd take me into the homes of his patients. He'd listen to them
carefully, both as a writer and as a doctor, and then when he left each
home, he'd sit in his car and write notes. I'd say, "What are you
doing?" And he'd say he was writing down the wonderful expressions he heard from them. He would later use them in his poems.
And some of the stories he heard from them he worked into those
wonderful *Life along the Passaic* stories, which are doctor stories,
really. He used to say, "The important thing is to *hear.*" I've found
that when I've used the tape recorder, at times it was because I
thought I wasn't a scientist if I didn't have everything tape recorded.
And then I'd remember what Dr. Williams said, and slowly I started
weaning myself from it. But it's hard because you figure you get
everything that way. And it has interfered at times, because I didn't
listen as closely as when I didn't have it.

Interviewer: So when you didn't have it, you'd just write things
down?

Coles: Afterwards. I'd write it all down. And I'd edit what I
heard—you edit the tape anyway—I think I was editing in my mind
as I was writing it down. You write down what you feel you really
want to remember. It's a complicated thing, how you do this work.

Interviewer: I imagine you must have libraries full of tapes.

Coles: I do. I have a lot of tapes, and then more recently a lot of
notes on my yellow pads. And often, even when I was using the
tapes, I'd sit down in the evening and write an essay in which the
important things that I heard were put together. Lately I've been

working in Northern Ireland, in Belfast with the Catholic and
Protestant children caught up in that struggle, and in South Africa
with the black children in Soweto and Afrikaaner children in Pretoria.
I found myself not using the tape recorder.

Interviewer: Not at all?

Coles: Just occasionally. I'd use it so I could listen to the voices,
for the use of language and dialect. I felt that I learned a lot just by
listening and writing down afterwards what I had heard, rather than
by trying to catch every word.

Interviewer: I carried several of your books home from the
Cambridge library last week, a very thick stack of books—and I
began to wonder how you are able to write so much. They had
nearly twenty of your books: the *Children of Crisis* series, biographies, criticism, children's books, poetry. How do you manage to do
all that?

Coles: I write on yellow lined legal pads. I write in the mornings,
early, just after my children have gone to school. I think about what
I'm going to write the night before. Then I sit down and by golly, I
write. I write on a quota basis. I try to write three to four yellow pages
a day, five days a week. And if you keep on doing that with some—
almost a religious—dedication, the books mount up over the years.
One of the reasons is some sort of a necessary feeling I have that I
must do this fairly regularly. The only time I stop writing is when I'm
out in the so-called field. That is, when I was in South Africa or
Belfast I didn't write much, other than the notes I was taking. But
when I'm at home either teaching or doing my work in this country,
visiting families—usually I don't visit the families until the afternoons
because the kids are in school all day—I will write in the mornings,
and that writing mounts up. If you stop and think about it . . . also I
have sort of a cramped hand, a cramped writing hand, so I would
estimate that I probably write eight hundred to a thousand words a
day.

Interviewer: Then do you revise a lot after that?

Coles: Yes. What I do is revise one time. All that is typed up. Then
I approach the typed version with a whole new personality. I look at
it as an editor—and I'm very tough with my own writing. Maybe
some critics would say not tough enough. But there is a difference. I
cannot edit my own handwriting. It has to be typed. And then I just

slash into it. As I say, maybe I should learn how to slash into it better. There is that very important second stage of the writing, though—it's edited. And then it's done.

Interviewer: You mentioned your friendship with William Carlos Williams. How did you come to know him?

Coles: As an undergraduate at Harvard I majored in a combined English and history field, and I wrote my thesis on Dr. Williams and his poem *Paterson* and the novel *White Mule* which enormously interested me. At that time, in 1950, Dr. Williams was not quite as celebrated as he later became in the sixties. He died in 1963, and when I was doing this writing he was a well-known poet but by no means well accepted in the academic circles, the university circles. The only reason I was able to work so well and congenially at Harvard on that subject, namely him, was because of Perry Miller, who was a professor of English and American literature at Harvard and was an enormous influence on me. He was an English professor, but I think it's also fair to call him a theologian. He was very much interested in the Puritan mind, and in the moral issues the Puritans struggled with, and he was interested in the literature which that generated. And that was my major undergraduate preoccupation. But I had read Williams' poetry and wanted to write about him, and Miller encouraged me to do so and was my mentor. I envisioned myself going to graduate school and becoming a student of Miller's in American literature. After I had written my paper on Williams, Miller encouraged me to send it to him. I got a reply from Dr. Williams, saying, "Any time you're here, come and say hello." And boy, I went down to New York fast. I then became a friend of his, a young friend of his. He was very, very helpful, as an older person. I talked a lot with him.

Interviewer: And he encouraged you to go into medicine?

Coles: Well, yes. I became so impressed with the dual life he lived as a physician and as a writer/social observer of sorts that I thought maybe I'd give it a try myself. So I started taking on premedical courses, and I applied to medical school. I was turned down by four or five of them, because they thought I was a little flaky, I think, although I did well in the premedical courses. They'd often ask me what kind of a doctor I'd want to be. I'd say that I wasn't sure but . . . and then I'd tell them what I'm telling you now. But at Physicians and

Surgeons, at Columbia, I was interviewed by a man named Philip
Miller—the same surname but obviously no relation to Perry Miller.
He was a biochemist. He interviewed me, and I told him how I'd
come to that point in my life. He said, "By golly, we ought to take
someone like you, even if you're not sure you want to finish medical
school." So they did take me. I had to struggle in medical school,
because I wasn't really adequately prepared for the sciences, and I
didn't do too well in them. But I managed to get by. I would visit Dr.
Williams, and I was very much interested in religious matters through
Perry Miller and through my own life. I would go to Union Theological Seminary, where I took a seminar which Reinhold Neibuhr gave
before he had his first stroke, which was in '52, I think. I guess I was
trying to combine my medical life as a student with these interests in
religion and in literature. That I think has been the struggle that I've
waged all my life.

When I finished medical school I interned at the University of
Chicago. And even then I remember as an intern, with my white
uniform, dashing out of the hospital because Paul Tillich was giving
some lectures at the University of Chicago. Also during that year, Dr.
Williams came, even though he'd had a stroke and was partially
paralyzed. He came and read in the Rockefeller Chapel there, read
his poems. It was a very poignant meeting for those of us who knew
him, because it was hard for him to talk. Yet there was something in
him that wanted to take that poetry of his and share it with others.
When I finished up that year I came back to Boston. The question
came up: what was I going to do with my medical training and
internship? I guess by this time I realized I couldn't go into pediatrics,
which was my major interest, because I wasn't tough enough. The
kids would undo me. They'd start crying and I'd almost want to join
up—cry. And that's not good. So Bill Williams suggested, "Why
don't you try going into psychiatry, child psychiatry, and get to the
kids that way." So I did. I took a residency at the Massachusetts
General Hospital, at McLean Hospital, and then at Children's
Hospital for a couple of years in child psychiatry. And by this time I
had become so immersed in child psychiatry that I tended to stop
reading a lot of the books in theology and even in literature that I'd
been reading. But then I was drafted into the Air Force under the
doctors' draft, and I went down to Mississippi where they put me in

charge of an Air Force neuropsychiatric unit. That was where my whole life really changed a second time, because the whole civil rights movement was getting going, and children were being marched into desegregated schools in New Orleans in the face of all the violence that was going on. I've described what happened to me in the first chapter of the first volume of *Children of Crisis*. This was kind of . . . This changed my life. I stayed there and got involved with these children, involved with the civil rights movement.

Interviewer: Were you particularly vulnerable then to getting involved in that conflict? You described in your book *Walker Percy: An American Search* that it was "a critical time" and you were "somewhat lost, confused, vulnerable, and it seemed, drifting badly."

Coles: I *was* drifting, I think. I guess I was trying to figure out how to combine this medical life that I had with my interests in literature and a kind of complicated religious background that I have. My mother comes from the Midwest, actually from Iowa. She is an Episcopalian. And my father comes from a Jewish background, from England; they've lost their religion for a few hundred years. They were Sephardic Jews who came from Spain originally, and had been in England for several hundred years. He's an agnostic scientist. So I . . . these balancing acts . . .

Interviewer: So you had a religious and a scientific background.
Coles: Exactly.
Interviewer: Were you a religious child then?
Coles: Oh yes! My mother took us . . . We were brought up in Boston, my brother and I, with a good deal of religious, Christian, faith, I think it's fair to say. I struggle with that. At times I guess I'm an agnostic, and at times I'm very much connected to the Old *and* New Testaments. I love to read Jeremiah and Isaiah and Amos, and I love to read Mark and Luke and Matthew and John and St. Paul. The Bible means a lot to me, and theology means a lot to me. Williams, by the way, had no interest in religion. He was a wonderful agnostic, exuberant, here-and-now person. And in a strange way that was a problem. Because I was drawn to T.S. Eliot's poetry, from college days on. And you know, Eliot and Williams had a rough time with one another.

Interviewer: *In the American Grain* by Williams is full of that.
Coles: Yeah, they really were antagonists. I couldn't figure out

how it was that at the same time I was both an admirer of Eliot's and an admirer of Williams'. Once I talked to Williams about this. He said, "Well, you're not me. You can have this kind of distance. I'm in the middle of a fight, you're an observer." But you know, Williams was partly Jewish, too. And later I got involved with Erik Erikson, who is also partly Jewish. So this continuity in my life is strange, this involvement with people who have juggled religious issues. Erikson had been an artist before he went into psychoanalysis, and I think I identified with this struggle to go back and forth between the world of science—in his case psychoanalysis, in my case medicine—and the world of literature. And religion too, because of Erikson's involvement with Luther and Gandhi. *Moral* literature as well as novelistic literature.

Interviewer: So if you had it over again, would you have gone to medical school?

Coles: Definitely. It was a very important part of my life. I got to know patients as individuals, and I still remember many of them I treated as an intern. I went back and did a year of pediatrics just before I went into the Air Force, so I guess I managed to get that pediatric side of me well built up, as well as the psychiatric side. I think a doctor has a marvelous opportunity to get to know people in ways that perhaps no one else can.

Interviewer: Did your medical training make you a better writer?

Coles: Well in my particular case it did. I knew Flannery O'Connor when she was sick, in the hospital and very ill. She was in Georgia, and we were living in Georgia for several years, when I was working in the civil rights movement and with school desegregation in Atlanta. I had a long talk with her in the Emory Hospital. Obviously writers use their imaginations and don't need to have access to anyone, other than the richness of their own minds which is more than enough for them. But because she had been involved with doctors in the struggle she waged against lupus, she said that she thought it would be a marvelous opportunity for a writer to be in these situations. And of course some writers have been doctors. One thinks of Chekhov and again Dr. Williams and Walker Percy. But clearly many writers have had no need for medical training to become the great writers that they've been. And obviously many doctors are not interested in writing. I think one thing that medical training offers, which is worthy of consideration by people with other interests, is that it's a really helpful antidote to social science. A person who has gone through the empirical training of medical school, and who understands the uniqueness of the individual which medical training reveals, does have an opportunity to do social science work in a way that I happen to think is very important, that is, with a respect for the humanities, for their concentration on individuality, their emphasis on irony and paradox and inconsistency and contrariness rather than the emphasis that social science training tends to place on theory and on abstraction and on trying to generalize almost at all costs. Sometimes the costs are very high.

Interviewer: Have you become more suspicious of abstraction and theory, of categorization into types and stages? It seemed to me, in going through your books, that there was a certain progression.

Coles: And you probably noticed a certain increasing animus against my own profession. Well, you're right. I started out as a psychiatrist, and I started getting psychoanalytic training in New Orleans at the New Orleans Psychoanalytic Training Center, which later became a full-fledged Institute. I was . . . I think maybe I still am a smug, self-centered person. But if I am, I was even more so then. Boy, it's embarrassing when I stop to think of the psychiatric arrogance I was a victim of. It took me a few years to comprehend. This was what going into the homes of ordinary black and white people in the South tended to confront me with—my own narrowness and blindness and smugness and narcissism. Here I met people who were facing a tremendous social and historical crisis, and who were acquitting themselves with dignity, or showing the fear and anxiety of people who are threatened in ways that I had never been threatened. My whole way of thinking about them, with all the psychiatric terms and all the quickness to judge people indirectly through psychiatric categorizations—all of that was of little use in understanding the lives of these people. I had to begin to think of a way of looking at them that was different from that of psychiatry. Of course what one realizes is that there are always George Eliot and Charles Dickens and Dostoevsky—and all the writers who have helped one over the years to understand human beings—who are waiting in the wings to help you to get to know the people you're talking with in these homes. So I think I became somewhat disenchanted with my profession, and I think I began to lose interest in its way of thinking—and in its language, which is rather prolix and self-important.

Interviewer: Do you feel just that the *psychiatric* categorizations are useless, or that no system of thought can explain the various ways in which people, both children and adults, respond to crisis?

Coles: Flannery O'Connor put it beautifully. She said, "The task of the novelist is not to 'resolve' mystery but to deepen it!" The danger with social science, the danger for that matter with any kind of intellectual process, is that we take ourselves too seriously, and that we forget the difference between products of our own thinking and the world itself. We impose our notion of reality on the world and see only our notion of reality rather than the defiant complexity of the world—and of course the mystery of the world. Now, I'm caught in the middle, as you point out. On the one hand, I want to clarify and observe and point out and understand, and in a sense simplify in the nonpejorative sense of the word 'simplify.' But on the other hand, I'm constantly impressed with mystery, and maybe even feel that there are certain things that cannot be understood or clarified through generalizations, that resolve themselves into matters of individuality, and again, are part of the mystery of the world that one celebrates as a writer, rather than tries to solve and undo as a social scientist.

Interviewer: If you had it to do again, would you have not trained in psychiatry?

Coles: I think I would have gone into pediatrics and maybe family medicine, if I had it over again. I'd probably do primary care medicine is my hunch. At that time they didn't have it. And the kind of public health they had when I was a medical student was a matter of memorizing the charts of the life cycles of some species of worm in distant Africa, while at the same time there we were, just a few blocks from Harlem. And we never went there.

Interviewer: In reading *Still Hungry in America*, I was struck by the passages in which you talked about the diseases you'd seen—the malnutrition, skin ulcers, the parasitic infestations, the untreated serious kidney and heart diseases. Do you feel a special obligation since you're both a doctor and a writer? How can you leave those people after you've seen the very treatable conditions that are making their lives miserable?

Coles: That's a very important ethical point, and the only way I

could answer that is to say that in the instances I have seen them I
have done something. That's been a part of my work, to get them
medical care. It's hard for me to write about that because it seems
rather self-serving to say, "Look, I treated these people," which is
what every doctor does. But the fact is that's what I have done. In
every region of the country that I've worked, I've gotten involved with
the existing medical situation. The kids and their families, I've come
to know them over the period of a year or two, and pretty well.
Visiting them I've come to know their medical problems, as well as
trying to understand their feelings and their attitudes toward the
world. And I have indeed gotten them connected to medical facilities
when that's been necessary. Now the other side of one's contribution,
at least one *hopes* it's a contribution, is that after all as a writer you
can call attention to the larger issues that these people are struggling
with. And in the case of hunger, my involvement in testimony before
the United States Senate, and that very book which came as a result
of that, was a part of the effort to get the Food Stamp program going,
and to get this seen as a national problem rather than a series of
individual cases.

Interviewer: So do you think your work has had a substantial
effect?

Coles: Well I don't know. To tell you the truth I wish it had a *more*
substantial effect. I've testified again and again before various
Congressional committees on migrant children, on the problem of
hunger and malnutrition, on the problems of ghetto kids, on
problems of school desegregation—a whole range of issues that have
affected families and children. Sometimes I think some of that
testimony has had some value, but at other times one despairs. But
one tries. The problems of black lung disease among miners—I've
testified again and again about that. And we have made some
progress there. Black lung disease is now recognized as a medical
entity that is connected to the occupational hazards of mining, and
the miners who get black lung disease in recent years have been
compensated for the disease. When I started this work in Appalachia
that wasn't the case, and I think part of the victory was due to
medical and social testimony from people like me. And there've been
a number of us who have offered that testimony—doctors and social
observers who were involved with mountain families who had miners

in the family, miners whom we got to know. Some of the legislation concerning migrant children drew upon the observations that some of us have made about how migrant children live and what their educational and medical problems are. I wish that migrant families were living much better than they are today. And the occupational health legislation which affects black lung disease, and very importantly, *brown* lung disease, that is, among the textile workers of North and South Carolina, I wish that there were more and better laws. So on the one hand one works with these issues, but one is also pretty . . . at times discouraged. Certainly discouraged during the Nixon years, but even now, one wishes that this country could do more for the marginal social groups that are getting a pretty raw deal.

Interviewer: In *Irony in the Mind's Life,* you quote from George Eliot's *Middlemarch:* "Who can quit young lives after being long in company with them and not desire to know what befell them in their after-years?" I was wondering about the kids in the first volume of *Children of Crisis*—whether you'd ever be going back to them?

Coles: I have been. I go back once a year to the South and visit some of those families. I suppose I could call it follow-up work, but it's really just visits to people who were so wonderful to us, who taught us so much, and offered us so much hospitality. That's a beautiful quote from *Middlemarch.* We have done that, my wife and I. And some of those kids of course we've followed so long they are obviously no longer children, but are themselves in their twenties or thirties and parents.

Interviewer: Have you written about it?

Coles: A bit in *Farewell to the South,* a collection of essays. There's a long introduction in which I offer some follow-ups. But you know, when you've travelled as much as I have, and lived in so many different parts of the United States—I've been in every American state, including Alaska obviously, and Hawaii, all fifty states, and worked in every region of the country, North, South, East and West—there comes a point when you can't follow up all the people you've met, unless you're in a state of constant manic ascension, with no sleep and moving around endlessly from airport to airport. But there always have been one or two families with whom we've been especially involved, and those are the families we've kept up with, just making a visit every year or so to say hello. I'm haunted though by that question of George Eliot . . . oh well, I'm haunted by George Eliot.

Interviewer: So you have seen changes when you've gone back to visit the people you first wrote about?

Coles: Some changes. I see some changes, and Lord knows, having been involved with SNCC and the whole civil rights movement, I've seen wonderful changes with respect to segregation and school desegregation, to the point that school desegregation by and large is more a reality in the South than in my own home town of Boston, and if that isn't an irony, what is? I've seen a lot of social and racial changes in the South, and I've seen some changes for the better among the people in Appalachia, but there are also things that haven't changed much. For instance, we lived in New Mexico for several years, and I worked on the reservations of the Southwest, and the problems of the Indian people are very severe and *not* getting better. I worked in Alaska with Eskimo families, and the problems that Eskimos face are now getting *worse* rather than better, due to the pipeline, the refineries, the influx suddenly of a combination welfare economy and a one-time glut of cash. They've suddenly been yanked out of a subsistence economy in which nevertheless they have a certain amount of dignity and personal sense of themselves as hunters and fishermen—and now what are they? So you see alcoholism, and you see a kind of passivity and dependence on the visit of the airplane once a week to the village with pizzas. You go into the villages and you hear Linda Ronstadt blaring forth on hi-fi and you see skimobiles and kids drinking Cokes and eating pizzas and potato chips, and you say, here's modern America in these Eskimo villages. And though there are advantages to this, there are also severe moral and psychological losses. It's a real problem, how the Eskimos are coming to terms with the sudden presence of technology and money and so-called "Lower Forty-Eight" civilization. The risk is that one gets condescending. The Eskimos themselves, some of them, will say, "Hey, listen, this is what we want, just like you people have wanted it." But there's a good deal of evidence that, in addition to what they have gotten out of this, that is in the way of cash, they've experienced a substantial loss in morale, and in their own self-respect. They weren't prepared for contemporary American life as most of us were, because it crept up on us gradually over a generation or two. Our ancestors came here and were part of building up whatever this country is—and Eskimos suddenly had it thrown at them. So it's a mixed answer I'd have to give you.

Interviewer: In the past twenty or thirty years, medicine has become more institutionalized and technically oriented; and relatively little interest is placed in the kinds of social issues you're so involved in. And very little interest in what one might call the medical humanities. Do you as a result feel estranged from the medical profession?

Coles: I don't know, I don't know that. You'd have to ask other doctors. One student here was interviewed for medical schools, and mentioned that he'd taken a course with me—this in conjunction with his own interest in writing. He was told by the people on the admissions committee that they didn't think he ought to go to medical school if he wanted to be a writer, and that if I happened to have pulled this off that was fine, but they didn't want people announcing before they even get to medical school that they were interested in going to medical school because of an interest in writing and the help this would give them as writers. And I can understand that; I mean, there's such a need for doctors, and I think they felt this was a little frivolous. Also I didn't go to medical school to get a medical education from which I would then draw upon as a writer. I went to medical school out of a real desire to become a doctor and live the doctor's life that I'd seen Dr. Williams living, and also that I'd seen an uncle of mine living, my mother's brother. And somehow later in life I connected these interests.

I've written articles for the *New England Journal of Medicine,* for the *Journal of the American Medical Association,* on writers—I've written on Flannery O'Connor and Dr. Williams for the *J.A.M.A.,* and I've even written about *Middlemarch* for the *New England Journal of Medicine.* And I've written for the *American Journal of Psychiatry* and for psychoanalytic journals—and I've done book reviews for many of them. So somehow, again, it's a tightrope. I've balanced this life in some way. I love . . . I still read the *New England Journal of Medicine* and I read the medical articles in it, not just the social comment. And I do think of myself as a physician, very much so.

One reviewer said I'm a writing doctor. And that was very well put. If I had more ability, I'd write novels like Walker Percy or I'd write poetry such as Dr. Williams did—but I don't have that ability, I just don't have the ability to do that. So I . . . if you don't have the ability you don't have the ability.

Interviewer: Haven't you published a book of poetry?

Coles: I have written poetry, and I've listened to children and pulled their words together in a form that I guess one would consider a kind of poetry. It's not the best kind, but . . . but I have written poetry and some of it has been published, and there is the book of poems drawing on the work with children.

Interviewer: Are you teaching now?

Coles: Yes. I teach a course in the medical humanities at Harvard Medical School, and I teach undergraduates two things. I teach an undergraduate course called "Moral and Social Inquiry." We start with James Agee's *Let Us Now Praise Famous Men*. We read George Orwell's *The Road to Wigan Pier*. We go on to read Flannery O'Connor and Walker Percy, Ralph Ellison, Tillie Olson, Dorothy Day's autobiography called *The Long Loneliness*, about the Catholic Worker Movement. And we end up with *Jude the Obscure* of Thomas Hardy, and *Middlemarch* of George Eliot. So it's a mixture of novels and social documentary writing and autobiography and moral essays. And we see some movies that connect with the reading we've done. We read *The Diary of a Country Priest* by Bernanos, and we see the movie that Bresson did. And then last fall I taught a seminar called "Religion and Twentieth Century Intellectuals." So I teach on both sides. And at the medical school what we read is William Carlos Williams's doctor stories, *Life along the Passaic River,* Walker Percy's novels *The Moviegoer* and *The Last Gentleman* and *Love in the Ruins*—all of which have a doctor in them. The first one is a future medical student, and in both *The Last Gentleman* and *Love in the Ruins* a physician is a central part of the narrative. We read *Middlemarch* which has Dr. Lydgate, and we read *Arrowsmith,* the old favorite, that unfortunately is read by too many medical students when they've been in high school or college. Anyway, we use novels to approach medical issues.

Interviewer: Do you read different kinds of doctors' writing— Céline or William Burroughs?

Coles: Céline is especially important, and I haven't used him yet, but I'm going to next year. I think he's a very interesting physician—that's for sure. Obviously it would be hard for some medical students, as he has been hard for a lot of readers, to take. But I don't regard Céline's fascism as the central issue in his life. I think the issue in his life is that of his disgust for the hypocrisy of the world, a world that he saw from the point of view of a doctor as well as a political person. He's an interesting writer, a very gifted writer. He would be a valuable addition to that course, you're absolutely right.

Interviewer: And Burroughs?

Coles: Burroughs I have trouble with. The trouble I have with him is that while politically I'm fairly liberal—quite liberal, I guess—culturally I'm more conservative. I used to have discussions with Williams about this. I guess I can go as far as Williams, not too much further. There's obviously a stodgy part of me culturally. I tend to want to assign nineteenth century writers like George Eliot and Dickens and Hardy to my students—because I think they were wonderful moral observers. Someday I would love to teach a course, maybe at a law school, on Dickens and the law, because the various kinds of lawyers that he portrayed, and the way he looked at a profession are, I think, still of great interest today. The moral insights he offers us about professional life are very shrewd. You go from *Bleak House* to *Great Expectations* to the lawyer in *Tale of Two Cities*. And of course, George Eliot, with Dr. Lydgate—you can teach a whole course around *Middlemarch* to medical students or undergraduates. The issue of what makes for the moral decisions of professional life, centered around Lydgate and what happens to him . . .

Interviewer: Have you become more interested in moral issues in recent years?

Coles: No question. I am increasingly interested in moral issues, and the ways that writers, that is novelists and poets, have come to terms with these moral issues. And I'm interested in what these people have to say to people like me, doctors and psychiatrists and intellectuals—though I don't like that last word—to people who are psychologically trained.

Interviewer: You say in the introduction to the first volume of

Children of Crisis that, "There seems no end to crisis in this world."
Is that the case?

Coles: (Laughs.) Or whether I've manufactured crises in order to
. . . to justify my writing . . .

Interviewer: Let me rephrase that. How many volumes of
Children of Crisis will there be?

Coles: Well, there have been five dealing with twenty years of
work in America. It is important to point out—I want to make an
editorial point here, maybe a self-justifying point—I didn't publish
my first book until 1967. And the work started in 1959. So for eight
years there were no books. I think if you were to talk with my editor,
Peter Davison, who is editor at the Atlantic Monthly Press, he'd tell
you that he really had a devil of a time getting me to write that first
book. Hard to believe it may be right now, but I was very reluctant
about writing at first, because I was so overwhelmed by the
complexity of what I'd seen, and the enormous difficulty I had in
doing justice to that complexity as a writer. Now maybe I was overly
ambitious in wanting to do justice to that complexity. I suppose I
could have carved out some area of it and written psychiatric articles
about that area. But I had and still have, over my shoulder, the
shadow of someone like George Eliot. Now I'll never be able to do
justice to that complexity, the way she did in *Middlemarch*. But by
golly, those are the models. She and Tolstoy and Dostoevsky and
Henry James, and one at least remembers them as writers. Finally I
did write those portraits and the first volume went to press. Since
then I've done those other volumes, dealing with the various parts of
the country where I've worked. I've been working recently in
Northern Ireland, where I think any observer would feel there's
"crisis" going on in the children's lives. And I've been working in
South Africa, also critically caught up in a racial struggle. And I must
say, though I've just turned fifty, and feel myself entitled to stop this
fieldwork, I can't do it. I love going into a new part of the world and
getting to know children, getting to know their parents and their
teachers, and just *seeing* that world, the way maybe Orwell did when
he used to do the kind of travelling he finally wrote up in *Down and
Out in London and Paris* or in the *Wigan Pier* book. I can't write,
again, as well as he; I don't have the gift for narrative presentation
that he had. But I do just love to look at the world and try to do

justice to some of its rhythms, especially through the eyes of its children. The other thing I would mention is the considerable interest I have in the art of children and in interpreting that art, which goes back to my mother's interest in art. My brother is very much interested in art, and teaches courses at the University of Michigan that connect literature and art. I think that if I've done nothing else in those volumes of *Children of Crisis* and in my other writing about children, I've tried to point out what children's drawings and paintings can teach us about their moral and psychological perceptions. This has been an interest now for over two decades. I've interpreted drawings and connected them to the lives of various children, whether they be black or white or Appalachian or Eskimo or Indian or Chicano children. I think some of that writing has been valuable both for my profession and for interested laymen. And I'd like to continue doing that in connection with children abroad, in Ireland and South Africa, because I think it teaches us something about the relationship between a political or historical crisis, and the ways that children grow up; more abstractly, call it child development or human development.

Interviewer: We talked about your mistrust of psychiatric categories and language. Yet with the children's drawings you do make interpretations, you do make generalizations in a psychiatric framework.

Coles: But you'll also notice that I'm always taking one step forward and at least a half a step backward, or at least sideways, by making the observations, and trying to put them in other contexts, and maybe even qualifying them or maybe even pointing out that they apply to these children but might not apply to other children— and that in any case they may be overwrought. And that my own writings may be guilty—probably are guilty—of the various sins that I criticize in other writings. And I use the word sin because I think the issue is moral. How presumptuous is the observer becoming? How godlike does he feel himself to be? And the best people in my profession—people like Erik Erikson and Allan Wheelis, who are my two heroes of sorts within psychoanalysis—they pointed out again and again the limitations of this work, and the need we have for understanding the dangers we get into in connection with our own arrogance, and in connection with gullible or hurt people who want to elevate us into positions we have no right to be put in, or to allow ourselves to be put in. Allan Wheelis points this out in a marvelous essay, "On the Vocational Hazards of Psychoanalysis," which is part of his really fine book called *The Quest for Identity.* He points out that we are put in a godlike position, and become intoxicated with our own self-importance.

Interviewer: After your work with children in South Africa and Northern Ireland is done, what next? Are you working on other biographies or criticisms?

Coles: The work in Ireland and South Africa and one or two other countries will take a number of years. I have a book on Flannery O'Connor coming out this spring. And I'm working, in a more intellectual vein, on the life of Simone Weil. She's a source of great interest to me as a moral philosopher, and her life as well as her writing can offer a lot for us to think about. There are certain people whose moral and intellectual example has meant a lot to me. I suppose I'm hoping that I'm given the life to do it, and in one way or another I'll come to terms with their lives. Not necessarily with long biographies, because I'm not really very interested in doing that. But in either intellectual biographies or essays or whatever. Erikson was one, I've done a book on him. I wrote a long paper on Anna Freud because she's meant a lot to me, her work with children. I've written a book in conjunction with a photographer about the Catholic Worker Movement and especially Dorothy Day. I've written some about James Agee, and I think I'll probably end up writing some more about him. Same goes for Orwell. Dr. Percy, I've written a book about him, and a book about Dr. Williams. And Georges Bernanos, the French Catholic novelist, has meant a lot to me. *The Diary of a Country Priest* is one of my favorite novels, and I'd be surprised if in some way I don't come to terms with that. And that just about exhausts the list. (Laughs.) And probably will exhaust my life.

Interviewer: What do all these people who are your heroes have in common?

Coles: What they have in common, I guess, is that they've struggled with moral and religious issues. They have had their literary sides, too—more than sides in some cases. And more than that, there is the issue of service. Orwell struggled with this in a certain way, and Agee, and hence the anguish in *Let Us Now Praise Famous*

Men, the issue of how much do you exploit as a writer, and what do you offer in return to the people you're writing about? This comes up if, as a writer, you are dealing with external reality, if your writing is not made up only of the internal or fictional, subjective experiences which you mold into characters and narration. And since I've been so involved with the world outside of me, this issue comes up: what does one owe the world? You brought this up very appropriately in connection with the hunger issue in the late 1960s. The hope is, if you're caught up in the civil rights movement or in the struggle migrants are waging for both personal dignity and a larger share of the economic world that they manage to hold up through their labor, that the writing and the testimony and some of the medical work at least pay back some of the debts that you've rung up from going place to place and asking people to tell you things which you then write up and tell to the world at large. It's a haunting question, though: what does one owe?

Conscience of a Psychiatrist
Phil McCombs/1986

From *The Washington Post* (Washington, D.C., April 20, 1986, pp. H1–4). Reprinted by permission of *The Washington Post*.

CONCORD, Mass.—Up the gravel drive and under the trees, Robert Coles' big yellow house sits on a hill, half an hour from Cambridge. Beyond a stone fence and a barn are woods. Coles' BMW sedan and Wagoneer are parked near the door, which he answers while restraining a dog. "Aran, that is absolutely *rude* behavior!"

Coles, the child psychiatrist and Harvard professor, celebrated documentarian of the disadvantaged, prolific author whose books include the prize-winning *Children of Crisis* series, a self-described Christian "searcher" who has been called "the greatest social conscience of his generation," is not unaware of the irony presented by the BMW.

Nor are his Harvard students, who go by the hundreds to hear Coles' preachy, passionate, often mesmerizing lectures on "The Literature of Social Reflection." That he should come from comfortable Concord in a BMW to wring his hands about the wretched of the earth has helped earn the course its nickname "Guilt 105."

And, as may befit an author of 36 books and 850 articles, he is sometimes referred to on campus as Robert "Never an Unpublished Thought" Coles.

"If you've read all *those* by now," he says in a phone conversation, his voice developing its characteristic high nasal whine, "you must have been to see an ophthal-*mahhl*-ogist."

His work, he says, is "compulsive . . . One reason I do this is I can't stand a lot of crap." Sitting alone writing, "I avoid a lot of people and situations."

Among those avoided are "intellectuals."

"I hate the word!" he groans. "I hate the people! I hate *myself!*"

Coles' recent books, *The Political Life of Children* and *The Moral Life of Children,* contain interviews with kids from around the world.

112

They received mostly favorable reviews, although *Time,* which had pictured Coles on its cover in 1972 as "the most influential living psychiatrist in the U.S.," now says his penchant for telling stories about children's lives without academic analysis shows that his "distaste for ideas and intellectual analysis is profound."

Coles admits to being "an oddball and a loner"—though he is hardly uninterested in ideas. As he moves into the later stages of his career, he says, he may be adjusting his gaze. At 56, the man who has spent a quarter-century probing the lives of children and families caught in social crisis now spends much of his time writing and lecturing on religious themes.

"It's quite clear," he says, "that I'm a religious freak . . . What else do you do when you get old and stop and think about what this life is all about?"

Next winter, Addison-Wesley Press will bring out Coles' *Simone Weil: A Modern Pilgrimage* on the life of the 20th-century religious philosopher; and *Dorothy Day: A Radical Devotion,* on the co-founder of the Catholic Worker Movement in whose "hospitality houses" for the destitute Coles worked while attending medical school.

Coles ushers Aran, and the visitor, inside. He is a wiry man, low-key, even shy. He has great personal warmth and puts you quickly at ease, suggesting how he has been able to charm intimate informa-tion out of Americans of many races, classes and ages.

With his unruly black hair, bushy eyebrows and ratty green sweater ("I'm such a slob"), he resembles photos of his hero, James Agee, whose 1941 documentary book on southern poverty, *Let us Now Praise Famous Men,* with photographs by Walker Evans, is a classic of literary sociology.

Entering his bright, book-lined study, Coles seems sad.

"I think I'm depressed because I'm thinking about my parents," he says, sinking into a chair. He holds out a handwritten letter from his friend Walker Percy, the novelist. "My parents just died, so he's telling me he's sorry."

A long sigh:

"They lived into their eighties and they had a good life. Still, it's hard. They were good people, and I must say, like someone out of another century, they lived together for 60 years, they were happy, and my brother and I dearly loved them. And all this *crap* about what's happened to the American family . . . children who don't have the kind of solid home life that I think they need. Their mothers and fathers are off in a million worlds. It's *not right.*

"You know, people think of me as a liberal, but on some of these issues of family, I've always felt myself to be quite conservative: character and moral life, not only moral thinking, but moral *living* . . . You wonder: So many people now, they bring up their children to learn to get ahead, they want them to learn to read before they even go to kindergarten, to get 800s on all the SATs and get into all these fancy colleges. But what is their moral life, what do they *believe* in?"

The BMW, the nice house, the upscale life style he enjoys—these are the kinds of facts Coles brings up in his classes, turning on himself. In a recent lecture he told how he toiled with migrant farm workers but "I couldn't stand it so I checked into a Holiday Inn." The workers wanted to go too, but Coles refused them.

"I'd be embarrassed, I'd be confused . . . They might even stop picking the crops after a while if they get used to this Holiday Inn life. And who's gonna pay the bill? The Ford Foundation will pay the bill! [But] pretty soon there won't be any of their [grant] money left."

The story gets a laugh, but Coles is serious in urging students to examine their privileged lives and somehow put them to good use in helping less fortunate people.

"What's wrong with feeling guilty?" he asks the students. ". . . Let's say that Jesus had a guilt trip. What was *his* problem? 'Hey buddy, take it easy! Don't worry about those people that need some bread! . . . What are you visiting the prisons for? Do you have a *hangup?* There must be some *shrink* over in Galilee you can talk to.'"

This is strong stuff at Harvard, where, says sociologist David Riesman, in a cosmopolitan, somewhat "corrosive" atmosphere, "Robert Coles is a point of reference for the noncosmopolitan, for the devout, for the student who isn't exactly with it in the going pieties and fashions of the moment."

Coles teaches another big lecture course on "The Literature of Christian Reflection," and seminars on "Dickens and the Law" at the law school, "Doctors in Novels" at the medical school, and "Moral and Social Inquiry Through Fiction" at the business school.

"In many ways, Bob is sort of like a pastor," says Phillip Pulaski, 32, Coles' assistant. "He probably is the most influential teacher at Harvard in terms of the impact on people's lives."

In his study, Coles has photos on the wall of his sons—Bob, Dan and Mike—and his wife Jane Hallowell. The two older boys are in Harvard and the younger one goes to high school and lives at home. The family has traveled and worked together over the years, and Jane coauthored two *Women of Crisis* books. Coles mentions her devotedly in his work as his guardian against academic abstraction.

It was Jane, he writes, who helped him see that 6-year-old Ruby Bridges—a recurring figure in Coles' books—was more than an object for psychological analysis as she smiled and prayed for hate-slinging whites who harassed her as she integrated a school.

At his wife's prompting, Coles saw Ruby Bridges as "moral protagonist . . . Was she not, utterly, and daily . . . the essence of what a human being can manage to be?"

"My life would be entirely different if it weren't for my wife," says Coles. "I would be in a psychiatric practice, probably in Boston . . . She's the one who wasn't interested in settling in a suburban home."

In 1958, after Harvard (class of '50) and medical school at Columbia, Coles found himself in the Air Force directing a psychiatric hospital in Biloxi, Miss. He saw blacks beaten for trying to swim at a beach, then mobs protesting school integration in nearby New Orleans. The South was exploding and Coles, with Jane's "idealistic and adventuresome spirit" as a prod, and her family money to live on at first, began studying children caught in the drama.

They were married in 1960 and began work on the first *Crisis* book, *A Study of Courage and Fear,* which studied children caught in the southern desegregation battle. It was published in 1967; subsequent volumes studied migrant farmers, sharecroppers, moun-tain people, southerners who moved to the northern slums, Eskimos, Chicanos, Indians and even the well-off and rich. *The Middle Americans,* not formally part of the series, deals sympathetically with the white working class.

Coles' method of "direct observation," learned from psycho-analysts Anna Freud and Erik Erikson, involved getting to know a few children and their families over months, even years. According to Jane, children and parents would "just begin to talk because of the way he is, and it was such a pleasure. Sometimes you'd have the feeling that a couple needed reassuring, instead of just a young psychiatrist from Boston, you know what I mean. It might have scared them. So, often I'd get into a gab with the mother."

When Coles would propound some psychiatric theory, his wife, trained as a high school English teacher, would say she had already read it in more subtle form in *Middlemarch*. Now Coles uses George Eliot's novel to show students subtleties of psychological observation that he says today's social scientists often miss.

Twelve years ago, when the family was living in Albuquerque and Coles was working on *The Old Ones of New Mexico,* a documentary book with photographs by Alex Harris, Jane fell ill. The treatments have damaged her hearing. "I can't teach because of this," she says. Her husband declines to discuss the matter, saying only that the family returned East at that "melancholy" time, and Coles got his steady job at Harvard.

Standing in her bright country kitchen now, Jane talks nostalgically about their work over the years, then leans forward and confides in a protective whisper, "He's the true heart of this [work], and you know that."

Coles' parents, an engineer from Yorkshire and an Iowa farm girl, instilled in their sons the notion that life is in the end a "mystery" best comprehended by holy men and Victorian novelists. They read aloud from George Eliot, Dickens and Hardy (none went to college, Coles likes to tell students), and his mother introduced Coles to Catholic novelist Georges Bernanos, whose books he now teaches.

His father, a Taft Republican with a liberal streak, introduced Coles to George Orwell's *Down and Out in London and Paris* while Coles was in high school. And once, when Coles came home beaming with "self-pleasure" at a good report card, he received a sharp lecture from his mother on "the sin of pride."

These early lessons deeply influenced Coles, and as he grows older he seems to be contemplating them with increasing intensity. Yet back in Biloxi, before marrying and getting down to his life's work, he went through a period when he was depressed and under psychoanalysis. He would speed over to New Orleans in his sports car for the fine food, jazz and girls. He also spent a lot of time watching movies.

Then came one of those unexpected, life-changing surprises.
Walker Percy's novel, *The Moviegoer*, set in New Orleans and
peopled by characters in various stages of existential despair, came
out in 1961. Coles was gripped by it and immediately recognized in
Percy his "spiritual kinsman."

Today Coles says Percy's influence has been beyond calculation.
Percy, a medical doctor and Catholic convert, writes novels that
critique contemporary life and carry an often disguised message of
Christian hope. In 1978 Coles profiled him for *The New Yorker* in a
series that later became a book, *Walker Percy: An American Search*.

During a telephone conversation, Coles showed how subtle and
pervasive the Percy influence has been. He offered to meet a visiting
reporter at the airport, saying he wanted to get out of the house,
drive around Boston, talk in bars and sit next to ordinary people.

Then, chortling at the prospect, he exclaimed: "We'll have a
'rotation!' "

The term, which Percy distilled from the work of the 19th-century
Danish philosopher Sören Kierkegaard, pops up in *The Moviegoer* as
a trick used by people who are in despair. Percy's character Binx
Bolling defines a rotation as "the experiencing of the new beyond the
expectation of the experiencing of the new."

A newspaper interview is not a new experience for Coles.
However, as it turned out, the existential pub-crawl that he looked
forward to with such relish in this case had to be called off because of
a last-minute speaking engagement.

In Coles' study, photos of Percy and of other Coles models, friends
and mentors peer down from the wall—Agee, William Carlos
Williams, Flannery O'Connor, Erikson, Anna Freud, Day, Weil,
Bernanos. Beside the brooding intellectual faces are photos of
sharecroppers, Eskimos and others Coles came to know as he
studied them.

Williams was an especially strong influence, and Coles wrote a
book on him (*The Knack of Survival in America*). While Coles was a
student at Harvard, he sometimes followed the poet and doctor on
his medical rounds of working class Paterson, N.J. Williams urged him
to shun abstractions and embrace particulars: "Catch an eyeful, catch
an earful, and don't drop what you've caught."

In fact, Coles has never been comfortable as a social scientist drawing the kind of general academic conclusions that social scientists draw.

As early as 1961 he wrote in *The Atlantic,* "When the heart dies, we [psychiatrists] slip into wordy and doctrinaire caricatures of life. Our journals, our habits of talk become cluttered with jargon . . . We embrace icy reasoning."

In *The Moral Life of Children,* he takes a swipe at Harvard Prof. Lawrence Kohlberg, who is widely known for his theories on moral development in children.

Writes Coles: "For Kohlberg, [Ruby] was a 'preconventional' or 'premoral' lass. Her prayers, her smiles, were, I suppose, mere gestures, not the careful responses of a truly reflective person—a Cambridge theorist, for example."

Says Kohlberg: "I think he's a fine guy and a sensitive guy who isn't very theoretically sophisticated . . . The fact that young children often perform heroic acts is in no contradiction with my theory."

In this February's *Boston Review,* William Damon criticizes Coles' "dabbling in psychological theory [and] gratuitous railings at social science." He says Coles occupies the "somewhat lonely territory between social science and journalism."

"I know some doctors who look down their noses at him, but I look down my nose at them," says Peter Davison, who edited the *Crisis* series and many other Coles books. ". . . Dostoevski would say he's a 'great soul.' "

As Coles' spiritual concerns intensify, they seem increasingly to point up what has become his radical critique not only of the social sciences but modern thought and culture in general.

"The social sciences," he says "have had much too easy a time of it with the gullible American public." Then this:

"Flannery O'Connor said that the task of the novelist is to deepen mystery, and mystery, she said, is a great embarrassment to the modern mind, and I think that is a wonderful statement, and I think it's a statement that it behooves all of us to live with and be grateful for, and, you know, having said *that,* I've said *'Goodbye!'* to American secular social science, and a lot of other things in the American secular world, which is hungry for certitudes, and formulations, and stages and phases, and wants *everything* categorized and put into labels and compartments, and wants an

explanation and a recommendation for when you take your next
breath, wants to be told at what day and what month and what year
a child should learn how to read, and how to have sex in 150 new
ways, and lose weight, and keep your cholesterol at a certain level,
and you can't even *die* without these people telling you the stages
you're supposed to go through!' "

He catches his breath.

Then, more quietly: "People are lost, and don't know it, and are
wandering in the wilderness."

"I never went South to be involved in the civil rights movement,"
says Coles. "I was already there and I came from a conservative
background. [I was in] SNCC [the Student Non-Violent Coordinating
Committee] and the Mississippi Summer Project, but I found some of
the stridency and the ideological positions being taken . . . something
I couldn't tolerate."

There were other things he couldn't tolerate as the years went by.

Reisman says that after Martin Luther King, Jr., was shot, Coles
publicly denounced the "inane revolutionary yearnings of . . .
affluent radical whites . . . He said what the black family in Roxbury
[a section of Boston] wants is a tough Irish policeman with a gun . . .
to shoot these black thugs or whites who cheer them on."

More recently, Coles caused a stir by reporting that only children of
affluent, liberal parents appear to worry about nuclear war; working
class children worry about money and other problems.

Yet, says Reisman, "No one could be more concerned with nuclear
arsenals." He dubs Coles "the internal conscience of the con-
scientious."

Coles tells students that criticisms of the left are part of the
intellectual tradition he admires. In a recent lecture he discussed
Orwell's "devastating assault on the socialist left" in *The Road to
Wigan Pier,* saying that Orwell, Agee and others "are constantly
looking with a skeptical eye at the world they themselves come
from."

Coles—who says he's "independent" politically—is not, finally,
easy to label, perhaps because in his work as a documentarian he
emphathizes with all sides. In his book on rich children, he showed
how early moral stirrings grow cold under the influence of mate-
rialistic parents. Yet in Albuquerque, his neighbors were "all

conservative Republicans. They were the most wonderful people in the world . . . I found them, in the everyday way, so much nicer and kinder than some of those liberal intellectuals that I knew from the Northeast."

Coles says despite his inclination to "be conservative on many social issues . . . I will never be a conservative politically [because] Jesus spent his life among the poor, and the Hebrew prophets were preoccupied with the poor, and I think *they* are the ones we have to attend . . .

"I don't feel myself part of the 'moral majority,' nor . . . part of the whole parading of religion that we see now in America. It's kind of awful the way that's being used now politically, it's kind of disgusting."

Coles told *Contemporary Authors* he is Episcopalian; agrees in an interview to the designation "Christian existentialist"; and adds that when he called himself "agnostic" in a book it was "in the sense that . . . doubt is part of faith." He says that going to church nowadays, where "everyone is embracing one another and saying hello to one another . . . makes me nervous."

In examining and castigating himself before students, Coles says, he seeks to raise issues in a way that "will, I hope, affect their lives . . . In teaching them I'm trying to teach myself. I'm in the same damn boat they're in—tempted by all the problems of materialism and ambition and greed." In a recent lecture, he introduced Thomas à Kempis, who wrote in the *Imagination of Christ* that, "He who knows himself well is mean in his own eyes . . . Be not, therefore, puffed up with any art or science."

"Here are these writers who've all been struggling with this," says Coles, "and I think we all ought to struggle with it. 'Unreflecting egoism,' George Eliot calls it in *Middlemarch*. How do you tame that? It's a lifelong challenge."

And a sorrow for Coles, who remains tormented by his struggle to reconcile his own position with the wretchedness he sees in the world.

"And how do you ever get out of that?" he asks, his voice growing low. "I don't know. I try to tithe myself, I try to share money [but] I'm still living comfortably . . . I used to have these conversations with

Dorothy Day and she'd say, 'If you want me to accuse you, you've got the wrong person.'"

Now, in his study, Coles grows almost inaudible, as if writhing in despair: "I can't do anything else. I *can't*. I couldn't live. I used to wonder if I could live the way she [Day] used to live, in those hospitality houses, and I'd go crazy."

What attracted Coles to the common, uneducated people he chronicled over the decades, he says, was the simple decency and morality he often found. And what was shocking, he tells students, is that he had to lay aside his education and professional training to understand them.

He still struggles for that understanding, looking ironically at himself looking at them: With respect to Ruby Bridges, that pioneer of integration in America, Coles tells students recently, an interesting "longitudinal irony" has developed.

Now in her thirties, Ruby works for a big company and wants, Coles says, to make "money, a *lot* of money, to help her family." She and her husband "are struggling, as we all struggle, to accumulate some kind of security for themselves."

She also has decided to send her children to private Catholic schools. [UPI quoted her as saying, "My son went to the (public) school that I started at and I don't like to down public schools, but he wasn't really learning the way he should have."]

Says Coles in his lecture: "I had a long talk with her—in a bar, where else? Who's right, who's wrong? . . . I've never figured out, at times, how to answer these questions."

Coles is a workaholic.

"We have no social life. I never take vacations. Who cares about Paris or Rome or London?" He takes walks with his wife, and still likes movies, especially with Clint Eastwood. "I can't stand that whole Woody Allen kind of movie."

For the next phase of his career, Coles plans a study of "how children get their religious and spiritual values; without reducing religious experience to a lot of psychological terms, which is the prevailing tendency even among the ministry."

In addition, he and photographer Alex Harris are trying to set up a center for documentary studies at Duke University to train social scientists, photographers and others. Says Coles: "The tradition of going out into the world, whether it be with a camera, with a tape recorder, with a pad and pencil . . . to observe how people are living . . . in a direct kind of contact with them, is terribly important."

Coles has just answered a letter from a 13-year-old. "I answer those letters with such scrupulosity," he says. "I feel it's an *absolute obligation* to respond . . . It's part of [my] role as a teacher."

Then: "You know the way Percy puts it: *'We hand one another along.'*"

Does Dr. Ruth Talk to Your Kids More Than You Do?

U. S. Catholic/1987

From *U. S. Catholic* (Chicago, IL, August 1987, pp. 22–29). Reprinted by permission of *U. S. Catholic*.

When Robert Coles's wife was expecting their first child, Coles showed up one day bearing a stack of books by noted "experts" in child rearing. His wife took one look and went back to her novel. "What do those writers know about taking care of babies?" she asked him. "They know how to write books, but does that mean they're good parents?"

Coles learned his lesson. Today he's burned up when he sees other parents making the same mistake he made. "Our self-confidence as parents has steadily been eroded by our naive faith in 'experts,' many of whom are probably off worshiping other 'experts.' Why read the Bible when we have Ann Landers and Dr. Ruth?"

So where can perplexed parents turn? To their kids. "Realize that you have something to offer a child that isn't a function of the last book you've read," he says. "It's you." Coles, a psychiatry professor at Harvard University and the author of several books, including the Pulitzer Prize winning *Children of Crisis* series, has some simple words of "expert" advice for parents: listen, and talk.

How did you get interested in studying the moral and spiritual lives of children?

Let me start by telling you that I was trained really not to be too interested in moral or religious questions, except as they could tell me something about a child's psychological thinking. I trained in pediatrics, child psychiatry, and psychoanalysis in the 1950s. That was when the American public, particularly the upper-middle class, carried on an idolatrous romance with Freudian psychoanalysis, which examined and treated emotional disorders by focusing on ego development, childhood traumas, and unconscious drives.

My education probably differed from most of the people I went to medical school with because, instead of science, I had majored in English. In fact, William Carlos Williams, one of the finest writers around and a physician himself, acted as a mentor of sorts for me in graduate school. Williams writes with a strong moral voice, which has always impressed me. It was he who inspired me to become a physician, although I was originally going to become a pediatrician, not a psychiatrist.

Why did you switch to psychiatry?

Actually, I became a pediatrician first; but I had trouble being tough enough to be really good at it. When I gave a child a shot, for instance, and that child started to cry, I would get too involved in the tears.

One day while I was still an intern, I heard Anna Freud, the founder of child psychoanalysis, give a lecture on children. I became quite taken with her and what she had to say about kids. This more than anything got me headed toward a residency in psychiatry.

A few years later in Boston came an event, a tragedy really, that made me wonder if reality could be understood best in psychological terms. I'm speaking about the last polio epidemic, just before the Salk vaccine became available. I had the opportunity to work, both as a pediatrician and a child psychiatrist, with all those children who would have died without massive iron-lung machines doing all their breathing. And that was an important experience for me because not only did I try to understand these children and work with them rather intensely, but the conversations I had with them were unlike any others I knew of. Never before had I heard such intense moral self-scrutiny from kids.

These children weren't prepared to be sick; most of them came from affluent families. Polio struck the well-to-do rather than the poor, by and large, because the poor had built up an immunity to it. And so I was suddenly in the presence of children who, out of the lap of luxury, found themselves stricken with a disease that was probably going to kill them. They wondered why they had become ill, what they had ever done to deserve this, and if a good God could have done this to them. They openly speculated about the meaning of life, particularly the value of the often brief life left to them.

Their questions were clearly not psychological, nor could I explain them away in psychological terms. I would have needed to have been an extremely cold, tough—and, I would think, bad—therapist not to notice or respond to what I saw.

Can a child make moral decisions?

Absolutely yes. I'm appalled at these schemes of morality which put children in the so-called "preconventional stage" of moral development. These theories imply that because most children lack an intellectually sophisticated moral life, they're not able to make difficult moral decisions. Yet it's common knowledge that a smart, well-educated person can behave like a skunk; and it's also no secret that a not-so-smart person or someone with little or no education can be very sensitive and kind. That goes for kids as well.

Maybe little 6-year-old Ruby Bridges, the first black child to desegregate a New Orleans public school, couldn't analyze complex moral theories; but she managed to pray every day for the mobs who taunted and threatened to kill her. Ruby came from a poor, illiterate family and was just herself learning how to read and write, yet I've rarely met anybody with as much courage. I've met many, many other children with strong moral convictions, even children who were dismissed all too readily as bad or delinquent.

One 9-year-old boy told me the other day that he likes to go to church with his parents because he likes seeing them on their knees. "Why?" I asked him. "Well," he said, "they're looking up to someone besides themselves." As far as I'm concerned, that's not a boy in a "preconventional stage" of moral development.

What's the source of this moral awareness? Where does it come from?

I think children have within them the same capacities that adults do: capacities for love and kindness and thoughtfulness. But we adults and children also have a mean and envious side to ourselves, which, by the way, 25 years of analysis won't necessarily get rid of.

I know for a fact that if I or my children choose to live ethically, we'll still struggle with our own egoism for the rest of our lives, unless we just want to give into it—and a lot of days I do. I'm wrapped up in

myself all too often. I find that when I'm driving I don't give people
the right-of-way because I'm "important" and feel like I need to get
where I'm going. And I can give a great lecture in a classroom on
moral matters, but then ultimately, just like everybody else, adult or
child, I'm faced with the side of myself which is low-down, two-bit,
and hypocritical.

One of the biggest favors we can do for our kids is to say, "Hey,
listen, being an honest, considerate person is hard stuff. It's going to
take some doing." I think somehow we don't believe in sharing with
our children the terrible awkwardness that we all get into. We want to
give our children the rose garden, but we're afraid to break the news
to them about the thorns. We parents don't even want to hint to our
kids that someday they are going to die, just as we will; that just as
inevitably as the sun comes up in the morning, our children will feel
pain and hunger and loss; that they may even be punished for their
good deeds and rewarded for their bad ones, at least in the short run,
but it's worth it anyway to lead a life of moral integrity.

*If I told my teenage son he might be punished for his good deeds, I
wonder how eager he would be to do them.*

To begin with, you wouldn't be telling him something he didn't
already know; you'd just be verifying it. People with any common
sense at all, be they 6 or 60 years old, know that if they speak out in
the name of an unpopular cause that not everybody is going to be
their friend.

When Ruby Bridges walked down the street with federal marshals
on either side of her, guarding her against the screaming segregationists, she was quite sure that her decision to go to a white public
school was not going to bring her massive popularity. We ought not
to underestimate our children's moral perceptions; at the same time,
we parents would be speaking out much more often on moral
questions if we recognized how carefully our children listened to us
and watched our moral behavior.

*Do the kids you've talked to through the years have an innate
sense of religion or awareness of God?*

Plenty of times they do; but not always. Some children, through
their religious lives, really make some powerful moral discoveries. But
it's also possible for children to use religion to justify some of the

most arrogant, immoral actions imaginable and to urge others to do the same.

I've spent years in Belfast where the so-called religions, Catholicism and Protestantism, are all too interested in prompting suspicion and hate. Obviously, I saw more of God's love in Ruby Bridges as she prayed for the mobs who taunted her than in some of the Irish youngsters who prayed that God would strike down their neighbors.

Do you think parents today are less confident about raising their kids? Or is it just me?

You're not alone; our self-confidence as parents has steadily been eroded by our naive faith in "experts," many of whom are probably off worshiping other "experts."

When our first son was born, I gave my wife five psychology books to read; but she refused to touch them. I thought, "What is her 'problem'? Why is she 'resisting' this kind of knowledge?"

My wife is a high-school English teacher; and, instead of my selections, she was reading George Eliot's *Middlemarch*. I said to her, "What are you reading that for? Here's Dr. Spock. Here's another book called *The First Year of Life*—doesn't that sound important? Shouldn't everyone who has a newborn child read that and learn from a noted authority in child psychoanalysis?"

"If I can't bring up a child without those five books," my wife replied, "we're in a lot worse trouble because it means I don't even have the instincts to take care of a little baby without looking up what I'm doing in somebody's table of contents."

And then she asked me, "What do those writers know about taking care of babies, anyway? They know how to write books, but does that mean they're good parents?"

Today I agree with her. It's all too easy for parents to swallow child-rearing books hook, line, and sinker. Why read the Bible or George Eliot when we've got Ann Landers and Dr. Ruth? Most of us don't even know who George Eliot is. But everyone knows who Dr. Spock is, or the author of *Children of Crisis*, or whatever guru happens down the turnpike next.

What does classic literature have to offer parents?

George Eliot in *Middlemarch* reminds us, for heaven's sake, to get a longer view of things: realize that you do have something to offer a child that isn't a function of the last book you've read. It's you! Eliot doesn't try to package reality into neat, little brown boxes or try to make parents feel insecure because they get confused.

George Eliot looks at the ordinary contradictions of life. She writes about many of the complexities, ironies, and inconsistencies of living that can't ever be outdated by the latest theories on child raising or sex education.

Biblical parables, stories by Leo Tolstoy, Mark Twain, and J. D. Salinger are all part of our cultural and moral heritage because they really capture what it means to be a human being. And so do Walker Percy, Saul Bellow, and Flannery O'Connor. These people can help us give ourselves and our children a rich moral education.

What would you like your children to learn from these books?

I would like my children to learn the same thing from those books that I do: that morality exists in everyone; and without following it, people become their own worst enemies.

I would like my children to come away from those books with a better sense of all of our mutual dependence on this planet, lest we all murder each other in a dark moment one day.

These books are filled with moral questions and a world where the consequences of one's actions can be clearly seen. Children ask moral questions about the world all the time; and parents mistake many of them for sexual concerns. How did we get here? Where are we going? What are we? What are we meant to be or to do? When children ponder these matters, they usually aren't only trying to learn about the birds and the bees; they're trying to grasp what it means to be human.

What kind of answers do they get?

Parents generally don't respond very well to these questions because their minds are usually somewhere else. Parents are more attuned to "goal-oriented" questions on sex or achievement. And we reap what we sow because kids quickly see that parents find their questions about how much television they can watch and what homework needs to get done vastly more interesting than their moral preoccupations.

I think that what children in the United States desperately need is a moral purpose, and a lot of our children here aren't getting that. They're getting parents who are very concerned about getting them into the right colleges, buying the best clothing for them, giving them an opportunity to live in neighborhoods where they'll lead fine and affluent lives and where they can be given the best toys, go on interesting vacations, and all sorts of things.

Now look at the implications of this. I think we correctly take it for granted that the media, especially television and the movies, exert an enormous influence on our children; and we're properly concerned about it. Before I traveled abroad to talk with children all over the world, I assumed the more any children saw TV, the more they were influenced by it; but it's not so simple.

For the last 40 years the children in Poland have grown up in a culture where the government totally controls all the media, the magazines, the newspapers, the television shows, the movies—in short, everything—in a way that would be inconceivable to us here in the United States. And do you know what? The Polish kids I met consistently ridiculed the messages they heard on television and radio, and they scorned the textbooks they were given in school.

Now I'm talking about 8-, 10-, 12-year-olds who were—despite all the media messages—extremely critical of the government. Why couldn't the state-run government brainwash the Polish kids? Well, they and their parents shared an alternative moral vision that couldn't be shaken.

But isn't that because they have something clear-cut and obvious to fight against?
Moral vision doesn't only come from what a culture fights against. Moral vision comes from what a people fight for, what they're willing to die for and live for.

I think the reason that our children are so vulnerable to television is that there are no opposing values for them to hold onto. So it isn't television per se, or the indecency or greed of the media—it's our lives. We can't just fob it off on others.

There used to be something in our society commonly called "soul-searching." It meant a legitimate preoccupation, usually among young people, to find out the deepest truths of their lives. But we don't encourage our children to do it anymore. Instead, we encourage them to consume: drugs, alcohol, sex, plenty of material possessions—just like Mom and Dad. And when our teens start carrying through suicide pacts in small towns and big cities, we all scratch our heads and ask, "But how could this be?"

Most of the parents I know don't fit your description; they're just ordinary people trying to support their families.

Parents work very hard these days; and they're acquiring things that they feel are important for their children. And yet vastly more important things are not happening. They're not spending time with their children, at least not very much. They're not listening or trying to teach them. They're not even trying to teach themselves anymore because, in many respects, they've given up on themselves. And, of course, the children will pick this up.

I teach religion for teenagers once a week; and last night the toughest kid in the class said, "It would help me so much if my parents would just talk with me about sex." Is the solution that simple?

Hundreds and thousands of children in this country can report that they practically never have any significant conversations with their parents about sex, or for that matter, about anything. And because of that lack of communication, we leave our kids to fend for themselves in an area that can have disastrous consequences for them: premature sexual involvement.

The theories of psychoanalysis and the Catholic Church agree on this issue, although for different reasons. It would be inconceivable to Anna Freud that there could be a reasonable justification for passing out birth-control devices or sex information to young, unmarried teenagers and telling them, "Here is all you need to be safe." Anna Freud would say, "No. They haven't developed enough to make these kinds of commitments and choices. They need more time; they need to learn internalized controls."

But what if they are already sexually active?

The liberal intelligentsia of which, I suppose, alas, I am a member, claims that these kids need birth-control clinics. The boys, they say, should use condoms; the girls should use other contraceptives; and if that doesn't work, give them abortions. But Anna Freud would say, and I would agree with her, that this is to sell our young people down the river because we parents don't want to pay the price of confronting teens with what we know about the psychological and spiritual effects of early sexual involvement. They might not listen to us, or it might be hard for us to do; but parents need to confront their teens with the hard facts.

Children and teenagers need to hear the honest feedback of morally committed people from all walks of life, including their parents. They do not need to be patronized with condoms and birth-control pills by people who have already given up on them.

Is this lack of communication between parents and children the biggest reason for the rise in teenage suicides?
I would be very reluctant to make any generalizations about teenage suicide. Obviously, each young person who kills or tries to kill himself or herself has a story to tell, and problems with parents do play a part in many of them. But I think it goes beyond this. When I read about suicide pacts, with four and five kids killing themselves in high school, it seems clear that there is something social and cultural in this. When reasonably privileged, middle-class kids engage in these pacts, I think suicide has become an accelerated version of other kinds of self-destruction, namely with drugs or alcohol, that are already taking place.

And all of this, all of it, I find as the most accurate reflection of the moral aimlessness that cripples every strata of our society. As I listen to the parents or friends of these suicide victims afterward, I get the impression they had no moral or spiritual center. They moved fom group to group, from fad to fad.

I'm not trying to downplay the psychological problems of young people who kill themselves here in the United States; but these seem to be free-floating psychological problems with no larger context attached.

I look at the children I've worked with in Rio de Janeiro, who have terrible psychological problems—who are, besides that, hungry and desperate—and yet these children aren't committing suicide. They're fighting for life. Isn't this a major irony?

But these children who are fighting for food have *that* to fight for. In South Africa the black children believe in freedom. In Brazil children believe in just getting through one day and finding some food. And many of them, by the way, get food and share it with other children in the most extraordinary manner.

And then I come back to the United States and see our children who also have problems; but what do they do with them? They kill themselves.

As a parent, can you give me an example of how you've tried to give your kids the moral direction they need?
I was in the 5- and 10-cent store years ago with one of my sons when he said he wanted me to buy him a toy machine gun. I said no. And then he said that he really wanted it, he really wanted that machine gun. So I switched it around. I said, okay, I'll get it for you.

So I bought him the gun—with a lecture.

He paid, and you paid?
Exactly. Some critics would say I was bribing him. And my answer to them would be yes. I wanted my son to remember this particular lecture, and I felt that buying this toy for him would help him to remember it.

But when we were coming out of the store, a friend of mine saw Bobby walking next to me with his toy gun. He came up to me in shock. "How can you buy your son a gun?" he wanted to know. "You! A child psychiatrist. What kind of example is that for the rest of us?"

I said to him jokingly, but I also was annoyed, "Yes, I love guns. The more, the better. In fact, I could shoot you with one right now."

Talk about a crisis in confidence. Parents can't follow their own best judgment these days without having the whole world down their throats. Everything is monitored and measured. There's no room for any judgment call without some self-righteous person coming along and advising parents to read such and such a book or try such and such a method.

But what I've found is that this moralistic hustle and bustle is really a misplaced moralism that doesn't really address the heart of raising a child. What parents need are some passionately felt convictions that they themselves have struggled with and made their own.

What kind of convictions?

From my point of view? That it takes grace in this world to really live well and that grace is from God.

Those methods of child rearing that we read in books come and go. One day it's don't feed your child too much ice cream because of the cholesterol; the next day it's something else.

In contrast, I would hope I'd be ready to die for certain things in connection with my own life and my children's lives. Not over whether they watch an afternoon soap opera or a program on Saturday morning that has violence in it or whether I do or do not allow them a plastic gun from the dime store, but over this: if I saw my child ignoring someone in need, whistling Dixie while someone was in trouble, I would want to cry for my child and for myself. And I would feel that this was a tragedy that had befallen both of us, a tragedy that no expert would ever get us "out of" or should ever try to get us out of. I would feel that my son and I together—for I would take some of the responsibility—had done a terrible thing.

How does grace keep us going?

I don't think we can ever understand how grace comes because it's "free" and can come at any moment. But the possibility for grace ought to be what keeps us going. In "Master and Man" by Leo Tolstoy, grace just came upon the master in some miraculous way as he realized that he could save his servant's life by giving him clothes and the warmth of his body. That moment that the master had with his servant didn't include a meeting with a psychotherapist, and he wasn't with someone who was trying to get him through the five stages of dying.

The same holds for the lawyer in Tolstoy's "The Death of Ivan Ilyich." The psychological transformation was utterly unself-conscious. How lucky people were back then! I'm sick and tired of all the excessive psychological preoccupation of our time. I'd like to see a lot more moral preoccupation on the part of all of us and a lot less faddish enchantment with the social sciences, especially psychology.

I remember meeting, when I was a busy medical student, a 32-year-old woman with four kids who was dying of cancer. Her husband was a factory worker. I can recall to this day my smugness and aesthetic displeasure at her tremendous enthusiasm for a piano player named Liberace. I came into that little room where she was

dying, and my first thought was "how crude" when I saw the
Liberace picture and little miniature piano by her bed. But as I
watched her listen to Liberace on a little record player that was
brought into the room, I began to realize that here was someone who
was dying, and somehow through that music, she was crying and
yearning for a life that she never would live. And the music of
Liberace was comforting her on a deep spiritual level.

I wish I could have appreciated it more at the time, blinded as I was
by my aesthetic judgment. But I know now, looking back, that she
was receiving an enormous amount of solace. I came in one day,
terribly overworked and with little time for her, and she said to me,
"Oh, you look so tired!" I moved away from her, thinking to myself,
"I can't take that; that's something my mother would have said."

But, in fact, she had been listening to Liberace, who in his music
had been talking about people who are tired and need some kind of
refreshment of spirit. So she looked at me and observed I was tired.

*What are Americans missing from their day-to-day relationships
with other people?*

I think we miss truths about people that could change our lives if
we knew about them. All we need to do is listen: people talk all the
time abut moments in their lives that have made them stop and ask
about the world and its significance. And that's what this woman was
doing for herself with Liberace; and that's what I couldn't notice or
give her credit for.

I met a man in New Orleans recently, a poor man who spends his
whole day shining shoes. He was so cheerful, so sweet—he
explained to me where I could do this or that. He helps people all
day long while he tries to make a living. How does he do it? Without
a college degree and maybe even illiterate? Is it remotely possible that
without an education and with practically no money, not even a
minimum wage, he's behaving this way? Now, this is someone with a
story.

Belief in God can help people act that way, can't it?

I think the shoeshine man's faith in God has something to do with
the way he acts; and I think God has faith in him, too. It seems to me
that God chooses to be with certain people for different criteria than
most of ours. Maybe, just maybe, he doesn't check over our

educational level first, or the years of psychotherapy we've had, or
our socio-economic status. Wouldn't that be a surprise?

It's the old biblical story of the first being last and the last being first.
I am not romanticizing poverty or urging its destructive characteristics
on anyone; but there is a tradition in this country of dignified struggle,
of an earnest, hardworking struggle that many families in this country
no longer know about. And because we don't know about it, or have
forgotten what it was like, we tend to miss a lot of truth and meaning
in the world that we could otherwise give to our children.

I'd like to tell a true story that might help you see my point. A
number of years ago I took my son Bobby, who had been studying
Greek and Latin, to see both Greece and Rome. While we were in
Rome, we were sent to an audience with the Pope.

On our way to the Vatican we took a cab driven by a man who
spoke English. He knew exactly where we were going, and he sized
us up pretty quickly. "Are you going to get a special audience?" he
asked. Proudly I responded yes. And he said, "Oh, you're going to
burn in hell for going there." Then he started pointing to Castel
Gandolfo, where the Pope has his summer home. He said, "Do you
think Jesus would live there? Do you think he'd go and have a
summer home and a winter home and live that way? Have you ever
been to the Vatican? Would Jesus live like *that?*" We heard it from
him for about 10 minutes. Finally I turned to Bobby and said, "This
guy's making me so nervous. For all we know, this guy right here
may be Jesus." So I tried to buy him out by giving him a big tip, and
then we went on our way.

When we were inside the Vatican seeing all the priceless paintings
and artifacts, my son turned to me and asked me why the church
doesn't sell them and give the money to the hungry people of the
world. I gave him a stuffy academic answer—that there was an
important heritage there that needed to be preserved. He asked me
immediately what I thought Jesus would do if he came back to
earth—what Jesus would do with all the wealth there. I had no
answer then, and I still don't.

Sometimes I think that all of us as parents, along with schoolteachers and others, spend a lot of time squelching our children so
they won't ask the kinds of questions my son was asking that day. I
think there is a tremendous natural moral curiosity in children. And I

think a lot of us adults are frightened by the implications of that moral curiosity: that some of our rationalizations and self-justifications will be exposed, along with our moral jeopardy.

It seems that in every generation there's somebody who says, "There's never been a worse time for the American family." Do you think this is finally it?

We love to say these things because then we get to focus on ourselves. This is our way of paying attention to ourselves and actually calling ourselves quite significantly important. "No one has gone through what we've gone through" and "Just look at us."

I wish that all of us would read the Book of Ecclesiastes in the Old Testament at least once or twice a week, particularly when we come up with these statements.

But haven't you stressed that there's a great deal of spiritual emptiness today?

I think there is; and there always has been. In Isaiah, everything that he says concerns spiritual emptiness and the swollen pride of the kingdom of Israel. Those Hebrew prophets were in the same kind of dire straits that we're in today.

I'm not saying we should whistle in the dark about this, but let's get some historical and spiritual context for it. The point is that human beings are always going to struggle. "The modern family is in terrible shape," we say. I think Isaiah would say, "Oh really? You think *you* have problems." Look at what Jesus had to contend with—lots of imperfect people there, too.

Has there been any one person who has influenced your moral values more than anybody else?

The first person who comes to my mind is Dorothy Day, the founder of the Catholic Worker House and my friend for the last 30 years before she died. I'll never forget a lesson I learned from her the first time I met her at the Catholic Worker. I had arrived, as a self-confident medical student to perhaps do some volunteer work. Grandly, I asked to speak to Dorothy Day. Who but the best? Somebody pointed me to the kitchen where she and everybody else were eating lunch.

Dorothy Day and another person were sitting there, deep in

conversation as I waited for them to finish. I already knew enough about psychiatry to recognize that the person she was with was disturbed, alcoholic, and somewhat incoherent. For all I knew, there may have been other calls or other people who wanted to speak to Day, or other pressing things to do, but nothing seemed more important to her at that moment than continuing this conversation.

When they had both finished their lunch and their conversation, they got up, and I approached her. She could have certainly guessed that I was going to address her and not her companion. But what she said to me was, "You wanted to speak with one of us . . . ?" *With one of us.* Well, that took care of me. I don't think Harvard had anything more to teach me in four years than she had to offer me right then and there.

And I think we're all capable of that kind of teaching with one another occasionally, children and adults alike. I've seen children reach out to other children, to soothe and comfort them, even in our narcissistic culture. I've also seen children be mean to one another and regret it.

So there's always hope. There is for any of us, God willing.

The Doctor Is In

Deborah Baldwin/1988

From *Common Cause* (Washington, DC, May/June 1988, pp. 25–29). Reprinted by permission of *Common Cause*.

It has been 20 years since the peak of the student protest movement, giving rise to countless nostalgic recollections of those idealistic times known as the '60s. Characteristic of the genre was the recent *New York Times* op-ed piece in which aging baby boomer Benjamin J. Stein, a Los Angeles lawyer and writer, rhapsodized about the good old days and asked himself—apparently without irony—why, with three cars, a nice house and a lovely family, he felt so lonely for the Revolution. If the notion that he ought to climb out of his hot tub and organize for social justice crossed his mind, he didn't say so.

There are those who would argue that the social movements of the '60s never ceased to be relevant—they just lost momentum, subsumed by the preoccupations of the Me Generation. Among them is Dr. Robert Coles, a social critic, child psychiatrist, award-winning author, Harvard professor and purveyor of a unique brand of ethical activism that could help cure the '80s of its own excesses.

To goad his listeners, Coles uses a blend of optimism and mordant observation, typified by this summation of the current crop of presidential candidates. "I haven't heard any of these candidates reach out to the young people of this country and reach out to people who might want to be asked, as the president did in 1960, to give of yourself to the country," he said in an interview in early March. "What they're all catering to is the side of us that wants to hear, 'We're not going to ask anything of you, we're not going to increase your taxes, we're not going to come up with anything, we're just going to give back to you anything you want—and then some.'"

One of Coles's underlying beliefs is that we begin life with all the right instincts, but somehow in the process of growing up they're often snuffed. We wake up one day in a beautiful house, with two kids and a high-paying career, and can't remember what it was like to feel moral outrage. By capturing and directing the idealism of young people, he asserts, we can cure spiritual numbness before it sets in for life.

Coles is perhaps best known for finding hope in some of the most hopeless corners of the globe. After decades of exposure to families living under the most difficult circumstances imaginable, he remains impossibly upbeat about the next generation's ability to endure and achieve. He has seen it in the grinding poverty of Rio de Janeiro's slums, in bitterly divided South Africa, in the bleak isolation of Appalachia and even amid warfare in Northern Ireland.

"I may sound naive," he will say by way of preface, launching into still another enthusiastic defense of the human spirit.

Coles seems to derive his own strength and resilience from two groups of people: children, whose uncanny powers of observation and innocence provide the basis for many of his books, and a handful of individuals—he calls them his mentors—who observed the human race at extremes of idealism and despair yet continued to "actively take on the world," as Coles puts it, remaining "in a non-sentimental sense hopeful."

The ability to always look forward, armed with the wisdom of children and saints, has turned Robert Coles into a social conscience for the upwardly mobile—a nagging reminder that there is a world outside the comfortable cocoons we create to protect ourselves and our families, and walking proof that a middle-class upbringing and an Ivy League education can lead to some career besides, say, L.A. law.

Thousands buy his books and crowd his lecture halls. Tell us how to find meaning in our lives, they say. Make us stronger parents. Give us a remedy for the poverty of mind and spirit that plagues us. Audiences are "hungry for knowledge about, in a way, themselves, and one another, and what's possible in this country," Coles concedes.

His response, which he delivers in thoughtful narratives suffused with insight, sadness and laughter, seems tailored for our times: Give of yourself to others.

The last eight or 10 years have been a "tough time" for many American families, Coles observes, not only because many have been hurt by changes in the economy, but because of changes in government programs and policies. "Look what's happened to the former activism of the federal government in dealing with civil rights problems," he notes, "and in dealing with the problems of the poor."

A withering critic of the slippery ethics and me-ism of the '80s, Coles says he is also alarmed by corruption in key areas of our society. "This is a scandal," he says. "I teach students. . . . And it's not pleasant to see young people wondering how long this will continue and how many more people will be caught up in this, whether it's in the federal government or on Wall Street or more recently in our churches." He finds equally demoralizing "the kind of sardonic, mocking attitude you hear" from some students, because it is a symptom of a kind of indifference and scorn that is perhaps the worst kind of corruption.

Why don't college students rebel, the way they did in the '60s?

"You know, they're a little tired of moral outrage," Coles says, "because the outrage is not attended, not heard. After all, the president of the United States puts his arm around an attorney general who has been repeatedly implicated in suspicious or questionable activities.

"Some of these ministers confess to all kinds of really scandalous forms of behavior, then they seem to go on. . . . And even on Wall Street the outbursts are new, and then somehow the whole thing doesn't seem to have an effect. . . . There's no sense of *national* indignation, political or moral, which can set the stage for the private indignation of these students. . . ."

In a matter of moments, however, he's bounced back again.

"During the darkest times in my life politically," he says, "it's been hard for me to get too discouraged because of what I hear from children, from students. You hear hope, you hear idealism, you hear a kind of innocence that's so refreshing, you hear humor and good intentions working their way into ordinary remarks.

"And I don't want to be Dr. Pangloss, and I don't want to say we're living in the best of all possible worlds, but I try to hear that side of our country's life, rather than what I hear when I turn on the television from my so-called national leaders . . . and our so-called authorities of one kind or another. They're a dreary lot, a lot of them."

Perhaps best known for his five-volume series, *Children of Crisis,* published between 1967 and 1978, Coles more recently was a recipient of a MacArthur Foundation fellowship. He used the MacArthur money to travel with his wife and three sons outside America for the first time, plumbing children's psyches in Nicaragua, Poland, South Africa and elsewhere in an effort to understand how they develop their political views. In 1986 he produced twin volumes called *The Political Life of Children* and *The Moral Life of Children,* which describe the impressive, often unpredictable spurts of moral and political development he observed among children both here and abroad.

Coles's unconventional approach, more like that of a documentary filmmaker than that of a psychiatrist, involves interviewing children at length, inviting them to draw and discuss pictures about themselves and their world and using these as the raw ingredients for long reflective essays. His goal is to let children describe the world as they (and not the experts) see it, while nudging his readers toward a greater awareness of the needs of others—vulnerable children in particular.

Bound together as books, Coles's essays are imbued with a self-conscious, almost self-deprecating air. Often he will use his own experiences as a way to reveal one of the greatest pitfalls of experts and intellects everywhere—pride. Often it seems as if the man with all the answers is still searching himself.

Coles grew up in middle-class comfort near Boston and graduated from Harvard without much notion of what he wanted to do. He still refers to the "serendipitous" nature of the events that led him from college to medical school to the civil rights movement—which he says he "stumbled into" in the early '60s—and into the work that has brought him critical acclaim and a popular following. Obsessed with the role of fate in the evolution of character, he has said that he is haunted by the realization that he might never have pursued this course, opting instead for a private practice and a conventional lifestyle, if he and his wife Jane (a schoolteacher who has assisted in much of his research) hadn't been able to turn to their families for some initial financial support. When they approached private foundations in search of grants for the kind of nomadic research they wanted to do, they got form-letter rejections.

Today, of course, big-name foundations invite Coles to guest lecture at their events. In future talks Coles says he hopes to persuade foundations to assist with a project upon which he has pinned great hopes—namely to provide grants to young people who want to work in community service but can't afford to because they've graduated in debt or have other obligations. The MacArthur Foundation, after all, gave Coles almost a quarter-million dollars so that he could spend five years on his study of children's political values. A similar amount might have supported a doctor's work at a rural health clinic, he notes, adding, "Why couldn't some of our foundations, and perhaps the federal government in conjunction with them, sponsor certain people for a stretch of time? Say to some doctors and some lawyers and some engineers and some schoolteachers and some social workers, 'Look, here's five years of support to enable you to do this kind of work in communities that need it.' "

All kinds of young people, including the privileged, would respond, he believes. In preparing the fifth volume of *Children of Crisis,* a study of the children of the well-to-do, Coles found many of them to be "very shrewd" about politics and the need for social change. "For two years now," he adds, "I have been teaching courses at the Harvard Business School—if there's ever a group of people you'd think are headed for heart-and-soul yuppiedom. And I'm stunned at how much earnest goodwill I find in some of those students." Coles estimates that more than half the student body at Harvard contributes some time to community service.

"I think idealism—and generosity of spirit—is a natural part of childhood," he says. "It doesn't matter what the family is, whether they're black, white, rich or poor. I found that everywhere; it's part of being a child or an adolescent, looking at the world with that kind of freshness. But, of course, you know that the heart dies—a lot of this idealism is not amplified by schools, by families or communities, or it is even discouraged."

The next step for those who have been involved in social, political and racial struggles, he says, "is to help a new generation of young Americans to not only get involved with the problems of this country through their activities, but to let that involvement help them become better educated both intellectually and, if I may even use the word, become deeper spiritually and morally through reflection on what they've actually done."

Coles advocates this variety of educated activism in the humanities courses he teaches in five different departments at Harvard. (He is developing a course specifically on community service which he hopes to start teaching this fall.) His lectures, linking the moral values in literature to contemporary society and its needs, gently prod the privileged Harvard student body to abandon the quest for materialism and conventional kinds of achievement—undergrads have dubbed his course "Guilt 105." His course at the Harvard Medical School has students working in clinics and hospitals for the poor; in seminars they integrate these experiences with what they've learned from great literature, which Coles believes contains a wealth of useful knowledge about moral values.

One of Coles's favorite novels is George Eliot's 19th-century masterpiece *Middlemarch,* a study of the influence of class and circumstance on "the unfolding," as she puts it, of various characters' moral development. The book is astonishingly contemporary in its observations, which include this insight into the way society wears down youthful idealism: "In the multitude of middle-aged men who go about their vocations in a daily course determined for them much in the same way as the tie of their cravats, there is always a good number who once meant to shape their own deeds and alter the world a little. . . . Nothing in the world more subtle than the process of their gradual change! In the beginning they inhaled it unknowingly; you and I may have sent some of our breath towards infecting them, when we uttered our conforming falsities. . . ."

As might be expected from a man who weaves 19th-century literature into his business school courses, Coles often seems old-fashioned. He is identified as a political liberal, but says he's a conservative on social and family issues ("and on economic issues a populist"). "I worry about where our values are going. I'm appalled by the pornography that our children, that all of us, have available," he says. In a recent essay in *Sojourners* magazine describing his current work with teenagers, Coles writes with characteristic wryness, "After spending time with sexually savvy 16-year-olds, I feel like retiring into a Norman Rockwell picture of the 1950s or maybe one of Frank Capra's film celebrations of American innocence. Still, I manage to give myself a lecture on the dangers of retrospective romanticism. . . ."

The side of Coles drawn to Eliot, Tolstoy and Dickens also takes enjoyment from the complexities and ambiguities of the human experience. Coles's own life is a good case in point. Here is a doctor who cannot bear to draw blood; a professor who is uncomfortable grading students; a founder of the food stamp program who dislikes federal bureaucracies; a member of a prestigious faculty who dislikes academia (and the professions in general). Coles is an educator and simplifier—a storyteller—yet reveres mystery and the unknown. He is class-conscious yet apolitical, having turned away from the government after his heroes Robert Kennedy and Martin Luther King were killed; an influential award-winner who rejects conventional measures of success; a loner who claims he would never have engaged in this "crazy mission"—his lifetime work—if it hadn't been for the support and approval of his wife Jane. He is a psychiatrist who rejects labels, pigeon-holing and popular theories about psychological and biochemical predeterminism; a contributor to *The New England Journal of Medicine*—on the subject of *Middlemarch;* a workaholic who often feels the tug of family; a religious believer who is often uncomfortable in church.

If presented with such a list, Coles's response would no doubt be a dramatic lurch of the eyebrows and an eye-crunching laugh. Fifty-eight years old, he is wiry, with dark wayward hair, an infectious sense of humor and an earnestness that makes him seem, well, youthful. He speaks *slowly* . . . and *rhythmically* . . . like *this.* He also tends to bend sideways when answering questions, as if making a conscious effort to repress a desire to preach.

Over the years Coles has perfected an ability to tell people things they may not want to hear. Impatient with the narcissism and materialism of our decade, he also casts a jaundiced eye at today's self-styled authorities—the pollsters and advertising geniuses who mold political campaigns, and the banal self-help books that let us avoid making difficult moral decisions about the way we live. "Parents who are not exactly sure what they dare to want for themselves or their children (besides the various objects incessantly paraded before them with wicked cleverness on the television screen or in newspapers and magazines) turn eagerly to psychologists and psychiatrists, members of the so-called helping professions," Coles once wrote disparagingly. "We want to 'analyze' everything, including our children's behavior, and at the same time we have convinced ourselves that we lack the authority to take a firm stand on much of anything—with respect to their lives or our own."

He has been described as shuffling up to podiums before audiences of well-to-do professionals, looking slightly disheveled, a little like TV's Lt. Columbo without the raincoat. (Like Columbo, Coles even makes frequent mention of his wise but rarely seen wife.) Then, without benefit of written text, he launches into powerful, seemingly impromptu language, reducing his audiences to pudding. This effect seems all the more remarkable given the sound of his voice—Peter Falk with a nasal Boston accent.

Working out of a quiet, orderly office on the Harvard University campus—a plaque on the wall proclaims it to be Franklin Roosevelt's undergraduate suite—Coles seems to enjoy the role of the tireless, guilt-inducing guru. A man of practiced patience, he seems unperturbed, for example, when a photographer he doesn't know can't resist breaking into a reporter's questions with some observations and inquiries of his own.

But then, Coles spends a lot of time listening to others thrash through their self-realizations. Students come to Coles constantly in search of meaningful alternatives to investment banking and the like. It is common for his former students to say, "He changed my life."

If Coles seems extra-patient with undergraduates—a recent campus visitor observed them to be largely scruffy and self-indulgent, just as she remembered from college 20 years ago—it may be in part because he has never lost his ability to identify with the young.

He has never let himself forget, for example, that once upon a time he drove a white Porsche convertible with red leather seats, in homage to teen rebel James Dean, and that he liked dating and going drinking.

Or that his parents and colleagues thought he was wasting his life because he wouldn't open a private practice and make money like everybody else.

Or that he leaned on a handful of extraordinary individuals who changed *his* life.

Coles says he became a doctor who worked with children "because *he* did," a reference to the poet and old-fashioned general

practitioner William Carlos Williams. Junior year in college he met
Williams and started following him on his rounds in poor neighborhoods in Paterson, N.J. Williams taught Coles that there's a
difference between moral ideas and moral conduct—a difference
between *thinking* the poor need help and actually helping them, for
example—a distinction that runs throughout Coles's work. Williams
also helped get Coles in medical school and years later, upon
discovering that the young confused pediatrician had an unfortunate
aversion to giving shots, helped to steer him toward child psychiatry.
"He was a wonderful person to know," Coles says, "and a great
inspiration to me. . . . Now there's an example of something, you
see; you come in contact with someone and you get to know him
and ultimately he changed my life."

It was also Williams who helped Coles understand the meaning of
his profound encounter with the most unlikely mentor of all, a six-
year-old black girl named Ruby Bridges.

Coles sought out Ruby, the daughter of impoverished, illiterate
parents, in 1960 when she was singlehandedly desegregating a
school in New Orleans. Accompanied by federal marshals as, twice a
day, she steadily threaded her way through jeering, hateful mobs, she
prayed for God to "forgive them because they don't know what
they're doing." As Coles tells it, he was a self-absorbed and
somewhat arrogant young psychiatrist who thought he could identify
a psychological condition for what turned out to be a six-year-old's
commitment to live what she learned in the Bible. Literally. After all,
as Coles notes dryly, Ruby wasn't in a position to take the steps he
might have chosen had they changed positions: call a lawyer, ask the
local police for protection, analyze the mob's pathology and then
write about it afterward.

It was a humbling experience, and one that crops up often in
Coles's books and lectures, not only because Ruby taught him about
moral behavior but because she also inspired him to pursue this
"whole new chapter" in his life—that of a documentary writer. Coles
says he'll never forget Williams's relief when he learned, "I'd found
my vocation—this long search was over!"

Other mentors include Dorothy Day, the purposeful, self-sacrificing
leader of the Catholic Worker movement; Erik Erikson, the Harvard
psychologist who understood children; and Walker Percy, the doctor
who writes moving novels about the South and once observed that

it's possible to get "all A's and flunk ordinary living." Coles says in a Faustian bargain he would gladly throw away all of his accomplishments—his three dozen-plus books and all the rest—in order to write one fictional work as instructive as Percy's *The Moviegoer.*

"Mentors, like parents, try to help us out," Coles says. "I hope one never outgrows the need [for them]. . . . Mentors are fellow soldiers on this pilgrimage that we all make—a trek—from birth to death."

Another mentor was Robert Kennedy, whom Coles traveled with in an effort to understand and document the effects of poverty and whom he remembers as "a compassionate American moral figure, trying to change the country in ways I respected." (Coles drafted Kennedy's final speech before his assassination—a call for federal programs to assist children in the ghetto.) Coles, who believes in the power of the transcendent experience, suggests Kennedy, who had a reputation early in his career as ruthless, may in fact have illustrated the capacity of the human soul to change.

"Our responsibility as a country or a state or a city or a community is to *be there* . . . when those moments take place," Coles says when discussing, in a different context, ways to tap students' instinctive drive to help others. "We can't program the moments—and who would want to—but we can be there so that those who for one reason or another suddenly become morally awake can find some way to express that."

Despite his close association with Robert Kennedy and the War on Poverty, Coles is no believer in big government, favoring instead the kind of help individuals can offer to others. "A massive effort ought to be made, individual to individual, family to family," he says, "perhaps helped along by government, on the local, state and national levels. How else do you reach the most seriously troubled families in this country? I don't think you help them necessarily only by setting up institutions. . . .

"Maybe I'm being naive about this," he continues, "but I have seen what individuals, even college students, are able to do with particular families in the Boston area and other parts of this country." If nothing else, volunteers can take the kids to a health clinic or find legal aid for a family's legal problems.

Of course burnout is a problem, but one way to fend it off, Coles suggests, "is for the whole country to say, this is what really matters to us. We're going to acknowledge you people."

How Dare We Call Ourselves Christians?

Mike Yaconelli and Bill McNabb/1989

From *The Door* (Yreka, CA, September/October 1989, pp. 14–19). Reprinted by permission of *The Door.*

Robert Coles, whose special interest is field work in social psychiatry, is a research psychiatrist for Harvard University Health Services, as well as Professor of Psychiatry and Medical Humanities at Harvard Medical School. He received his AB from Harvard and his MD from Columbia University College of Physicians and Surgeons.

Dr. Coles is the author of more than 900 articles, reviews, and monographs. Some of his 38 books include *Children of Crisis* (in five volumes); *The Middle Americans; Walker Percy: An American Search; The Moral Life of Children;* and *The Political Life of Children.*

So far, just your average guy.

We were impressed with one thing. Dr. Coles did receive the Pulitzer Prize in 1973. We had no idea that the Pulitzer Company gave away prizes. We've always admired Pulitzers, especially people who can play them. Dr. Coles really must know how to pound those pipes.

Mike Yaconelli and Bill McNabb talked with Dr. Coles in his musty, crammed, three-room office at Harvard (the same rooms where some guy with a weird middle name (Delano) lived for awhile). Mike and Bill found Dr. Coles to be brilliant, witty, mischievous, passionate, deeply committed, and possessed with the worst voice in the history of Doordom—raspy, nasal, shrieky (shrieky?), and saturated with a strong Bostonian twang. His laugh is somewhere between a wheezing asthmatic attack and whooping cough. We wonder, honestly, if that isn't part of God's economy. Coles' accomplishments are so . . . flawless . . . yet his voice so . . . well . . . flawed.

Regardless, Dr. Coles spoke with power and authority—neither of which came from his voice, but rather from his work, his presence, and his life.

Door: Do you worry about this country?

Coles: Yes I worry about this country.

148

Door: Why?

Coles: We have very little kindness.

Door: We have to admit, you surprised us with that answer.

Coles: I mean it. This country isn't a community. We have too many factions, too many divisions, too much distrust, and not enough love for one another. I am not talking about soppy, sentimental love; I am talking about a genuine respect for those who are different. I am talking about toleration for differences.

Door: Kindness seems so . . . so obvious.

Coles: Really? Here I am at Harvard University which is supposedly a big-deal place, and there is plenty of mean-spiritedness here. There are groups of students who direct their bile, distrust, and skepticism toward other groups, and that is very sad. After all, if we can't demonstrate kindness and respect toward one another *here,* with all our supposed intelligence and good fortune, is it any wonder it is not so obvious outside of here?

Door: Let's talk about "outside of here." What are most Americans worried about?

Coles: For *most* people in this country, life means getting by. How to make a living and how to stay out of debt are very much on the minds of most of us.

Door: Getting by is what most people worry about?

Coles: We forget that 70–80% of the people in this country don't have money stashed away. They live day to day. They are struggling to make a go of it and stay ahead of the bill collectors. For them, economic survival is—and should be—important.

Door: Worrying about money should be important?

Coles: For people who are struggling to make a go of it, economic worries *are* important, but I didn't say they are the *most* important. In the homes that I've worked with now for 30 years, I have noticed what seems to be weighing all of us down, whether we are rich or poor, is the question, "What does life mean?" That kind of question a philosopher would call an "existential" question. A religious person would call it a "religious" question. I would call it a personal and human question, but I think America has always implied that questions like that are important. You know, "life, liberty and the pursuit of happiness."

Door: The happiness question?

Coles: Well yes, in a way. I have talked with people who have a hell of a lot of money and are very unhappy morally and spiritually, and I've talked with poor people who have just about nothing (and most have to struggle with racism as well as poverty), and yet they seem very happy. I don't want to romanticize the suffering and impoverished, but they are happy because they can answer the question of meaning with a sense of moral satisfaction. They believe they are here for a purpose. They have ideals they strongly pursue and they have, I must add, a faith that is evidenced not just by church attendance, but in their daily lives.

Door: What is it about faith that seems to answer the question of meaning?

Coles: We have to start with the Hebrew prophets—Jeremiah, Amos, Isaiah and others—who positioned themselves *outside* the gates of the powerful, the privileged, and the all-too-often arrogant ones who ran things. Then there was Jesus who lived among the humble. He ministered to them, taught them, and lived with them. I have to say that one of the most unsettling paradoxes among the wealthy nations is the continuing presence of Christianity among the wealthy and powerful.

Door: Paradoxical? In what way?

Coles: Given the way Jesus lived. It's not the wealth I object to. But Christianity was a religion of suffering, of exile, and pain—even scorn. And then Christianity became a state religion, a political religion, and many of the people who espouse Christianity, even those who are priests and ministers, live lives of great comfort. I wonder if that's what Jesus had in mind for us. I cannot get it out of my mind what Jesus said. He reminded us that the first shall be last and the last shall be first.

Door: Hmmmmmmm. There are a lot of people here at Harvard who probably fit in the "first" category.

Coles: You mean the first who will be last?

Door: Uh . . .

Coles: Which is why people like me should be listening to the women who scrub floors and the men who dig ditches who are called "poor" or "last." I have the feeling they have a lot to tell us that we wouldn't hear from the big shots who teach at Harvard . . . including myself.

Door: Then why don't you give all this up and become poor?

Coles: It is a paradox. I used to ask my parents the same question and my mother would remind me of a concept that came out of the New Testament. She would say, "This is the way we are being tested. This comfortable life is a very mixed blessing. We have additional responsibilities and additional dangers facing us."

Door: Uh . . . that sounds like a clev—

Coles: —I know, I know. It sounds like a clever rationalization on my mother's part as well as mine.

Door: Well, yes it—

Coles: —If so, she'll pay for it in hell, as we all will. Meanwhile, it was the basis for considerable introspection on her part. I hope the rest of us will follow suit. By the way, how comfortably do *you* live?

Door: Uh . . . let's um . . . move on to another subject. What made you decide to become a psychiatrist?

Coles: I stumbled into it.

Door: Stumbled into it?

Coles: I had trouble sticking needles into little children.

Door: We didn't ask why did you decide to *go* to a psychiatrist.

Coles: Originally I had decided to go into pediatrics. But I had trouble being forceful enough with crying and hurt children. I couldn't stick needles in them without being undone. Pediatric surgery was out of the question.

Door: Again, your fear of hurting children?

Coles: Well, yes, but there was a more important reason.

Door: Yes?

Coles: I'm sloppy.

Door: Not a great quality for a surgeon.

Coles: Right. So when you get a combination of a befuddled slob who does not have the necessary toughness *and* is a little mixed-up himself, you've got a psychiatrist.

Door: A mixed-up psychiatrist?

Coles: Of course. Those who heal are in need of healing themselves. No news in that.

Door: Is it futile, then, to search for ultimate answers in psychiatry or psychology?

Coles: The futility is in searching for ultimate answers in the entire secular culture. Psychology happens to be a temporary, secular religion. How long will it last? Fifty years? Secular religions come and

go. Today it's psychology, tomorrow it will be weight reduction, or
cholesterol, or getting to the moon or Mars. Who knows what our
culture will be preoccupied with next? But *none* of this is going to
give us answers to the moral/spiritual questions that we ultimately
hunger for. Psychology isn't equipped to answer those questions.
Psychology gives us some information about the mind. But the mind
is not the soul.

Door: Psychology, then, can help a person's "mental health?"

Coles: We shouldn't even use words like "mental health." The
question is not "What is mental health?" or "Do you have mental
health?" The question is what do you *do* with your life? What do you
do with your mental health? Do you take it to the Bahamas and lie
under the sun with it for the rest of your life? Do you accumulate $10
million with it? Become a yuppie with it? On whose behalf, in other
words, is our psychological "mental health" being lived?

Door: But even ministers today are becoming psychologists.

Coles: That is paganism.

Door: "Pastoral counseling" is the term for it.

Coles: What can we do? It's paganism. My mother was dying here
in Massachusetts General Hospital. A minister came to see her. *He*
wanted to negotiate her through the stages of dying. *She* wanted him
to say a prayer for her. She was reading Tolstoy. She knew she was
dying. *He* wanted to talk about anger and denial but *she* wasn't
angry and she wasn't using denial. She just wanted a prayer.

Door: Is this all part of the same syndrome—we all want to
worship the expert?

Coles: The *secular* expert. Who are these secular experts,
anyway? What do psychologists and psychiatrists know about the
Christian life? What do they tell us? Take good care of yourself?
Massage your ego? We wouldn't want to have too many ego
problems, because then we might, God forbid, feel a little haunted
and driven like all the Christian saints were.

Door: Christian saints like Paul.

Coles: Ten years of psychoanalysis they would recommend for
him.

Door: What do you think of the Church?

Coles: Just look at it! Look at the history of the Church! A litany
of horrors! Fraudulent popes. Fraudulent bishops. And look what's

going on in the United States. Not only do we have fraud on Wall Street and fraud in the universities, but fraud in the name of religion. It's very sad. I go to an Episcopal Church which shall remain nameless. Two years ago I went to this church on Good Friday. I like to go to church on Good Friday between noon and 3. Those are important hours on Good Friday. *What did I hear?* I heard the minister talk about Freud. On *Good Friday* I'm hearing a talk about Freud? This is not what I should be hearing on Good Friday. Another nail on Jesus.

Door: That brings up ano—

Coles: —Let me finish my screaming. I go into churches and everyone seems to feel so good about themselves. Everyone calls themselves a Christian nowadays. How *dare* we call ourselves Christians! It's only for Jesus to decide whether we are Christians or not. I don't think He's made a decision in my case, and I'm afraid that when He does I am going to be sent straight to hell. I don't feel I can call myself a Christian. I can't be satisfied with myself. We all seem to be pretty content with ourselves in church, and that makes me sick. I think all of this contentment makes Jesus nervous.

Door: If you are uncomfortable calling yourself a Christian, what do you call yourself?

Coles: I am spending my entire life searching for *how* one becomes a Christian. I don't believe I will *ever* find that answer short of death. I believe our entire lives ought to be given to that search. And if there is a church that will take us stragglers and searchers in, then I'll come to that church. I want a church that will say to me, "We're not giving you a ticket. We're not giving any guarantees. This is a place for the troubled and confused, we welcome you with a smile, but don't take it for granted."

Door: You realize, of course, that there are a great many people who are concerned that you are hesitant to call yourself a Christian and who are very concerned that you are still searching. They are concerned that you haven't "accepted Jesus as your personal Saviour."

Coles: I accept Jesus as God become man. I accept Him as the One who lived in such a way that the rest of us have to spend the rest of our lives trying to be worthy of Him. To announce oneself as a Christian is fraught with danger because the question is not whether

one is a Christian, but whether one *lives* the way Jesus would have
us live. It is a matter of being, not declaration.

Dorothy Day painted on the side of the Catholic worker building
an exchange between Gandhi and a Western reporter. The Western
reporter asked, "Mr. Gandhi, what do you think of Western
civilization?" Gandhi replied, "I think it would be a great idea." I say
the same thing about Christianity. It would be a great idea if we all
tried to live it out with one another. But to say, "I am a Christian,"
often sounds like you are saying "you should be in awe with me
because I've made that statement."

Door: You are against people calling themselves Christians, then?

Coles: I've nothing against one saying it as a hope, a yearning, an
ideal. I am not adverse to saying to you myself that I'm a Christian, if
by that you understand I mean that I believe in Jesus Christ and in
His life and in what His life means to us everyday. But I am
desperately afraid of saying "I'm a Christian" for fear my chest will
start sticking out with pride. If I am saying that so you will admire and
approve of me, then I am in danger. I am also afraid that when you
hear me say I am a Christian you will stop putting important moral
challenges to me because you will think, "He's already converted." I
am in danger if I think I have ended my religious problems in life by
showing up in church for an hour on Sunday and announcing, "I am
a Christian." Baloney.

Door: Baloney?

Coles: Do I behave like a Christian when I'm driving my car? Am
I a Christian when I walk by someone who is in trouble and I think
what I am doing is so important that I can't stop for anyone? Am I a
Christian when I come home from work in a sour mood and I don't
give my wife the time of day?

Door: We have to admit we're surprised by the emotional fervor
you are expressing today.

Coles: And I am a psychiatrist, right? And the "shrink" world of
which I am a part has encouraged a cool, clever, distanced view of
our emotions. We are supposed to be nervous about our emotions
and cover up our nervousness with psychological impassivity and
neutrality.

Door: Um, yeah, that's kind of what we were trying to point out
. . . uh . . . we think.

Coles: It's pitiable. It's disgusting, actually, because it's not human. We are creatures of emotions and lusts and affections and yearnings. If we are removed from those by a veneer of coolness, then we are lost.

Door: Where does our self-worth come from?

Coles: We have to be able to give as well as take. This secular society, including the psychologically informed part of it, emphasizes the taking. What *we* need. What *we* deserve. Then we are just left with ourselves. We are left with that endless predicament that Narcissus was left in—which is the curse of curses—staring at ourselves in pools. It is very lonely. Very sad and very lonely. We need to see our worth affirmed in the lives of others—to build for others, feed others. We have to find something to do on behalf of others, otherwise we're just stuck with ourselves. And then we become stuck *on* ourselves, which is, of course, conceit.

Door: What most impresses you about Jesus?

Coles: One of the most startling and incomprehensible aspects of Jesus' life was how little, if any, meanness was in it. He lived His life making Himself vulnerable to others, giving, being pushed around, suffering, and ultimately being killed. Others were mean to Him. Others doubted Him. Others betrayed Him, made Him suffer, and killed Him. His response was to turn the other cheek, to shower them with love and goodness. And that was the difference between Jesus and us. We still have a potential for sinfulness, a potential for meanness. We can't get rid of it even by declaring ourselves Christians. If we have the fantasy or illusion that by declaring ourselves Christians we are going to get rid of our mean or self-centered qualities, we are conning ourselves more than if we took cocaine or heroin. We have to struggle with these emotions all of our lives. Whatever help we can be to each other through this struggle is our challenge. Walker Percy said at the end of one of his novels, "We can hand one another along." That's what Jesus did. He offered Himself to us. He offered His hand to us and said, "Here I am. I will always be here for those of you who want to reach out to me." Sin never leaves us. We don't have any choice in the matter. We cannot be rid of our sinfulness on this earth, so long as we are human beings, but we can do a better job of struggling against that sinfulness with the help of Jesus and one another.

Learning by Doing Through Public Service
Arthur Levine/1989

From *Change* (Washington, D.C., September/October 1989, pp. 19–26). Reprinted by permission of the Helen Dwight Reid Educational Foundation. Published by Heldref Publications, 4000 Albemarle St., NW, Washington, DC, 20016. Copyright 1989.

This past summer, when President Bush was proclaiming national service as part of his mission and nine bills on the service issue were pending in Congress, *Change* Executive Editor Arthur Levine conducted the following interview with Robert Coles about the role and meaning service can have in the lives of the nation's college students—and faculty. Coles, who is the author of the five-volume *Children of Crisis* series as well as *The Moral Life of Children* and *The Political Life of Children,* is Professor of Psychiatry and Medical Humanities at Harvard and has been actively involved in community service as a teacher and a volunteer since the 1960s.

Levine: I have been told that you are the most eloquent speaker in the country on the topic of community service for students. Not to put any pressure on you, but why is service important?

Coles: Service is important for many reasons. Educationally, because I think it is a tremendous way for students to learn sociology and anthropology, psychology and social ethics, and, in a sense, to learn about others and about themselves in the most effective way I know. One does learn by doing as well as by reading. Education is not only a function of books, but a function of experience and connecting what one reads with ongoing observations and experiences.

Service is also important, I think, morally and ethically, which, after all, is part of what I think universities are about. Harvard in the nineteenth century, for instance, used to say its mission was to develop the character of its students. One of its primary missions. I

156

am just old fashioned and conservative enough to believe that's
important, and that part of the mission of a university can be to help
develop the character of its students. And, by the way, the character
of its professors, because community service is important, not only
for the students. It would be tremendous to have us professors doing
this kind of work alongside our students, learning with them and
being part of that world of learning by seeing and doing and hearing.
We, too, could benefit from the kind of soul searching that goes on
when one is in a particular set of circumstances with others—finding
out about their lives, maybe trying to make a difference in those lives,
and also, maybe, perhaps having one's own life thereby changed.

Levine: It shocks me how hot the topic is getting. As of July, nine
different bills were pending in Congress on national service. Do you
have any sense of why this topic is so hot right now?

Coles: We have had such a cold spell, now the pendulum is
swinging from cold to hot, to pursue your image. There has been a
kind of ebb tide of involvement, a moral ebb tide of sorts, that we
have been remonstrated with recently, namely, that we should pursue
our own interest and our own paths and be relatively unconcerned
with others. This culture of narcissism and this emphasis on the "I"
and the "me" has begun to wear thin in people, as, I think, in-
stinctively it does. I think people are not only egoistic by nature; there
is also a side of them that reaches out to others and thinks of others.
Perhaps we go back and forth in our personal lives with those two
sides of ourselves, and maybe politically, as well.

Levine: So do ideas like "a thousand points of light" seem
appealing to you at the moment?

Coles: "A thousand points of light"? That expression and what it
is about has always been a part of America. I think the phrase
expresses a particular president's quiet, tactful notice to the country
that this kind of value—that is, the value of thinking of others as well
as ourselves—was going to make a difference to him and was going
to be a part of his mission as a president. I think Bush is pursuing it
and will pursue it. I do not think it is totally a political sham or a
brazenly frivolous bit of rhetoric. I think he means it, and I think he
will probably put some political capital into it, just as I think those
representatives and senators mean it. At least, I hope so.

Levine: I sense that it is real. It is the beginning of the nation's moving into a more progressive agenda.

Coles: Right. After all, for 20 years this country has struggled with disappointment and loss and a feeling of betrayal. We lost our president in the early '60s. Another president was driven right out of office. We watched the deaths of Robert Kennedy and Dr. King and Malcolm X. We lost another president who had to resign. We lost a one-term president due to a complex series of foreign policy tragedies and perhaps his own ineptitude. So, we have had a lot of trouble in this country politically.

And then we got a president who for two full terms sent the message, "Hey, let's just stop all these notions of reform and let's see what we all can get for ourselves." Reagan endured politically and his ideology, I think dominated an entire decade. I think now that is over and maybe the country is going to go back to some of the spirit—and I hope not the mistakes—of the '60s.

Levine: If you could design a service program for the nation, what would it look like?

Coles: I would like to see students of all backgrounds with their teachers involved in the projects where we are all needed—with the elderly, with children who desperately lack educational opportunities, on projects that would help the country ecologically and environmentally, in prisons—wherever there is a need for the kind of energy and intelligence that I hope both students and their teachers have.

I would like to see college students teaching in some of the schools. I teach, for instance, at a college and a medical school, but I also teach in a fourth-grade class in Cambridge. Those elementary school classrooms desperately need the kind of skills that college students have. Moreover, it would not hurt to have an occasional professor come in and help out. That professor might even learn something from these children, who are pretty sharp about what they see, including what they see about university life, because some of them walk right through the Harvard Yard on their way to school.

I would also like to see the range of activities be matched by the range of participation. I would like to see rich students as well as poor and middle class students doing community service. But this is a major problem. I would hate to see community service limited to minority students, for instance, who work out of their own sensitivity to their own personal experience. I would hate to see legislation written in such a way that only the poor students are being prompted into doing the service because it offers financial benefit.

Some of the students who need community service the most, I think, come from well-to-do backgrounds, students who are so geared to competitiveness and greedy self-assertion that we really are in serious moral jeopardy. Community service is a means for us, perhaps, to get some kind of moral assistance. That is just as much our need as, say, psychological assistance.

Levine: I like that imagery. I do not think I have heard it before. What age is appropriate for service?

Coles: In some of my work in this country I have seen high schoolers help elementary school kids, but I think the best is college students. And graduate students, by the way; let's not neglect what medical students and law and business school students can do. I have worked with medical students who are working with the poor and the needy in Boston, with alcoholics, with the street people, with the homeless, with prisoners, with troubled children, and they are doing wonderful work. Law students can help people who have legal problems.

So, I would encourage voluntarism from maybe high school age on. I worked with high schoolers who have done tutoring, and it has been very helpful both to the children being tutored and to the high schoolers who have done the tutoring. Maybe I might wait until the junior year in high school, but I would not write off the high school years. I would encourage community service activities in our high schools as well as in our colleges and our graduate schools.

Levine: What about young people who are not in college? I am thinking that one finds in college a population more white than of color, richer rather than poorer. What about all of those young people who do not make the transition into college? Is there a service role for them?

Coles: That is a very good and important point, lest public service become connected only to the, relatively speaking, elite. When I worked in Appalachia in the late '60s and early '70s, a marvelous group of volunteers there, the Appalachian Volunteers, were very sensitive to this. They had a wonderfully idealistic notion of their participation in this voluntary effort to work at some of the problems of the region—the educational problems, the environmental problems, serious environmental problems—the destruction of the landscape, really, by the coal companies. They tried to make connections with coal miners and with factory workers and with farm people—the younger farm people, the younger coal miners, the younger factory workers. And I thought that was a very important idea. They did forge some alliances with some working-class, blue-collar young people who helped participate in the more environmental aspects of community service. This is something that could be done.

Maybe blue-collar youths are less interested in some of the cerebral sides of community service—the tutoring programs—but they have very serious concerns, I think, about the environment, about pollution and the nature of the water, the nature of the land, acid rain. I think they could be enlisted, and this would be important for the country.

When I worked in New Mexico, many of the young people I got to know had no interest at all in going to college. They were interested in blue-collar jobs, or whatever. But they had a sense of injustice, a sense of injustice connected to land use, to water use, to the quality of the air. Those are aspects, I think, of what community service might be in this country and ought to be. We ought to make an effort to get such young people involved. It would really pull the country together in a way that perhaps it needs to be pulled together, so that we do not have class against class and group against group, an elite against a group that feels neglected or ignored.

Oftentimes, when intellectuals talk about young people, they do not think of young people who are working in factories or on farms or in blue-collar jobs. Instead, they think of young people as college students and as future professional people. This is rather a narrow view of young people. I would hope that any community service program would include not only those young people in the colleges and graduate schools, but those who are not, as well.

By the way, it's at the high school level that we could really anticipate these class divisions. We could make efforts in high schools that are not primarily geared toward college admissions committees.

Levine: Very interesting. Now, let me ask you a few questions about mechanics. In your national plan, would there be incentives?

What types of incentives? At some point, if you add incentives, it is not service anymore, it is paid work.

Coles: I have mixed feelings about this. On the one hand, I think there are some young people who really want and need those incentives, for all sorts of reasons. They need incentives about living successful lives, because some of them are demoralized and confused and without aspirations; yet they have to learn how to struggle out of their particular set of social, economic, and racial circumstances. Maybe they do not think there is any chance that they can successfully do so. But, having said that, I think there ought to be incentives for the well-to-do, too.

Maybe we ought to think of different kinds of incentives for different kinds of people. After all, we compel students to take languages; we compel them to take writing courses—there is a tradition of compulsion in our universities. Maybe we ought to think about the needs of some students just as we think about the tradition of scholarships and GI Bills. Perhaps some students do need some financial incentives or rewards, but those incentives or rewards do not necessarily have to destroy the sense of achievement and accomplishment that goes with voluntary service, Not necessarily.

Other students perhaps need different kinds of incentives. Perhaps they need the incentive of the college's saying, "Hey, this is what we stand for, and this is what we want you to be part of. We want you to be literate in many ways—educationally, morally—and we are going to put our money behind that. We will give scholarships to those who need them, and we are going to tell others that you need it, too. You have to learn how to speak Latin or Greek or Spanish or whatever. And, by golly, you are to go out there and do some work because it is educationally and morally part of our mission."

So let's flexibly reach out to all these constituencies with various "incentives."

Levine: Does a federal program make any sense in light of the kind of flexibility you are talking about?

Coles: The federal government has been a great prodder of the private sector and of the universities. The government pours money into the coffers of the universities, encouraging them in all sorts of ways, and I do not see why it cannot encourage them in public service, too. The more control the private sector has, including the university private sector, the better. The government has always been an important facilitator, and its cash has been welcome in many other areas. I mean, federal money is so earnestly sought for the humanities, for the sciences, for the social sciences. The universities have shown themselves able to survive this infusion of capital wealth from Washington without its destroying their integrity; they seem to welcome it. If they suddenly said, "We do not want it" now, I would want to know why.

Levine: There is talk in Washington of tying public service to, let's say, housing stipends, so you could use whatever money you make in service to buy a house; tying it to student financial aid, so students do not get any financial aid whatever unless they have done service. There are a lot of schemes. Do any of them stand out for you? Any to which you would say, "Yeah, let's go do that"?

Coles: I have mixed feelings about all of them. On the one hand, I hate to have financial aid so tied to service that students feel embittered. Do you know what I mean? That students feel, "Gee, I have to do this to get that money, but I do not want to do it, and I am really furious." Here is where, I think, the colleges and the universities have a mission. If the government is going to say, "This is what we want," the colleges and the universities have got to make clear to the students that it is not just the government behaving in a rather predatory and arbitrary manner. The universities have got to say, "Hey, we want this, too, and we *really* want it. And we want it out of our heart. And even if the government told you that they are going to give you these stipends without this kind of rider, we are telling you that this is an important part of your education, and it is an important part of our educational mission." There ought to be some way of getting that message to students.

Levine: In a lot of ways the universities and colleges are much more important actors than the federal government would be in the scenarios we have been talking about.

Coles: I wish our universities were more connected to this. The initiatives ought to be coming from them. They ought to be running down this road saying, "We not only want to be parties because we smell money around the corner, but we really believe that this is an urgent need of ours, an urgent intellectual need, an urgent moral need, and urgent educational responsibility that we, perhaps, have not taken as seriously as we might have over the decades and generations."

Levine: If a college were to come to you next week and say, "Yes, you are right. We think there is a moral requirement. Our students have got to do some of that. An intellectual requirement." What would you tell them to do? Do you have a favorite program that you would set up; some way you would organize this?

Coles: I would immediately go to some of the nearby schools and find out what kind of help they need from reasonably educated people. I would go to nursing homes. I would go to hospitals. I would go to places where the homeless are fed or find out whether there are homeless who are not being taken care of. I would then pull together my colleagues on the faculty and the students who are interested and see whether we could not respond to those needs.

It is terribly important—and I want to emphasize this as strongly as I know how—it is terribly important for more of us teachers to participate, to do the tutoring, to work in the soup kitchens, to visit the nursing homes or the jails; to bring our intellectual skills to these people and whatever nurturance and moral, intellectual, and emotional support we can offer to other people. In so doing, we have a lot to learn that will help us to become better teachers. So, I would begin to talk to the faculty as well as the students and, pretty soon, I think we would have a cadre of people, both teachers and students, out there helping others—being helped as we help others because service is a mutual thing. It is not only helping others; it is being helped. Because we learn, we affirm ourselves in certain important ways, I think, psychologically and morally. We have everything to gain by doing this as human beings and as citizens and as people who are trying to learn about the world.

After all, what is an intellectual? An intellectual is someone who presumably acquires a body of knowledge in his or her head about the world, and this is one way of doing so.

Levine: Here is the question I've wanted to ask you all along. The students out there doing service—are they reading anything in addition, and, if so, what does the reading list look like?

Coles: Students who are doing these activities also need time to reflect upon what they have experienced, and there are wonderful books that can help them do that. By the way, not only do the books help them reflect on the experience, but the books help enrich the experience. The books give them pause for thought; after they have discussed some of these novels or poems or short stories, they go back to their work feeling a bit more savvy, maybe a bit more whole and healed, a bit wiser, even, and therefore better able to teach or work in the soup kitchen or whatever.

I have a reading list. Some of Tillie Olson's short stories or Raymond Carver's short stories. Tolstoy, struggling as he did with what it means to be old and sick and dying and to hold onto life and know that it is ebbing away. William Carlos Williams' poetry and stories talking about working-class people and their struggles and hopes and worries and doubts. Ralph Ellison's *Invisible Man*, trying to render what it means to feel invisible to others by virtue of one's race, and what it means to be blind—because for every invisible man, there is a blind person who does not see him. When you have read those books, I think you feel a bit more; I think you are somewhat better equipped to deal with some of the inevitable moments of doubt and inadequacy and hesitation and fear that are going to afflict people doing certain kinds of community service.

The book reading, I think, helps as one is going through the experience; conversely, the experience brings to the book reading a new intensity of intellectual response. So, it is a mutual thing. You can read Tolstoy or Dickens or Hardy in one way in a college library, emphasizing the symbolism and their use of language and imagery. But you can also get from those books a moral message, and that moral message is always intensified when one is having experiences very similar to those described in the novels.

Dickens' evocations of poverty, Hardy's evocations of what it is for someone to be an outsider and yet want to go to college and feel that he will never be able to go there. Tolstoy's struggles, not only to understand the poor, but to understand the arrogance and the selfishness and smugness in himself that kept him from understanding the poor and seeing them. On and on it goes.

There ought to be room in voluntary service and community service for the people involved to sit down and reflect. I do not mean overly self-conscious psychological analysis. God save us from that. But just plain old moral and personal reflection using novels, using short stories, using poems, and also using the experience itself.

Levine: What is the best way to organize a student service? Is immersion best? Do we say, "Go do this for a term full-time?" Do we tell them, "Do five hours a week for your four years of college"?

Coles: I would organize the service eclectically, with different possibilities. Some students may want to take a year or two off and do this full-time. Others may want to stay at school. I would respect diversity here, diversity of opportunities and diversity of participation. Different kinds of people doing different things.

Levine: Are you already doing this?

Coles: Yes. I work with students who are doing voluntary community service in the greater Boston area. They tutor, they work with the elderly, they work in soup kitchens, and then we have a seminar in which we sit and read Raymond Carver stories, William Carlos Williams poems. We read some social science like Anthony Lukas' book, *Common Ground,* and we read James Agee's *Let Us Now Praise Famous Men.* We read some of Orwell's documentary writing, *Down and Out in London and Paris* and *The Road to Wigan Pier.*

Then we take up the matters that these writers take up. Namely, how does an outsider get involved in the community? At what personal cost or pain? How do you feel when you are working with others and having trouble doing so? What do you do with the sense of shame or guilt that may come upon you? How do you reach others who are different from you and establish relationships with them?

These novelists, these essayists, help us to have these discussions because they render some of the dilemmas, they render some of the experiences that the young people are having in these stories.

After those discussions, the students have an opportunity to go through the experience again, remember what we talked about, and perhaps feel a bit stronger and more savvy about what they are going to do.

Levine: How many students do you have in your class at a time?

Coles: I have a seminar of 20, and then I give an undergraduate lecture course called "The Literature of Social Reflection," which has about 600 students in it. The lecture group then breaks down into sections of 20 students, so we have about 30 sections. I try to visit every one of those sections, but that is back-breaking work. The sections are led by a whole cadre of graduate students, medical students, law students, School of Education students (a lot of them, as a matter of fact). They discuss—as I do with my own under-graduate seminar—the reading, and they also discuss the community service.

Levine: Are the students required to do community service?

Coles: It's voluntary. About half of those sections are so-called "community service" sections, made up of students who are going to bring their community service work to the course as a topic of discussion.

Levine: How long have you been doing this?

Coles: About 10 years.

Levine: Was there a period in which the numbers were smaller, when fewer people were interested in the topic?

Coles: Suddenly, over the last four or five years, the community service participation has been growing. And last year I introduced my own special community service course in the seminar.

This fall, in the Harvard Extension School, I am also going to teach a community service course for people working in Cambridge. Some may be school teachers or community activists, maybe lawyers or doctors who have been involved in community service work and want to discuss it. A whole range of professional people exist to draw upon, but one can also draw upon ordinary working people who want to take a course in the Extension School.

For five years I have also worked with the medical students of the Urban Health Project, in which medical students work in the summer between their first and second or second and third years. For that summer they work in soup kitchens, or as tutors, or with the homeless, or with alcoholics, or whatever—doing voluntary work—but we also have weekly discussions about their experiences. I assign reading to them—short stories or novels or documentary literature from Agee and Orwell.

Levine: And there are no second-party payments for this?

Coles: No second-party payments. This is all heart payments.

I've another interesting thing to tell you. I know a group of Harvard Business School students who this summer are working at commu-nity service. They organized themselves and they are working with schools—with agencies that work with vulnerable people whether they are the homeless or troubled children. I find it remarkable.

Levine: That is wonderful. Teaching investment strategies to poor kids?

Coles: Who knows? Maybe the experience will wean some of them away from Morgan Stanley and they'll spend their time working in the development office at Covenant House, a wonderful place in New York City where street children are rescued.

Levine: What a nice notion. How much of this have you been responsible for? I understand that you have taken these initiatives with the students. Perhaps that is what we need, a Robert Coles on every campus.

Coles: There are a number of people like me all over the country who would like to get involved. This is what I meant earlier: we need professors to get involved. Wouldn't it be great if we had deans and presidents and professors working alongside the students? What a tremendous educational moment in American life!

Robert Coles

Charles E. Claffey/1989

From *The Boston Globe* (Boston, MA, December 19, 1989, pp. 72–73) Reprinted by permission of *The Boston Globe*.

Dr. Robert Coles' office at Harvard is a small, first-floor suite in Adams House in which Franklin D. Roosevelt spent his student years from 1900 to 1904, a historic fact commemorated by an inconspicuous plaque on the wall.

"I got rid of all of the Harvard and Groton stuff," Coles explains, alluding to photographs of the president's college and prep school days that had augmented the plaque when he moved in several years ago. In their place now are photos of Roosevelt in situations more consonant with Coles' system of values: in an open touring car, chatting with farmers and mine workers—FDR in the field, among the people.

Coles, the child psychiatrist, educator, prolific writer, spiritual seeker and Pulitzer Prize winning author of the *Children of Crisis* series, recently celebrated his 60th birthday and, almost concurrently, the completion of the eighth and last of his books on the young: *The Spiritual Life of Children*.

"This marks the end of 30 years of work," Coles said of his latest book, which will be published next fall. "I don't know what I'm going to do next. Maybe I should retire," he suggests with a characteristic self-mocking laugh.

Coles, of course, is kidding. He is a restless, driven man who could never seriously entertain the notion of retirement. He has written 50 books and more than 1,000 articles and has traveled extensively: through the American South, Alaska, Central and South America, northern Ireland, Europe, South Africa, the world.

In an age of every-narrowing specialization, he is a generalist who resists pigeon-holing. He is also something of a paradox: an intelligent, reflective, well-educated member of the scholarly and professional elite who dislikes intellectuals, although it could reason-

168

ably be inferred that he is one himself. He is equally at ease in
Southern shacks or working-class barrooms and in Harvard's lecture
halls or in auditoriums with his fellow psychiatrists. He is also, by
Harvard faculty standards, a loner.

"He's a maverick in the sense that he embraces so many fields,"
says David Riesman, the Henry Ford II professor emeritus of social
sciences at Harvard. "He is very hard to classify. He is also a
maverick in the sense that he has sacraments of his own that are not
always those of the prevailing party's."

When court-ordered busing brought racial violence to Boston in
1974, Coles nettled some members of the local liberal establishment
by suggesting that the problem of desegregation was as much one of
class as of race. "I thought it a bit odd that liberal intellectuals living in
the suburbs should be lecturing working-class people in Boston
about their prejudices," he says.

Coles finds class a significant factor, too, in the shaping of the
attitudes of American children about the possibility of nuclear war. It
is the children of the upper and middle classes who evince the
strongest fears about nuclear annihilation, concerns they pick up
from their parents, he writes in *The Moral Life of Children*. The
children of blue-collar families and the poor do not think much, if at
all, about nuclear war, nor do their parents, he found, because they
are too busy fighting for economic survival to worry about larger
issues.

He admits to feelings of conflict between his way of life and his
humanitarian concerns for the poor. He lives in upper-middle-class
style: he drives a BMW (the humble model, a two-door sedan of the
300 series) and lives in comfortable surroundings in Concord. "I
don't know what to do about it," he says. "I can't get rid of it. I don't
know that I want to. I wish more people had this kind of life."

As a professor of psychiatry and medical humanities at Harvard, he
can, and does, teach anywhere in the university he chooses,
including the medical, law and business schools.

For the past 11 years, he has taught an undergraduate course
called "General Education 105: Literature of Social Reflection," a
course better known to students as "Guilt 105." It is the most popular
course at Harvard this semester with an enrollment of 850.

His reading list features writers whose work encourages self-examination: Tolstoy, James Agee, Ralph Ellison, William Carlos Williams, Simone Weil, George Orwell, Flannery O'Connor, Tillie Olsen, Georges Bernanos, Thomas Hardy and Raymond Carver.

"I try to connect literature with life," Coles says. "And I hope through this mix of social observation and documentary work that I can encourage students to make this connection.

"Some of the minority students feel I react more to middle-class white kids than to minorities." Coles pauses for a few moments before continuing: "I chose these writers because they're great writers, writers who happen to be white. I teach Ralph Ellison because he's a great writer."

Coles said he has received complaints from black students who told him they don't care for Ralph Ellison and his novel *Invisible Man,* because the author (the novel was published in 1952) refers to people of color as Negroes, not blacks. He said some gay students have caviled because the reading list does not include any books by gay people.

"I'm not interested in 'cause' writers," Coles says. "It's a literature course."

In an article last month in the student newspaper, *The Harvard Crimson,* a minority woman student complained that Coles' course was ethnocentric because its reading list was made up of predominantly white male authors.

The student, Gloria M. Custodio, wrote that Coles' lectures "do seem designed to produce guilt. This sense of guilt is not productive or constructive, the kind that sparks a reexamination of societal structures and behavior. This guilt is self-complacent, rooted in the fact that we Harvard students were born privileged and 'those people' weren't. And that's as far as social reflection goes."

Coles said of the *Crimson* article, "I see what she's trying to say. It's hard to direct a course to all the different people in it. But she didn't mention that I teach women writers such as George Eliot and Dorothy Day, and black writers such as James McPherson."

He has been criticized, too, for what some at Harvard consider his obsessive drive to get his observations and ruminations between hard covers. He turns out books with such frequency that some refer to him as Robert "Never an Unpublished Thought" Coles.

On a recent morning in Harvard's Sanders Theater, Coles was

delivering one of his twice-weekly lectures in the literature of social reflection. He eschews neckties and sport jackets, preferring instead the informality of a shirt (he favors proletarian blue), with sleeves rolled above the elbow, and chino or corduroy slacks and chukka-style boots.

Coles was discussing the 19th-century Danish philosopher Sören Kierkegaard and his influence on Walker Percy's novel *The Moviegoer,* and relating these writers to an incident that had happened one afternoon as Coles was driving home on Route 2 to Concord.

A potato chip truck had overturned, spilling its contents onto the highway. Motorists had halted and were milling about, smiling and chatting with each other as they snatched a few bags of the illicit goodies from the road.

"The people were looking happy for a change. They were seeing each other as people. They took a couple of bags of chips and then went back to their BMWs." The incident, Coles continued, represented an example of Kierkegaardian "rotation"—moments of joy or sadness. "It's some moment that singles us out, that causes us to take stock and ask about our lives."

The students laughed when Coles, lest he represent himself as impervious to the temptation, confessed that he still recalls vividly taking home a few bags of chips and presenting them to his family.

His lecture style is loose, sometimes digressive, interesting and informal. "I think of them as anti-lectures," he says to a visitor who, unbidden, critiques his performance.

David Riesman says he knows many of Coles' former students "who have had their lives changed by him—by what he has them read. He doesn't assign these books to be raced through but to be made part of one's consciousness."

Riesman also recalls an incident that tells something of Coles' moral courage and grace under pressure.

"After the assassination of Martin Luther King, there was rioting at Harvard, and the kids were yelling 'Burn, baby, burn.' Coles gave a lecture to the students in one of the big halls and he upbraided them for their attitudes. He said that black women living in the black areas of Boston would like nothing better than to have an Irish policeman sitting on their doorsteps. He told the students that their attitudes were disgracefully condescending and out of line.

"I thought that was very characteristic of him," Riesman said. "He has always had a keen eye for the blindnesses of the enlightened."

If Coles considers that one of his missions is to try to induce students to understand themselves better through literature, to realize that there is more to living than just making money, it is probably because his own life has been so profoundly influenced by a certain few writers.

He says he would have liked to be a novelist, but he doubts that he possesses the creative imagination. "I wish I could write like Raymond Carver," he says of his latest literary favorite.

Coles was raised in Boston's Back Bay and in Milton, one of two children of a Jewish father from Leeds, England, and a Protestant mother from Iowa, both avid readers. He graduated from the Boston Latin School in 1946 and then entered Harvard College.

He majored in English, expecting to become a high school English teacher. He soon became enamored of the poems, novels and short stories of the literary New Jersey physician William Carlos Williams. Perry Miller, his adviser at Harvard, encouraged him to write his thesis on Williams. The experience changed his life. He corresponded with Williams and they became friends. Williams affected him so profoundly that "I went through what they call today an identity crisis."

When he confessed to Williams that he was confused about what direction his life should take, Williams encouraged him to think about medical school. "Try medicine, why don't you!" Coles quotes Williams as telling him. "Lots to keep you busy, and lots to make you think. The great thing is—you get to forget yourself a lot of the time."

Coles muddled through premed courses at Harvard. When it became time to apply to medical school, he found that many places did not take him seriously. With the help of one "very patient, kindly, and, I now realize, properly puzzled interviewer," he was admitted to the Columbia College of Physicians & Surgeons.

Coles floundered at medical school. He had difficulty working in labs and dissecting cadavers. He was so discouraged that he almost quit, but Williams told him to stick it out and he did. He continued to read a lot. He also discovered the Catholic social activist Dorothy

Day, and ended up working on weekends in her soup kitchens. He
would go on to write a biography of her.

After graduation, he tried pediatrics as a specialty, but decided
before long that he did not have the "iron in me to be the best friend
a sick child needs."

Again, Williams intervened, suggesting that Coles try psychiatry.
He took his residency in psychiatry at Massachusetts General
Hospital and Boston's Children's Hospital.

The doctor's draft was then in effect, and Coles found himself in
1959 as an officer at Keesler Air Force Base in Biloxi, Miss., in charge
of a 40-bed neuropsychiatric unit.

At the same time he was undergoing analysis with Dr. Kenneth
Beach, director of the New Orleans Psychoanalytic Institute.

"Beach used to ask me why I went to the movies so much. I never
knew why until I discovered Walker Percy's novel *The Moviegoer* in a
bookstore in New Orleans in 1961. I read the book and I was just
stunned. I was the same age as [the protagonist] Binx Bolling, 29,
and like Binx I was trying to figure out my life."

Coles and Percy eventually became close friends, and Coles wrote
his biography, excerpted in *The New Yorker* magazine.

For the next few years, after his discharge from the Air Force,
Coles and his wife, Jane Hallowell, worked in the South with black
families—with children entering desegregated schools for the first
time, and later with migrant workers in Appalachia.

He was involved with the Student Nonviolent Coordinating
Committee (SNCC) and the civil rights movement and knew such
leaders as Martin Luther King, Jr., Ralph Abernathy and Julian
Bond.

Peter Davison, Coles' primary editor at Houghton Mifflin, has
known the psychiatrist-writer since 1959, when Coles' first published
piece, "A Young Psychiatrist Looks at His Profession" appeared in
the *Atlantic Monthly* magazine.

"I think there are two important things about him: he's a person of
great compassion and he is very devoted to his family," Davison says.
"On the other hand, he is a person of great anger and indignation.
So that when he writes out of compassion he writes one way, and
when he writes out of anger, it's in another way."

Davison adds that one of the things that fascinates him about Coles is "the way in which he can become one with the person he's talking to, or the class, or even with a group of 1,500 or so people. A niece of mine was a student in a freshman seminar of his and she was ready to sell all she had and go work for the poor. He must have affected thousands of people with that same degree of tender concern."

Coles credits his wife, who has written a few books with him, with helping him in his field work. "She has more moral passion than I have. I would never have persevered in this work if it hadn't been for her. We would go into these homes in the South and she would be wonderful with the parents. Some of them had never seen a white doctor. She helped me to earn the trust of these families."

He notes that one critic has described his work as a "cottage industry," a characterization with which he does not argue. "Our kids have gone with me to Brazil, Tunisia, Sweden, Hungary and Alaska. They have lived in New Mexico and Appalachia, and they spent two summers with me in Belfast. They did interviews, helped with research projects. They became field workers."

Their children are Robert, a student at the Duke University Medical School; Daniel, a student at the Dartmouth Medical School; and Michael, an undergraduate at Harvard who is taking premedical courses.

In the study of his home, where Coles writes, the walls are filled with photographs of his icons: Agee, Percy, Bernanos, Orwell, Simone Weil, Sigmund and Anna Freud.

He talks for a few minutes about Robert Kennedy and "how much he meant to me. He was such a person in those last years of his life. I traveled with him, got to know him. He was a wonderful combination of compassion and toughness." Since Kennedy's death, Coles adds, he has had very little interest in politics.

As to the future, he says he would like to write a biography of Anna Freud, with whom he maintained a long friendship. He is also considering a possible television project that would allow him to bring some of the people he has worked with to the attention of the public.

The moral and spiritual nature of so much of his work naturally leads to questions about his own religious inclinations. "I'm a wanderer. I go through periods when I go to church regularly and periods when I don't." He and his wife sometimes attend the Episcopal Church in Concord, where their sons were baptized.

Coles offers no theories about the riddle of life. He continues to be awed by the "complexity of life and of human nature, the ironies and the paradoxes and inconsistencies—and the mysteries."

One of his favorite quotations comes from an essay of Flannery O'Connor: "The task of the novelist is to deepen mystery and mystery is a great embarrassment to the modern mind."

Robert Coles

Dulcy Brainard/1990

From *Publishers Weekly* (New York, November 16, 1990, pp. 41–42). Reprinted by permission of Dulcy Brainard and *Publishers Weekly,* Cahners Publishing Co. Copyright 1990 by Reed Publishing USA.

In 1960 Robert Coles was a young Air Force doctor stationed in Mississippi. Trained in pediatrics and child psychiatry, he was finishing his psychoanalytic education, reading Walker Percy and, as a New Englander raised in the tradition of liberal intellectualism, trying to understand the culture of the South.

"Had I not been right there," he writes in the introduction to *The Spiritual Life of Children,* the eighth and final volume of his Pulitzer Prize-winning study of children begun 30 years ago, "driving by the mobs that heckled six-year-old Ruby Bridges, a black first-grader, as she tried to attend the Frantz School, I might have pursued a different life."

Child psychiatrist, teacher at Harvard, author of more than 50 books, Coles remains best known for his investigations of children's lives and the books that witness "the attention children give to a world which at times doesn't give them credit for such attention."

The first volume in the Children of Crisis series, *A Study of Courage and Fear,* comprises extended (often over years) conversations with children and their families, black and white, who were directly involved in the desegregation process. The following, similarly structured books, containing interviews with other groups of children with the limitations and demands of their sociological backgrounds, are: *Migrants, Sharecroppers, Mountaineers; The South Goes North; Eskimos, Chicanos, Indians;* and *The Privileged Ones. The Spiritual Life of Children,* out next month from Houghton Mifflin, continues in the direction Coles headed with *The Moral Life of Children* and the *Political Life of Children* (both published in 1986).

"This is a circle, a journey," Coles says, settling into a comfortable chair in the room where he writes at the back of his sprawling yellow clapboard home in Concord, Mass. He is wiry and narrow-shouldered, with a focused, amiable presence and a raspy voice that readily erupts in a short barks of laughter. Outside wide windows, beyond the books piled on deep sills, the early morning light intensifies the mottled bark of old apple trees, the red barn, the just-turning colors of the leaves in the woods beyond.

"The five *Children of Crisis* volumes look at children as they are connected to historical and regional events. Then I started to become—as George Eliot said, although she used the word with some sarcasm—more *theoretical,* and shifted to children as they are defined by their moral, political and spiritual lives."

Asked what he believes he's produced in these studies, Coles pushes at his rolled-up sleeves, runs fingers through metal-gray hair and deliberates at length before answering. "I think I've spent these 30 years trying to show the importance of the kinds of observations that Freud, and especially Anna Freud and Erik Erikson, have made about the nature of childhood. I have learned that childhood is connected not only to the drama of the family but with race and class and nationality, with religious and spiritual life, with neighborhood, regional life and ethnic life, and with events that take place historically, such as racial struggle. In other words, that childhood is the mirror of the world in all of its complexity and ought not be regarded as a phenomenon occurring within one particular home setting."

While he says that he "maintains a loyalty to the psychoanalytic paradigm" in his approach, Coles's studies go against the grain of many works published by his peers in his deliberate avoidance of elaborate formulations and what he calls "overwrought generaliza-tions." In his books, the children are their own witnesses. They describe their experiences, thoughts and expectations to Coles, who, quoting extensively, presents the speakers, their settings and ideas, and, most markedly in *The Spiritual Life of Children,* his own responses, to the reader.

"In Europe this is called phenomenological inquiry; it is a legitimate, well-respected tradition. In America, we have these absolutely dreary sociological categorizations that impose on life's complexities the most naïve kinds of structures and templates—it makes me want to yawn or vomit.

"I tell you, if I hadn't found this way of working, I might have left the whole world of psychiatry and been an English teacher, which is what I started out thinking I'd be, or in public health. It was tough. For three or four years I couldn't get grants for what I proposed to do."

Obtaining funding for this latest book was hardest of all. Writing to 15 foundations of his interest in exploring the religious experiences of children, he was turned down very quickly by all but the Ford and Lilly Foundations. "Even the Ford Foundation called it 'a further exploration of the moral life of children.' Only the Lilly Foundation was able to put it in writing: 'Spiritual and religious lives of children,'" he says.

Yet no one was more aware of the thorny, often personal difficulties and hands-off response raised by the topic than Coles himself. "We have been taught to be secular in our liberal upper-class educated culture." To some, religious belief equals neurosis, he suggests: "Something for the ignorant, the masses. For someone of my background to take this seriously, to find these children who are not crazy or kooky but are leading ordinary lives and let them testify to their faith is a step, believe me."

Raised by a religious mother who took him and his brother to the Episcopalian church every Sunday and a father who waited for his family outside in the car, Coles came to this book fully aware of his own secular leanings. He admits that "at times I couldn't stand some of the sentiment and sweetness and unqualified faith that I heard from some of the kids. I badly needed the skepticism of those agnostic and atheist kids who were ready to throw cold water on the others and keep some tension going. I think that's a part of religion anyway, part of Jesus's life and the Hebrew Prophets; that struggle with doubt and misgivings and betrayal."

It's a struggle he admits to readily: "It's the story of my life, this back–and–forthness between faith and doubt." He touches a copy of *The Diary of a Country Priest,* one of the few volumes he keeps on his desk. "I mean, if even that priest couldn't resolve it, how could I?" He underlines the question with an eloquent shrug.

A picture of that book's author, Georges Bernanos, is hung with two dozen or so other photos on the wall behind him. The gallery includes writers James Agee, Walker Percy and Flannery O'Connor, photographers Walker Evans and Alex Harris, psychoanalysts Erik Erikson and Sigmund and Anna Freud; interspersed among them are anonymous figures of ordinary people.

Nodding toward the wall, Coles observes, "These are the people who taught me to do this work. I could have wrapped up some of my stuff as 'discoveries' or 'formulations.' The books would probably have sold better as people rushed to get answers. And I would have felt like a first-class imposter. I have to live with myself and"—he points to the pictures—"with them. They would laugh me out of the room."

The continuing reality of those figures—"my jury"—has been another life-shaping force. Profoundly influenced as an undergraduate by William Carlos Williams, he acknowledges similar debts to Dorothy Day and his time with her in the Catholic Worker movement; and to Erikson, with whom he taught at Harvard and whom he credits with encouraging him to write directly about his early encounters with children.

No less influential are the writers—he often mentions Tolstoy, George Eliot—whose works have taught him not just how to work, but how to live. "My heroes, after all, are novelists."

Not surprisingly, he's written biographies of many of those represented on the wall, including Erikson, Percy (to whom *Spiritual Life* is dedicated), Williams, Day, Simone Weil and Anna Freud, the latter due out next year. ("This will be the end of my biographies too, by the way. It's a series of circles I've completed.") He's tried his hand at children's stories too, written when his three sons—two now in medical school, one in pre-med—were young; written two books of poems; plus the *Women in Crisis* volumes with his wife, Jane; and commentary to accompany photographic studies, such as *The Last and First Eskimos.* Collections of essays focus on aspects of psychiatry, e.g., *The Mind's Fate,* or on literary topics, as in *That Red Wheelbarrow* and last year's *The Call of Stories,* in which he testifies to the centrality of fiction in his life and the lives of his Harvard students, many enrolled in his literature courses at the medical, law and business schools.

A more recent hero is Raymond Carver. He's teaching a seminar at

Harvard now on Carver's fiction and the paintings of Edward Hopper, focusing on themes of isolation and alienation and the way writers and painters evoke them.

The new volume has precipitated his first book tour, which, arranged for December and January to fit around his teaching schedule and his family's vacations, will take him across the country. "For years Walker Percy, whose daughter has a bookstore in Louisiana, told me that booksellers are my intermediaries, and I owe it to them to visit their stores. I'm going to some of the places where I've worked and used the bookstores. I think this is important."

An agentless writer, Coles has been with the same editor since he began publishing. Poet and writer Peter Davison was an editor at Atlantic Monthly Press when Coles's first published article, "A Young Psychiatrist Looks at His Profession," appeared in 1961 in a special supplement to *The Atlantic Monthly* magazine. A few years later, Davison went to Atlanta and met Coles, who had begun his research with children involved in desegregation. Atlantic Monthly then gave Coles a grant from funds supplied to promising new writers, and in 1967 published the first *Children of Crisis* book. In the mid-'80s when Atlantic Monthly moved to New York, Davison elected to stay in Boston, bringing Coles with him to Houghton Mifflin.

With a laugh, Coles makes it clear that *The Spiritual Life of Children* is "*my* final volume—I have not exhausted the topic. If I were to do another project like this it would be five or six years working with kids, and I just decided no. Maybe it's a mid-life or old-age crisis, but this is very demanding work, to go from home to home, school to school, neighborhood to neighborhood, church to church. I'm blessed so far with good health but I'm not sure I could sustain the effort."

Instead the 61-year-old Coles has leapfrogged to the other end of life. "I'm interested in the elderly who manage to make a go of it, living with resiliency and independence no matter how old and sick and troubled. I've begun having some conversations with elderly people around Boston and in the South," he says.

The modest appraisal implied in "having some conversations" is typical of Coles's assessment of his work. Calling his 30 years' effort "a kind of documentary child psychiatry" and "a series of photos, a series of stories," he describes himself, with some ironic discomfort, as a "novelist manqué. That's about the best definition there may be for me. I pick up what I think are illuminating and suggestive experiences that the children have and then share with me, which then become my experiences, which I then offer as a writer. Then you take that and it becomes part of *your* life and it helps you think and feel and see and know. I'm hoping to do as the children do, to suggest and hint and illuminate—these are the words—rather than hand down paradigms and laws.

"I don't have the novelist's gifts, but I have that set of mind—not the sociologist's—and the novelist's sensibility: to show, not to tell."

Childhood's Chronicler

Al Sanoff with Joannie M. Schrof/1990

From *U.S. News & World Report* (Washington, DC, December 3, 1990, pp. 66–69). Reprinted by permission of U.S. News & World Report, Inc.

At first glance, it seems a classroom like many others, a room filled with 4 and 5-year-olds busily pasting pieces of colored paper on bottles. But there is something odd about the scene. In the midst of the children kneels a man in late middle age with sticky white paste all over his fingers. Clad in chinos and a blue work shirt, he chats with two of the children as he pastes. An outsider might surmise that the man is a visiting grandfather or a community volunteer. In fact, he is Robert Coles, a psychiatrist and professor at Harvard University who has told us more about the diverse and complex lives of children than any other scholar of his generation.

The methodology used in that classroom is vintage Coles. He is a man who, at age 61, has spent most of his adult life venturing into the world of children at their level to find out what is on their minds. Virtually no environment in which young people live today has eluded him. Ghetto households, migrant camps, distant Alaskan villages, Indian reservations—Coles has immersed himself in them all. For three decades, he has traveled the nation and the world interviewing children and documenting what he has learned in books rich in empathy and insight.

Now, with the publication this month of *The Spiritual Life of Children* (Houghton Mifflin, $22.95)—the eighth and last book in his series about children—Coles is ending the major research undertaking of his career and moving on to other, shorter-term projects. He leaves behind pioneering work on the lives of "children of crisis"— oppressed youngsters whose experiences had been virtually ignored by other researchers. He has woven a rich tapestry of childhood, shattering myths and stereotypes that had persisted for generations. Coles has demonstrated, for example, that contrary to the received

wisdom of child psychiatry, young people are surprisingly deep
thinking and are able to ponder complex moral and political issues.
In his new book, Coles shows children grappling with such profound
questions as the nature of life—and death. He has also been among
the first to debunk the long-held view that children are fragile
creatures ready to wilt under the slightest stress. His work with black
children who integrated Southern schools in the '60s played a key
role in convincing psychiatrists that children have surprising psychological strength. Coles has documented "the capacity of children to
extract from their environment what they need, even under terrible
circumstances," says Yale's Dr. Albert Solnit.

The example Coles has set may be as important as the specifics of
his work. The Harvard psychiatrist has demonstrated that it remains
possible, even in an age of narcissism and greed, to live a life of
caring and compassion, a life so dedicated to others that sociologist
Father Andrew Greeley once was moved to call him "a secular saint."
Greeley later amended that, saying, "I'd remove the word *secular.*"

To know what animates Robert Coles, it is necessary to look no
further than the den of his home in Concord, Mass. There, on one
wall, hang the pictures of writers of moral passion—George Orwell,
William Carlos Williams, Walker Percy, Flannery O'Connor, James
Agee—who have inspired his work. Next to them are pictures of
heroic social activists—Simone Weil, Dietrich Bonhoeffer and Dorothy Day. Only two images of psychoanalysts are on display, both
people whose work has centered on the young: Anna Freud,
daughter of the gray eminence of psychiatry, a woman whom Coles
came to know and admire, and Erik Erikson, who helped Coles chart
his life's work.

It is fitting that literary moralists dominate the den. Although Coles
brings psychoanalytic insights to his meetings with the young, the
"highfalutin theorizing" of psychiatry is not his stock in trade. For
Coles, it is not neuroses or suppressed sexual drives that are
important; it is the uniqueness of each individual. "The truths that I
have learned from Percy, O'Connor, Williams, those are the truths
that I have found in my work—complexities, ambiguities, ironies," he
says. "My work has brought me back to human particularity, brought
me back to my years as a student reading Conrad and Tolstoy—a

time in my life when I had been told by English teachers, 'Beware of generalizations about human beings.' "

This emphasis on individual lives has drawn fire from some critics who argue that Coles's research and writing are insufficiently scientific and that he relies on detailing lives as a substitute for tough-minded analysis. But Coles would have it no other way. "We have such an appetite in America for labeling people," he notes. "We want fast, inclusive, easily remembered categories. Psychology, psycho-analysis and psychiatry are secular religions, and people want the priests of these religions to just give them the stages, the cycles, the phases. I've spent a lifetime resisting that."

Coles, who won the 1973 Pulitzer Prize for two of his volumes about children, brings to his work a rare blend of qualities: The anthropologist's passion for field research, the moral outlook of a clergyman and the sensibility of a poet. "Coles is in a category by himself," observes Dr. Lawrence Hartmann, president-elect of the American Psychiatric Association. Also setting him apart is that he has studied normal children. They may be youngsters confronting abnormal situations, but they are not the troubled patients most psychiatrists treat. Instead of focusing on what is wrong with children, Coles probes what motivates them, what frightens them, what enables them to persevere, and then lets the youngsters speak for themselves in his books, quoting them in lengthy, often poignant passages. He has told readers, for example, that migrant children tend to see everything as temporary and view life as a constant series of trips, citing a child who said to him, "I love the yo-yo, because it keeps going, up and down, and that's what I do." He has also documented stories like that of John Washington, a mediocre student from a poor black family who decided, against the better judgment of his parents, to become a pioneer and transfer to a previously all-white Atlanta high school. The boy's life was threatened, he was called hateful names, yet he did well academically and subsequently went on to college. Such stories, Coles suggests, show that "there are possibilities within us, and this allows for hope. Our job in society is to respond to those possibilities."

It was from his mother, a Midwestern progressive, that Coles inherited his sensitivity to those less well off. She was a humble woman who taught her son to shun arrogance and to look inward.

"My mother used to say, 'We must scrutinize ourselves as well as others,'" he recalls. From his father, a conservative Republican, Coles learned to be a keen observer. During long walks, his father would point out different neighborhoods and the types of people living in them. The political conflicts between his parents helped Coles to develop an understanding of diverse viewpoints. "From them, I got my ability to go back and forth between whites and blacks, between people of different backgrounds," he explains.

The self-effacing psychiatrist seems perfectly suited to working with children, yet his life's work came about purely by chance. He had no notion of becoming a physician, let alone a psychiatrist, until he met poet and novelist William Carlos Williams. Coles had written his undergraduate thesis at Harvard on the poet and, at the suggestion of his thesis adviser, sent Williams a copy. Williams urged Coles to drop by if he were ever in the neighborhood. That neighborhood happened to be Paterson, N.J., where Williams spent most of his days not writing poetry, but as a pediatrician. Coles hustled off to Paterson and accompanied Williams on house calls. He was charmed by the gruff yet sensitive man who suggested that Coles, then considering a career as an English teacher, go to medical school. Williams helped Coles get into Columbia University's College of Physicians and Surgeons. Later, when Coles found himself uncomfortable in pediatrics because he hated drawing blood from a baby and causing the infant to cry, it was Williams who suggested Coles try psychiatry. Most of all, Williams provided Coles with the model for his life, the model of the physician-writer.

Despite the influence of Williams, Coles could have ended up as just another child psychiatrist had the Air Force granted his wish in 1958 and sent him to the West Coast or abroad. Instead, he was shipped to an Air Force base hospital in Mississippi. It was there that he encountered, and later became part of, the civil-rights movement. He began to study stress in young blacks entering desegregated schools. At first, he thought the study would simply provide grist for a psychiatric journal article, nothing more. For a time it looked as though even the article would not materialize because the children and their families were wary of this stranger who had come to question them. Fortunately, his wife Jane encouraged him to press on and to relax and be more friendly. Coles shed his coat and tie and began to chat rather than question. Gradually, the children opened up, and what had started out as a short-term venture ended up paving the way for 30 years of research, a journey that his wife and three sons traveled with him virtually every step of the way as they moved from one part of the country to another.

For Coles, each meeting with a child represents "an existential encounter." To help him in these interviews, Coles frequently totes a box of crayons. He asks children to draw for him in order to get them to put down thoughts they have difficulty verbalizing. But he interprets the pictures only after he has spent time with a child and can look at the artwork in context. A drawing may depict the anxieties of a rich child—one banker's son drew a truck with the sign "Don't rob me!" on the side—or the feelings of inadequacy of a minority child. The first child he worked with, a black girl named Ruby Bridges, began drawing herself with only one ear or eye, while the white children in her pictures were strong and physically intact. "A picture can tell so much about a child's hopes and worries, his view of parents, sibling, school, teachers, society," says Coles. Schools should put more emphasis on art, he believes, as a way to stimulate those children who have difficulty doing conventional written school work. "We've got to learn how to turn kids on in ways that they can be turned on," says the psychiatrist.

The soft-spoken, almost shy interviewer of children turns into a charismatic speaker when he ascends the lecture platform at Harvard to teach "The Literature of Social Reflection," otherwise known as General Education 105, which was the most popular undergraduate offering last year. The course, which centers on the lives and literature of the writers he admires, is laughingly referred to as "Guilt 105" because Coles emphasizes the importance of living a life of moral concern. Students have entered the course smugly bent on careers in law or business and have left questioning their plans. "The course can cause students to have a midlife crisis at age 20," says Whiz Hutchinson, a section leader.

Coles is as unconventional in hiring graduate assistants as he is in the rest of his life. He is not interested in those moving in lock step toward a doctorate. He seeks people who know something about life, and so the instructors include a novelist, a housewife who is a social activist and Hutchinson, a private-school teacher who drives 240 miles round trip just to be there.

Coles, who also teaches a freshman seminar and a small class at the medical school, is amazingly open with students. He tells them about his own search for meaning and about his ambivalence at being at a "big shot" institution like Harvard. His closeness to students launched Coles on his new research project, studying people over 80 who are able to live on their own. He was drawn to this group because some of his students were doing volunteer work with older people and asked Coles to go along. Coles is fascinated by the survival instinct of older people and wants to find out what keeps them going. He has already begun interviewing elderly people in Durham, N.C., where he has an affiliation with Duke University, a link that enables him to return regularly to the South, a region with which he feels a special bond because it is where his work began.

As Coles examines another phase of the life cycle, he is finding that the elderly often shed the pressures and aggressive drives of middle age and return to the innocent and reflective side of childhood. Many play central roles in the lives of grandchildren. "They're the quiet mediators, the repositories of wisdom. They hand on traditions and hover over children in a way that young people don't resent as much as what parents do," he suggests.

Coles will never forsake the young. He vows to continue visiting programs for children and to remain a volunteer teacher in Boston-area elementary schools. But with his new project Robert Coles is now closing the circle of life.

Robert Coles with Studs Terkel

Studs Terkel/1990

An excerpt from a live, WFMT radio [Chicago, IL] interview conducted by Studs Terkel on December 20, 1990. Permission to publish from Studs Terkel. Transcribed and edited by Jay Woodruff.

What is God? I can picture a kid asking that question. The kid could be a sharecropper's kid, a poor white kid, a black kid in the South. It could be a Hopi Native American child, an Eskimo child, a rich kid going to some Episcopalian prep school. And they all ask "What is God?" Who is the observer? Child psychiatrist and author, and poetic always: Dr. Robert Coles. The number of books he's written, especially on the subject of children and their psyches and their physical lives, is unmatched by anyone. *Children of Crisis* is a remarkable series dealing with kids of all strata of our society, and other societies as well. His most recent book might be something of a synthesis of some of the others: *The Spiritual Life of Children.* In it are some paintings we have to talk about by the children themselves. We begin right off the bat with the subject of religion or God. And a kid, a girl, boy, no matter where she is in society.

Coles: A big part of their lives. They're human beings, they want to know where they came from. They want to know where they're going, if any place. They look up at the sky, at the stars, at the moon. And they say what is this all about? I've had so many children say to me, "Is there anyone behind the sun or the moon watching us?" Or, "How does God choose who's going to be born and who isn't?" Or, "What's going to happen to us when we leave this earth?" We all know this as parents or school teachers or relatives of young kids. We know that they ask these questions. And these questions define our humanity. We're the creature of language and awareness who wants to know answers to these great puzzling questions of origin and destiny. And religious life and spiritual life, I think, address those big questions.

Terkel: Why am I here? I'm sure you heard that very often in different forms from the kids.

Coles: I started out hearing it when I was a pediatrician, working in the Children's Hospital in Boston. We had a polio epidemic, the last one before the Salk vaccine. And I'll never forget some of these kids who suddenly were paralyzed. Some of them even in iron lungs. They would ask questions right out of the Old Testament, out of Job. They'd say "What did I ever do to deserve this? And why has God chosen me to be sick?" And some of them would tell me, "I think I'm going to die, and I wonder if I'm going to go any place. And my mommy and daddy say 'Yes, you're going to go to heaven if you die, but you're not going to die.' And I think I may die. And I want to know where this heaven is." And I'd say to them, "Well, I think we all want to know where this heaven is." These kinds of exchanges get you thinking.

Terkel: I suppose these kids, up against it, are angry at God, too.

Coles: There's a lot of that. I met some kids, of course, once I started working with the school desegregation struggle in the South in the early 60's, some of the black, and even the white kids who were poor; they would ask, "Why is it that we're living this way? What did our parents do that we end up this way?" And then, of course, they address God and say, "What did we ever do that you put us in this situation?"

Terkel: You're dealing with the subject of religion in an untraditional way for a psychiatrist. I mean Freud's way of looking at religion was something of another nature. That is a negative way to look at it.

Coles: It's all too negative.

Terkel: In *The Spiritual Life of Children* you refer to a Dr. Rizzuto, who is answering him. You side with her.

Coles: Absolutely.

Terkel: Would you mind explaining that.

Coles: She's a psychoanalyst who dared take on a lot of the psychoanalytical orthodoxy and say, "Hey, look, Freud didn't understand religion." In a sense, in her own way, she was doing with Freud what Ruby was doing with that mob outside the Frantz School in New Orleans in 1960. She was saying, "Listen, Sigmund Freud, I admire you, I'm a psychoanalyst too. But let's not hate blindly. Let's not dismiss our spirituality and religion and call it a neurosis and call these people sick. Let's try to understand what this is about." And she does so in a beautiful way. She says, "Look, we're all trying to ask questions. We're all trying to figure out life. And this is a kind of a spirituality which should not be called neurosis. And let us understand this as an aspect of our humanity, which is kind of nice." It gave me a lot of strength. It gave me some sanction to do this work.

Terkel: You were with Native American children. They're more of sky and nature and trees and God, all a bit more interrelated than they would be with a non-Indian.

Coles: The Hopi have a view of the world that very much resembles what a lot of us are coming to realize as we look at the environment and worry about nature. They've always had enormous respect for the land and the water and the sky. And in a sense their notion of God is what we would call the naturalist notion of God: that God lives in the world around us and indeed is the world around us. If we treasure whatever we call God, we have to treasure the world which is God. And to hear this in 7–, 8–, 10–year–old children as they look at the sky and appreciate the weather and notice the clouds and the configurations of clouds, worry about what's happening to the water or the land, is to realize that a lot of what we're coming to now belatedly in American middle-class secular life, has been anticipated for us by other groups by generations.

Terkel: B. Traven, the mystery writer, wrote a short story called "The Conversion of Some Indians." It's about this very point. It's about an old Catholic priest, a padre, a kindly good man wants to convert them. He's talking to them for days. They're listening and listening and listening, and then they come back with the answer. "You're a good man, but your God was spat upon and humiliated. And he was killed at the age of 33. Is that the way you treat your God? Our God rises every morning and warms us and we look toward him. In the evening he sets with the cool and we feel good. I think we'll stick with our God."

Coles: I had a moment with an Indian child, a Pueblo Indian child, in New Mexico, that I'll never forget. We were taking a walk. I'd done an interview with him. And suddenly, across the sky, we heard a tremendous noise. I thought, gee, it sounds like thunder, and then I realized it was a sonic boom. Some of our Air Force planes stationed in a base there near Albuquerque had been doing some missions, and they broke through the sound barrier. The kid looked up and he saw a look of perplexity on my face. And he said, "The crazy Anglos. They're beating their drums again."

Terkel: And, of course, he was right on both counts. The crazy Anglos. What they are doing to nature.

Now, maybe I'm wrong, but I found the rich children's view of God a little more abstract than that of the less affluent kids.

Coles: I think abstraction has come readily to more affluent people because maybe they don't want to look too closely at the reality which they *own,* which other people suffer from. I've noticed a lot of privileged kids basically have been taught pieties, and have been sheltered from a lot of earthy experiences that some of these poor kids have had. The irony of it is their earthy experiences resemble Jesus' earthy experiences. And the experiences of the Hebrew prophets who stood outside of the gates and denounced arrogant power, and therefore were humble. So I think the whole Judeo-Christian tradition is spiritually closer to the lives of ordinary people who struggle everyday with these mysteries, not in an abstract or pietistic way, but just from day to day trying to make a living and trying to figure out what this suffering and vulnerability is all about.

Terkel: I think you're on the button. It has happened so many times. In the 30's, during the organizing of the CIO, there was a circuit writer, Claude Williams, in the South. And Claude would use the Bible as a workingman's book.

Coles: It *is* a workingman's book.

Terkel: Yes it is. You know there was an Art Young cartoon, a picture of Jesus, just the profile, as it would be on a post office wall. And it simply said "Wanted, agitator, He stirreth up the masses." That's what some of the kids see, and they meld Jesus and God very often.

Coles: They sure do. A lot of the kids who are in this book would point out to me very, very carefully, that Jesus lived a very tough life, just like those Indians pointed out in that Traven story. This was a very hard life, and they feel sorry for him. They wonder how people who were rich and powerful felt toward Jesus when he was alive. That's an embarrassing question, isn't it? When you start wondering about that, you can get into trouble.

Terkel: I'm sure you run into black people who will very often tell you "Jesus, of course, was black. How could anyone have a light skin if he comes from Egypt? How can he be blue eyed?"

Coles: This is the narcissism of everyday life, which has each of us taking God and making him our own.

Terkel: *The Spiritual Life of Children* includes all these pictures, paintings of God and heaven and hell. But there's one . . . Marguerita, a little girl who lived in the favela slum in Rio. Asked about God, she says, "Well, God is all I have."

Coles: I met another girl in a favela in Rio who at 13 had already learned to sleep with rich men. Who had been homeless and basically a street kid. And in my profession we'd probably write her off as seriously disturbed, and call her all these psychiatric names. But you know what I found out about her? A nun told me that she brought 50 percent of the money she made, doing this sleeping in the Copa Cabana in Ipanima with rich men. She brought it to the nun's soup kitchen, and gave her that money to feed other kids. And I thought to myself, how many of us will do this? Talk about a moral life.

Terkel: That is a great parable.

Coles: I thought there is a moral life that doesn't come from an affluent home. And it doesn't come from going to church. And it doesn't come from all the props that we need with ourselves and our kids. I've never known what to do with that story other than to be in awe of having heard it.

Terkel: What did you do in getting the pictures?

Coles: I would ask these children if they would draw some pictures for me. I asked them to draw pictures about heaven or hell, what they imagined those places to be like; About God or about the devil or any of the biblical stories that they remember. I've accumulated thousands of children's drawings and paintings as an important part of how I do my work. You don't even have to speak the language of the child. You can just sit there with crayons, painting and drawing pictures together with them.

Terkel: Looking at this next one, number two, entitled "Religious and Non-Religious People."

Coles: This is a drawing done by a Swedish boy. What he essentially shows in this picture is a doctor working on a patient. He shows two people with their hands clasping one another's hands, reminiscent of the Sistine Chapel, of Michaelangelo. So this is the possibility, in his view, of a spiritual and religious and moral life, in which people help one another and try to heal one another. Then he draws pictures of a concentration camp, a Nazi flag, and people waiting basically to be destroyed by a gas chamber. He draws another picture of someone shooting someone, or hitting someone. Basically what he's saying is there are people who do good in the world, and there are people who are hateful. And this is the difference, in his view, of the religious versus the unreligious life.

Terkel: You see it all very clearly. Three and four: "Jesus Helping the Blind Man" and "Jesus and the Leper."

Coles: Beautiful moments of healing, of God as a healer. And, in the case of the leper, as God who is willing to associate with people whom the conventional world ostracizes or criticizes. I've had some children say to me, "You know if Jesus were around he would worry about people who have AIDS and he'd try to heal them. He wouldn't try to run away from them or call them bad names."

Terkel: This one of Jesus helping the leper is right on the button. It could be AIDS.

Coles: The children are willing to make the connection between the way Jesus was with the lepers, and the way we ought to be with people who have an illness now that is hurtful to them and threatens their lives. But also seems to threaten some of us. In a different way it threatens us the way it threatens the people who have AIDS.

Terkel: Some of these I'd call representational paintings. "Moses and the Tables of the Law; God's Paw."

Coles: This is a Jewish kid who warned me the Jewish people are not supposed to represent God visually. But he couldn't resist, in some way, giving some physical incarnation to God. So what he did was depict Moses receiving the Ten Commandments on top of the mountain. Then he drew kind of a paw and he said, "I'll call this God's paw. And it's handing over the Ten Commandments to Moses." It's a very touching picture. There's another one called the "Planet where God Lives." This was done by a kid who had seen lots of Star Trek and movies. He has the kid basically in a machine because he's got a wheel. He's going up into space. There is this planet where he has different colors. This shows you that kids connect all the technology now, the exploration of space, to their spiritual lives. They figure, "Well, if you keep on going up in these machines, high enough and far enough, maybe one of these days you're going to stumble into God."

Terkel: There's also another of Christ healing. "Christ Raising Lazarus From the Dead." He's sitting up in the coffin.

Coles: The interesting thing about that one is that Christ looks like he's Superman. He has that cape of Superman. And that's another fusion of contemporary mythology with ancient storytelling. There's another one called "The Crucifixion," which I find so haunting. It's Jesus on the cross and there's electricity in the air—those yellow slashes going through the sky. What I find so haunting about that picture are those four flowers drooping. It shows you a child saying the natural world can somehow respond to the troubles of mankind. It's a kind of a Hopi sentiment there, of intimacy in the natural world.

Terkel: You see the crucified Christ about to ascend to the heaven. But these four little droopy flowers, four of them.

Coles: They're in mourning for what's happening to Jesus. It's very touching.

Terkel: And, moving along, "The Saved and the Damned."

Coles: Lots of kids, by the way, have talked to me about the saved and the damned. I've asked them who they think gets saved, and who is damned. They come up with statements worthy of the great populist tradition! They'll say, "Well, people who were good to other people are going to go to heaven. But there are a lot of people who don't care about other people. And they're not going to get there."

Terkel: What you call theological populism.

Coles: Theological populism in children. We need a little more of that in adults.

Terkel: Here's another drawing, "The Second Coming."

Coles: That's showing God, in a sense, in the old Greek tradition of being the one who arbitrarily decided who's going to be saved and who's going to be damned. Which in a way haunts all of us: namely, how do you know whether you're doing the right thing and whether you're headed for some kind of happiness or whether you're headed for some kind of suffering, if there is another life. Oftentimes, even in this life, we don't know what we're headed for. And this, in a way, is children acknowledging that fate and luck are a big part of life, a big part of life. Good luck, bad luck.

Terkel: "The Second Coming" also has a musical choir. There's music.

Coles: Well, music is a part of our destiny.

Terkel: "Hell and Heaven," the different views. "Lot's Wife." And Lot's wife is hollering "Help."

Coles: I watched a child drawing Lot's wife and suddenly I began to wonder what kind of a person is this child drawing? Suddenly I realized, in a beautiful moment of poetry, the child had rendered Lot's wife as a salt shaker which had arms and legs.

Terkel: And hollering "Help."

Coles: Yes, because Lot's wife is supposed to turn into salt. So in this child's mind she turns into a salt shaker.

Terkel: "Heaven and Hell," and the views and visions of it. That comes up very often. What is your vision of heaven and what is your vision of hell?

Coles: I've heard some very poignant responses. One girl said to me, "Heaven is a place where people are nice to other people." I thought, "Wow, I want to go there." And then I said, "What's hell about?" She said, "Hell is where all the people are who haven't been nice to other people."

Terkel: Throughout there's this recurring theme of self-criticizing on the part of the young. The imagination, but also this lyrical, this poetic aspect of it.

Coles: I think poetry is a part of childhood. Lots of times children lose that poetry as they get older. They conform. They become all too automaton-like in the way they think and feel. There's a novelist, Elizabeth Bowen, who described what goes on for all too many of us, in the title of a novel which she called *The Death of the Heart*. And we lose that heart-felt responsiveness to other people. You hear in children, and you see in the drawings they do, the openness and vulnerability they feel to themselves and to other people, their own ups and downs. And Lord, that's a good side of what human beings can be. It's nice to witness it. It would be nice if some of us learn from it too.

Terkel: And by the way, they associate Bible stories with events in their lives. Very often they use a Biblical tale.

Coles: Definitely. Recently I heard a child talking about the greenhouse effect. She'd heard her parents talking about the greenhouse effect, and the parents said that because of the greenhouse effect and the environmental changes the water is going to start flooding the coastline, and we'll have more and more flooding at a more northern latitude. And she said, "Maybe we'll all end up in Noah's Ark again because of what's happening to the environment." She was taking environmental concerns and connecting them to an ancient story, and in a nice way trying to understand what was happening.

Terkel: So the child understands the power of metaphor.

Coles: The power of metaphor, the power of narrative, the power of symbol. The power of storytelling. What is the Bible? It's a series of wonderful, moral fables, stories. Stories. They tell stories.

Terkel: They also ask, when terrible things happen, does God really care?

Coles: The old pediatrician in me remembers children sick and vulnerable asking questions and connecting themselves to Job. And in general trying to understand through biblical stories their own story.

Terkel: You describe them as pilgrims. In a way there's a quest here. You speak of the quest.

Coles: There is a quest. I think children are like the rest of us. They want to know what their destiny is. They want to know where they're going. They're looking ahead. They're visionary in that sense. They're asking what will happen. In a sense they're moving themselves in their minds through space, through time, toward what they know will be the end of a life. We all know life ends, and so they have a sense of themselves as being in motion, not only physical motion but moral motion, even spiritual motion, as they try to figure out, not only the concreteness of specifically what they're going to end up doing and where they're going to live, but what kind of people they're going to be and what kind of life they're going to live. In that sense I regard them, as I think they regard themselves, as pilgrims, young pilgrims.

Terkel: And there's a quest.

Coles: Seeking the quest, seeking for some meaning in life, for some significance in life. That's what we are: people who want to find that.

In the book, a girl who I thought was very much like Dorothy Day was trying to give someone some directions. She was trying to help an old lady find her way to a house she was seeking. This girl was doing the traditional good deed for an elderly person, and I thought for all we know this person could be like Dorothy Day, who was also trying to find the direction for herself, and has inspired so many of us to find direction. I saw that girl and I thought of Dorothy Day. Maybe because I thought this girl has the same kind of moral capacity that Dorothy Day had. This is where youth and old age, and indeed all of us, come together as seekers, as pilgrims: people, as Walker Percy put it, "handing one another along" in this journey.

Youngsters Have Lots to Say about God

Richard N. Ostling/1991

From *Time* (New York, January 21, 1991, pp. 16–17). Reprinted by permission of *Time* magazine.

Q. You talked with hundreds of children all over the world for your book *The Spiritual Life of Children*. Are you now more inclined to see all religions as one, or are the lines sharply drawn?

A. The lines are drawn. Jewish children had a strong interest in righteousness; I could hear some of those Hebrew prophets in their words. Christian children were true to an interest in the Incarnation, which at times strained their faith, and in the redemptive tradition that somehow Jesus arrived here to save us and that this salvation, when earned, would be theirs. And I found among children brought up in Islam a distinct emphasis on obedience and submission.

Q. Did you run into surprises?

A. I was surprised by the energetic interest that children in secular America could bring to spiritual reflection. I didn't have to prompt these children or work as hard as I thought I would.

Q. A footnote says you "hesitated long and hard" before doing *Spiritual Life*. Why?

A. First I had to come to terms with the way psychoanalysis treats religion in a cavalierly condescending, and at times outrageously intolerant, manner, plus some plain old ignorance.

Q. Are children merely echoing what their parents or clergy teach them?

A. There's a big part of that, of course, not only in religion but in politics and, I might add, in psychology. Having said that, I've heard children in a wonderful fashion echo that Tom Sawyer-Huck Finn-Holden Caulfield tradition of American literature, bringing feisty skepticism and originality to spiritual matters. They have pointed out to me that the churches and synagogues and mosques can betray the original spirit of the faiths those children have been brought up in. Lots of children have commented on how Jesus lived, his association

198

with outcasts and unpopular people, his poverty, the fact that he was
a carpenter and his friends were peasants, that he didn't go to college
and get fancy degrees, didn't have a lot of money, didn't associate
with big-shot people.

Q. Are most children really interested in spiritual questions?

A. They're interested, out of their humanity, because they know to
ask what [Paul] Gauguin asked in his 1897 Tahitian painting: Where
do we come from? What are we? Where are we going? Those are the
great existential questions of artists, philosophers, novelists, histo-
rians, psychologists, and the questions of children and of all human
beings.

Q. So we adults can learn, religiously, from children?

A. Look, psychoanalysis says we have a lot to learn from children.
The spiritual interests of children have a lot to teach us as well. I have
listened to children of eight or nine or 10 getting to the heart of the
Bible. I have found in elementary schools a good deal of spiritual
curiosity that does not reflect mere indoctrination. This is an
interesting capacity children have, and I think we ought to pay
attention to it.

Q. How should schools deal with it?

A. This is one of the great problems in American public schooling.
Many teachers are afraid to bring up moral, let alone spiritual,
questions for fear that they are going to violate the Constitution. It's a
tragedy, intellectually as well as morally and spiritually. This might
relate to the educational problems among some children. A large
number of the schools' assumptions are basically materialist and
agnostic. There's a kind of culture conflict between the families and
the schools. That conflict may have some bearing on what children
learn and what they don't learn, and on how children behave in
school.

Q. Might it have a bearing on parents' support and enthusiasm for
schools?

A. Definitely. And not only in so-called Fundamentalist areas but in
the suburbs and certainly in the ghettos as well, where the black
spiritual tradition is not welcome in schools.

Q. What could be done?

A. Children could be taught history that connects with their actual
history, namely the history of the great religions, what those religions

have been about, culturally, aesthetically, intellectually, morally and spiritually. That learning could inform the moral lives of those children, and classroom life. There is also an intellectual vacuum. Children aren't being taught what religious life stands for and what these various traditions have to offer us, even as they are being taught what Freud or Darwin stands for.

Q. I understand you teach a course on religion that has the largest enrollment at Harvard.

A. That's my course on the literature of social reflection, which has in it a good hunk of religion. Last year it was the largest course, but this year it's No. 3 because I cut down the enrollment. I also taught a course for a number of years on the literature of Christian reflection. I hope to go back to it. That course was not an indoctrination into Christianity. It simply reminded us that religion has given us a great narrative and lyrical tradition that the secular world has a lot to learn from. By the way, there's a great spiritual and moral hunger among a lot of these secular college students.

Q. Tell me more.

A. The hunger is often displaced into secular preoccupations, namely politics, psychology, health, support groups, child-rearing preoccupations, sometimes literary and artistic interests, what have you. These interests are part of the search all of us undertake for some kind of meaning in life. I just think those fundamental existential concerns are never going to go away.

Q. Isn't religion often used negatively?

A. So is everything else. So is intellectual life. Look at the sectarianism in the name of psychoanalysis, the way we've learned to hate one another. Look at the Ivy League colleges. The meanness you find there rivals Belfast. Religion becomes a scapegoat. We see clearly the hatred in the name of religion, but we don't see so clearly the hatred generated in the different departments within these fancy universities or different political worlds. There's no sphere of human activity that lacks smugness, arrogance, self-importance, divisiveness and all the other sins we're capable of. And I say *sins*. If you look at what the religious tradition tells us, it warns about this sin of pride. No amount of secular progress, social or economic or educational, has so far enabled us to get beyond that darker side of ourselves.

Q. Are you officially a member of a religious denomination?

A. No. My children have been baptized in the Episcopal church, and my wife and I used to go with them fairly often. I have trouble finding a home in religion. My father was a scientist, Jewish with some Catholic background. My mother used to take us to the Episcopal church, and my father would never go in. He'd sit outside and read the Sunday papers. He was very skeptical of religions. He thought they all basically betrayed their ideals, and I think he was right. That's a part of me, along with some yearning for faith. For all my political liberalism, I'm fairly conservative on religious matters.

Q. Do you believe in a supernatural God?

A. Sometimes I do, and at other times I have my moments of doubt. I regard those moments of doubt as part of the struggle that we all have for faith.

A Conversation with Robert Coles

Peter Costa/1991

From the *Harvard University Gazette* (Cambridge, MA, January 25, 1991, pp. 5–8. Reprinted by permission of the *Harvard University Gazette* and the Harvard University News Office.

Robert Coles is a child psychiatrist, Pulitzer Prize winner for several volumes of his *Children of Crisis,* and author of *The Spiritual Life of Children* (Houghton Mifflin, 1990). Peter Costa is director of the University Office of News and Public Affairs. The following is an edited transcript of the conversation between Coles and Costa.

Costa: In 1960 you served as a physician in the Air Force in Mississippi and you witnessed the racial struggles of the South, the sit-ins, the protests, the beginnings of the civil rights movement and its effects on the children whom you saw there. Did witnessing these events lead you to your work with children?

Coles: I had been trained in pediatrics and child psychiatry before I went into the Air Force under the doctors draft when all physicians had to put in two years in the military. This applied to everyone until about 1965. So I was prepared to work with children by training. In fact, the first research I did was with children in the Children's Hospital who had polio. It was the last epidemic before the Salk vaccine. In the course of working with them as a pediatrician and as a child psychiatrist I began to notice some of their moral and even spiritual concerns as they lay there sometimes dying or certainly paralyzed and frightened about what would happen to them. I think that prepared me for what I saw in the South.

I witnessed the early struggles of children to get into desegregated schools, often involving the need for them to walk by mobs of hecklers, some of them threatening to kill them. I think it was this earlier training and experience in working with children under stress that enabled me to visualize myself talking with a new group of children under a different kind of stress, namely the horrors of social and racial stress in the face of real tension and enmity between white and black people in Mississippi and Louisiana.

I was in charge of an Air Force psychiatric hospital in Biloxi, Mississippi, then and I used to go into New Orleans to medical, psychiatric, and psychoanalytic meetings and it was these travels from Mississippi into Louisiana that enabled me to witness school desegregation because I drove by one of the schools that was desegregated. I saw hundreds of people massed in front of the school, screaming and shouting and threatening one little black child who went into the school all by herself because the entire white school population was withdrawn by the parents of these children. Here you had a situation out of a Franz Kafka story because you had a little girl all alone in a school building with a mob telling her everyday that they were going to kill her. When I saw that happen, my mind went back to the children I met in Boston who were facing a different kind of ordeal, and to my conversations with them and I thought to myself, maybe if I got to know a girl like this little girl, whose name was Ruby Bridges and who became a heroine of mine and, I would say, a teacher of mine, I would learn a lot from her and maybe I could be of some help to her and her family. This began this work.

Costa: Was it Ruby who walked past the angry mob smiling, and when a white women asked her, "What are you smiling at?" she looked up and said she was smiling at God?

Coles: Yes, this is the girl. This is the girl whose religious and spiritual interests I heard and took note of, but I'm afraid didn't pay as much attention to at the beginning there in the early '60s as I might have, and perhaps should have, had I not been trained in psychoanalytic psychiatry. That field has not exactly been known, at least in the past, for its major interest in religious and spiritual matters, at least interest in a positive sense.

Costa: I was struck by an anecdote in your book about the nature of psychoanalysis and what are legitimate areas of inquiry. You were working with a young boy from a privileged family. The boy was a computer freak, quite brilliant and wanted to talk to you solely about computers and information processing and things of the intellect. And you told him that psychoanalysis is not meant to be an exploration of the intellect or the soul. Do you have to set aside your psychoanalytic training to discuss spirituality?

Coles: There is a growing number of psychoanalysts who see a connection between psychoanalytic matters and spirituality, and for that matter, I think Freud himself implicitly saw this all the time. For instance, his written exchanges with Einstein are essentially moral and spiritual in nature. His explorations of Moses have a spiritual side to them. His interests in creativity and in the soulfulness of certain writers bring him closer to spiritual matters. After all, he was an intensely moral figure who stood for certain values and principles and made those values and principles very clear to the world, and I suspect much clearer to his patients than many of his followers have been willing to be with their patients.

Costa: You've interviewed thousands of youngsters all over the world in different cultures. Do most children reflect adults' views of God, or did you find any that had original ideas of God?

Coles: I think original for them in the sense that these children were not prepared by studies in theology or philosophy or religion to come up with the thinking they've come up with. In that sense their thinking shows that there is a certain kind of common thinking that perhaps all of us have when trying to struggle with these common problems we all have: mainly, how do you figure out the meaning of life and what do you do with the limited amount of time you have on this planet.

I've found that a lot of children do not learn their ideas about religion and spiritual matters only from their parents, although, indeed, the parents are a major influence. They also have a lot of conversations about such matters with friends, with other relatives, with grandparents, especially, by the way, in certain cultures such as in black families and in Spanish-speaking families in America and in other countries where grandparents have much more significance than they do in many American families. And from teachers, from athletic coaches, from people they meet—adults, and people of their own age—in the course of their lives, and often just from their own musings and speculations. I've talked with children who tell me that they look out the window sometimes, at the stars, the moon, the sun, the clouds, and the configurations of the clouds, and wonder and speculate and think. Some of these speculations I find extraordinary.

I have a longstanding interest in theology going back to when I was taking psychiatric training here in Boston at Massachusetts General Hospital and Children's Hospital. I audited a course that Paul Tillich gave in systematic theology in the '50s here at Harvard. I remember him discussing with us Karl Barth and a lot of his theological interests in not only human beings' search for God, but God's search for us. I thought that was an interesting way of putting it. I've often gone back to those moments here at Harvard when I remember some of the remarks that I've heard from children. I especially think of one girl who said to me, "You know, God must be very lonely at times and he must try and make friends with some of the people he's going to send down to the earth and then when he does send them down he must miss them and he must try to keep track of them." As she developed this extraordinary line of speculation about God I thought, "My lord, this is worthy of Karl Barth." This child's speculations are, indeed, worthy of Karl Barth, and maybe some other theologians too.

There's a kind of resourcefulness, richness, texture, subtlety, and nuance to a lot of these speculations that you hear from children which I think entitles them to be called in their own right—apart from the influence of their parents and others in the adult world—seekers, pilgrims who are interested in the eternal questions that we all have about life. Here we are with an infinity of time and space before us and after us. We wonder about what we are doing, and this, children are eminently capable of wondering about as much as we adults are.

Costa: From a psychiatric viewpoint, do you think having a sense of spirituality or religion or religiousness contributes to a child's health?

Coles: We all have some sense of spirituality or religiousness even if we are agnostics or atheists and deny an explicit or even implicit interest in conventional religion or conventional dogma as it's handed down by the various religious groups. I go back to those questions, for instance, that Gauguin asked when he painted that triptych of his in 1897 that hangs in the Boston Museum of Fine Arts. He titled it, "Where Do We Come From? What Are We? Where Are We Going?" To my mind, that's what spirituality is. It's the capacity for awareness that we all have and the capacity through language to ask these important existential questions. In that sense I think every one of us has a religious or spiritual side. We may not practice a religion, we may not believe the dogma handed down, but we ask the questions and we wonder. It's that wondering and it's that musing and it's those philosophical sides that children have as well as adults that I call spirituality.

Costa: You asked many of the children to draw or paint God. Did most of the children portray God as a smiling, bearded deity?

Coles: No. God varies in many ways by the background of the child. I noticed when I was working in Europe that God was blondish with blue eyes in Sweden, and slowly the hair color and the eye color changed as I moved down through Hungary toward Italy. Then when I crossed the Mediterranean Sea I started talking with children in Israel. In Tunisia, God had a distinctly different coloration among those children who were willing to draw God. Of course, Jewish and Islamic children do not draw pictures of the deity.

Costa: You never asked a child of Jewish or Islamic faith to draw a picture of God.

Coles: I could have gotten into some of the difficulties that Salman Rushdie got into. Some of these children were prepared to violate some of these tenets because they were tempted to and had in their own minds pictured God, regardless of the injunctions that they not do so in an engraving sense by drawing or painting. Some of them even wanted to draw a little circle to represent God, at least in a geometric sense.

But they were willing and anxious to draw pictures of Moses and other Hebrew prophets and of Jesus and his comrades. But the child's racial background, religious background, even socioeconomic background, and the child's personal life definitely influenced the way the child thinks of God and will picture God. Christian children were very anxious to draw pictures of Jesus and, indeed, of God. There was a great deal of variation depending on where they lived and what their neighborhood was like and who they usually see and therefore what colors come naturally to them as they pick up the pencils and the crayons and the paints.

In my work over the last thirty years drawings and paintings have been extremely important. I learned long ago when I was training to be a child psychiatrist how helpful it can be when talking with children to ask them to draw pictures. In the book *The Spiritual Life of Children* the drawings and paintings that are part of the book are very important because they really give the reader, even as they gave me, access to the way children's minds work as they attempt to imagine what—really for all of us—is almost unimaginable, namely, what God looks like. It's quite a task for anyone whether you're a child or an adult to picture what is beyond any human knowledge or experience.

Costa: Tell us about the boy who had the interesting visual representation of the Trinity. I think he saw the Holy Ghost as a rainbow.

Coles: This was a wonderful way of trying to give some visual life to what is obviously the intangible. He said to me once, "I just don't know what this Holy Ghost is. I've asked the nuns and I've asked the priests and they tell me close your eyes and imagine and it will come to you and if it doesn't, then don't worry about it." The boy once told me, "I closed my eyes and I couldn't see anything and then I told my mother and father that I couldn't see anything and I was trying to think about what the Holy Ghost looks like. Then suddenly I thought to myself I know what the Holy Ghost is. The Holy Ghost is a rainbow and my mother said, 'Where did you get that idea?'" And he said, "Well, because the Holy Ghost knows everything and sees everything and a rainbow has all the colors and it covers the whole world because it is a huge arc."

What this boy was really telling me—we had further conversations about this—is that he had somehow managed to find a concrete symbol for this very, very elusive conceptual matter. I thought to myself this is worthy of anyone I have ever met at Harvard, professor and student alike.

Costa: Catholic nuns, as discussed by the young people in your book, got a bad rap—or maybe a deserved one—as being extremely stern. One student said that if the nuns are so strict, then God must be even sterner.

Coles: I have a great deal of affection not only for the Catholic church but for certain nuns whom I've known very well, and I've spent a lot of my life working in a Catholic workers soup kitchen and knew Dorothy Day very well so I don't come off this with any animus. But it so happens that the Catholic children I worked with most closely in Boston were going to a particular school where they were both getting a lot from these nuns and being very well educated by them. But the nuns were very stern and I think some of their sternness came across in the conversations I had with some of the children. Mind you, they were very respectful of these nuns and very admiring of them in certain ways, but there's no question that the nuns handed on to these children a very stern, tough, demanding, and somewhat ascetic God. And not those nuns alone because some of the children I worked with in the South who came from a fundamentalist Protestant background also struggled with some of that Christian asceticism that they had picked up in Sunday School.

Indeed, when I talked with Jewish children of the Orthodox persuasion in Israel there was a good deal of that there among them as well. This has always been an aspect of the three religions I've studied through children, namely, Islam, Christianity, and Judaism, that ascetic, puritanical side. But, of course, there are other sides to religious life and I've gathered that from children as well. The more joyous, celebratory, and sensual side of religious experience.

Costa: There was one chapter in your book which I think your fellow psychiatrists and psychoanalysts would worry about, and that was describing those rare but real instances when some children experience a visionary moment. How do you as a psychiatrist differentiate a visionary moment from, say, a psychologically dis- turbed moment?

Coles: I remember having a long conversation with Anna Freud about this, and she pointed out to me, "You know, there's a continuum between the normal and the pathological, and the real issue is how far we walk down that continuum. Some footsteps are fine, but, of course, as you move further and further away into the realm of the psychopathological then they all start worrying. The visionary side of our lives is not to be confused with the hallucinatory side of disturbed people's lives.

Costa: I would be remiss if I didn't ask you this question: How does God look to you?

Coles: It depends on my mood, it depends on the particular day, maybe even the time of day in my life. I often think of God when I think of my parents. I think of God when I think of my mother's wonderful smile as she put her hands on my brother and me and encouraged us and handed on to us some of the treasures of her own

moral and intellectual life, namely, George Eliot's *Middlemarch* or
Tolstoy's *War and Peace*. I think of God coming across to me through
my mother's smile and her loving kindness or my father's highly
refined moral sensibility. I think of God sometimes when I remember
my father in the last years of his life doing volunteer work with fellow
elderly people in Boston, and visiting them and bringing meals to
them. I think of this as a God-like moment. My father and some other
elderly people sharing stories with one another. His goodness being a
part of their lives and a lot of what they offered to him being a part of
his life.

I think of God when I think of some of the children I've met and
what they've said to me, which comes across in this book. I think of
God when I think of some of the elderly people I've met whose
thoughtfulness and sensitivity gives me pause and gives me some
meaning in my own life. In other words, I think of God through his or
her people who are in their own ways incarnations of whatever the
deity is.

I think of God when I think of some of the teachers that I have had,
some of the Harvard professors that I have studied with, such as
Perry Miller, Erik Erikson. I think of God when I remember my
friendship with Dorothy Day. If God somehow isn't connected to
Dorothy Day, then I don't know what God is. And why shouldn't I as
a human being in my visual life and in my intellectual life and in my
imaginative life and in my emotional life connect God with someone
such as Dorothy Day.

Costa: You are unique, except for William Carlos Williams, who
was your great mentor, to be a literate doctor who can communicate
to others in emotional and imaginative ways, and still not jettison the
science of being a physician. How did you come to harness those
two horses?

Coles: This has been a lifelong struggle for me. The answer is
implicit in your question. I wrote my college thesis on William Carlos
Williams, and then Perry Miller, my professor here at Harvard,
encouraged me to send it off to Williams with some resistance on my
part because I was afraid he wouldn't like it. From [Williams] I got
back a little note on one of his prescription pads saying, "Not bad—
for a Harvard student!" Then he added a little footnote: "If you're
ever in the neighborhood, drop by." Well, a week later I was down in

New York, with fear and trembling, calling him up. I got his wife on the phone and she said, "If you want to come over here, Bill will be coming home and maybe you can have a cup of coffee with him, even some supper if you want to stay with us." So, of course, I made a beeline for the bus and went over there to Rutherford and that's how I met him.

The next day he took me on his medical rounds and I met his patients in Paterson, the poor, humble, working-class people whom he'd given his life to as a physician, up and down those tenement house stairs, meeting them, knocking on the doors, visiting them, often not being paid by them, struggling to do what he could for them, and struggling with all the problems he had as a hard-working doctor who also wanted to write, and obviously did write. I shifted my whole life around because of this. I became so taken with him and so admiring of him that I thought this is how I'd like to spend my life, at least being the doctor side of Williams because I never thought of myself as a writer and I never thought of myself as having the ability to write other than to write college papers.

So I took the premedical courses and went to medical school and while in medical school I used to visit him a lot and he did become a wonderful mentor in my life. Those conversations gave shape to my whole sense of what life ought to be about. So I went into pediatrics—because he had basically been a pediatrician—and then went into child psychiatry. In fact when I started my work in the South he was still alive—he died in 1963—and I shared with him some of my experiences with some of the first black and white children I met during the school desegregation struggle. He was the one who told me to try to take these observations and offer them to readers as stories. He said, "Don't write this up in psychiatric jargon, don't write it up as if you were a social scientist. Those children are telling you wonderful incidences. There is a narrative voice in you that I hear as you describe what you've heard from these children and they have narrative voices. You be the intermediary between those children and what they are going through and what they have to tell you and what you have learned from them, and what you have to offer readers." With that kind of advice from him I think my writing career began because I tried to do what he suggested I ought to do. That's, in a capsule form, a summary of how one particular stumbling, bumbling person trying to find some meaning in his own life happened upon this particular way of combining medical and psychiatric research with a writing life.

Costa: You've written more than a thousand articles and more than 50 books. In 1973 you won a Pulitzer Prize for your writing about children. What do you see as your next goal in your work and in your writing?

Coles: I'm now doing interviews with elderly people who managed, despite their medical infirmities and their vulnerabilities—social, economic, racial—to be independent and live on their own. I'm very interested in independence and resiliency, whether it be in children or other people who are older and I'm trying to do some interviews in the North and the South with elderly people—black, white, rural, urban—to try to figure out how, perhaps against great odds, elderly people manage to live a life of dignity and resiliency. I think this will keep me busy for a while.

I guess, in that sense, I'm continuing a tradition of documentary child psychiatry and documentary psychiatry and mingling the kinds of observations that people such as James Agee, Walker Evans, and Dorothea Lange did . . . mingling that with the kind of medical psychiatric training that I've had and then trying to write it up in some kind of a reasonably coherent and understandable manner.

A Conversation with Robert Coles

Lynne V. Cheney/1991

From *Humanities* (Washington, DC, volume 12, number 2, March/April 1991, pp. 4–9.) *Humanities is an official publication of the National Endowment for the Humanities, and as such is in the public domain. Lynne V. Cheney is chairman of the NEH.*

How storytelling can provide moral insight was one of the topics NEH Chairman Lynne V. Cheney discussed recently with Robert Coles, Professor of Psychiatry and Medical Humanities at Harvard University. Dr. Coles is the author of fifty books, including the *Children of Crisis* series, for which he won the Pulitzer Prize.

Lynne V. Cheney: I want to tell you how much I have enjoyed *The Call of Stories.* There is a young man at the end—I think you call him Gordon—who talks about characters like Jude Fawley [in *Jude the Obscure*] and Jack Burden [in *All the King's Men*] and how they're alive for him and how, when he has tough moral decisions to make, he thinks of them. I've quoted that passage so much because it's such eloquent testimony to what literature can mean for a person's life.

Robert Coles: Oh, thank you. That is sometimes forgotten by some of us critics who take literature and turn it into an object and then analyze it. We forget that people are capable of not only using those books intellectually, but taking them to heart.

Cheney: You have been pretty outspoken about some of the more recent trends in literary scholarship. I have a speech you gave to the National Council of Teachers of English in which you talk about deconstruction.

Coles: Well, I understand that there are some valuable parts to the kind of literary analysis that is called deconstruction, which is in a sense a catch-all phrase. I understand the intellectual will that's involved in deconstruction, and I even applaud it. In a sense I

212

compare deconstruction to the kind of psychoanalytic intellectuality that I'm all too used to in my own profession—these efforts to figure out in an abstract way symbolic meaning and to get to the bottom of certain intentions on the part of writers, or patients, for that matter. But sometimes in this rigorous analysis, the overall meaning of either a life or a story is forgotten. Sometimes there's a certain comic extravagance, shall we call it, that gets going in this kind of analysis, whether it be the psychoanalyst working with a patient or the literary critic working with a text.

If I want to be really mean, I could quote you something that Raymond Carver said. He was asked by an interviewer—I'm quoting directly—"Do you know much about the deconstructionists?" The interviewer was a man named John Alton and he asked him that in 1986, and Carver's response was, "Enough to know that they're crazy." I don't go that far, but I think at times it's kind of funny and I sometimes think of Kafka and think of what he would do with some of these efforts to take over these stories and at times turn them into nothing.

Cheney: You've also spoken about the diminishment to art that results when the critic becomes more important than the storyteller.

Coles: Unfortunately this happens. It's not very surprising to those of us who have been parents and have seen children fighting things out with one another; sometimes I'm afraid that we never do outgrow our childhood. In that sense, ironically, some of the deconstructionists who uphold Freud so fervently and reverently might remember what he observed when he saw people fighting things out and becoming very rivalrous and claiming property vis-à-vis one another.

Cheney: And setting out to undo the older generation.

Coles: Setting out to undo the older generation and claiming that there is some wisdom that is very special to them as the new generation.

Cheney: You were an English major as an undergraduate.

Coles: I was. I majored in English, and my tutor was Perry Miller. What a great man he was, and what a privilege it was to study with him! I took a course that he started in 1949 called "Classics of the Christian Tradition," and in that course he used not only some of the great texts of the Christian tradition such as St. Augustine's *Confessions* and Pascal's *Pensées,* he'd draw upon poems of Robert

Frost or Emily Dickinson and he'd encourage us to read novels. He's the one who encouraged me to do my thesis on William Carlos Williams.

Cheney: I remember reading that he encouraged you to do that because Williams was not merely unremarked, he was held in rather low esteem by certain members of the Harvard faculty.

Coles: Williams was held in very low esteem by the august Harvard faculty. I always tell my Harvard students that they should keep their eye out not only for the books that the Harvard faculty write, but the ones that they don't write. The English faculty of Harvard in 1950, when I was writing my thesis on Williams, was not known particularly for its humility.

Cheney: But you've tried to help them in that regard.

Coles: Well, I'm risking becoming arrogant myself at this point. But I must say, it was awful. I worked hard on that thesis. It was on the first two books of *Paterson,* which had been published in 1947, 1948. And then I had a terrible time with two teachers who went over that thesis with no great enthusiasm. But Miller told me, "You've learned something from this that's more important even than what you learned from Williams, who is not only a great poet and storyteller, but a great populist with a tremendous feel for ordinary people and their language and the rhythms of their lives and the tensions they have in their heart. You've learned the distance between such a writer and some of us who live in these fancy university buildings. If you've learned that and can stay close to that kind of knowledge, then you've gotten your money's worth out of Harvard." I'll never forget him telling me that, and I'm almost giving the message word for word.

Cheney: You then began to spend time with Williams after you finished the thesis.

Coles: I did. That's a little story in itself. Perry Miller suggested that I send the thesis to Williams, and I will never forget that moment. I looked at him and I said, "Well, I can't do that." And he looked at me with the kind of knowledge that a good psychological skeptic has and he said to me, "Well, I guess you just don't have the postage." I looked back and suddenly saw what my mother used to call the sin of pride working full time, and I said, "Well, I guess I can get the postage together if I try hard," and I did. It must have been about 10 cents in those days. I sent the thesis off and I got back a memorable little note written on one of his prescriptions.

Cheney: Oh, how wonderful.

Coles: And it said, "Dear Mr. Coles, This is not bad—for a Harvard student!" Then he had another line, which was, "If you're ever in the neighborhood, please drop by," and underneath was "Bill Williams." A week later I was in Manhattan with my heart beating very fast, and I called that number in Rutherford and I got his wife, Flossie, on the phone, and she told me that he was out in Paterson with his patients but that if I wanted to come over, she was sure that he would be glad to see me, which was just very nice.

Cheney: And you went on house calls with him and . . .

Coles: I went over there and he took me on his rounds and down to Paterson, where I met some of his patients, and that was the beginning of a whole new life for me. I started taking premed courses and decided to be a doctor.

Cheney: And then a psychiatrist.

Coles: Well, I was originally in pediatrics, and that's a story that connects with him. I used to have trouble with some of these children in the sense that I had to do some very difficult procedures on them, and they'd start crying, very agitated, and I told him about this and how upset I got. He looked at me and he said, "I guess you don't have the iron for that kind of work." He said, "Why don't you try the psychological side of children's lives?" and that's how I went from pediatrics into child psychiatry.

Cheney: And you spent twenty years working on *Children of Crisis.* Have I got that part right?

Coles: You've got that right. What happened is, I went into the Air Force in 1958 under the old doctor's draft, and I was in charge of a military hospital in Biloxi, Mississippi, Keesler Air Force Base. I was in charge of the psychiatric unit there. It was a big neuropsychiatric unit, and this was in the late fifties, early sixties, just when school desegregation started in New Orleans; I was right there, and that marked the beginning of a whole new life for me. I had worked with children who had polio in Boston in the Children's Hospital in the last epidemic before the Salk vaccine. When I saw what was happening to these children on the streets of New Orleans, trying to get into schools that were totally boycotted and surrounded by mobs, I decided that I was interested in not only medical stress, but this kind of social and racial stress. That was the beginning of the whole research that started then and continued through the sixties and seventies, talking with children, black and white children in the South, and then extending it to the children of migrant farm workers and Appalachian children. Then we went out West and lived in New Mexico for a few years, and I talked with Spanish-speaking and Indian children, and then we went up to Alaska and talked with Eskimo children. Then the final volume, volume five, has to do with the children of well-to-do, middle-class and higher families. So it was a whole American journey that took place in those decades of the sixties and the seventies. In the last ten years I've been doing work with children, trying to figure out how they get their moral values and their political values, their sense of what it means to be a member of a particular country such as the United States or England or Northern Ireland. We've worked in Latin America and Africa, too. And the last volume, which is the end of my whole thirty years of wandering around, is called *The Spiritual Life of Children*.

   Cheney: That sounds fascinating.

   Coles: And that'll be the end. But in between, I've been involved with certain writers like Walker Percy and Flannery O'Connor, and they've been an important part of my life because they help me to figure out what I myself believe in and what matters to me.

   Cheney: I've never been psychoanalyzed or been to a psychiatrist, so I don't know much about your profession, really. But it does strike me that you're unusual.

   Coles: I guess I try to take child psychiatry and psychoanalysis and bring those disciplines into the world of children and parents and teachers. I work in schools and homes and neighborhoods rather than in a clinic or a hospital. I've never had a private practice, so I've tried to just do that work out there in the world, which is what Williams used to do. He would visit those patients and get to know a lot about them medically, but he also got to know a lot about them culturally and spiritually and intellectually. Somehow he took that knowledge and put it into his writing, and he was a great inspiration. I don't have his gifts as a writer, but I certainly would like to think that I've followed in his footsteps a little bit.

   Cheney: You really are a storyteller. It occurs to me when I look at your books that you not only bring psychiatry into the world of children, you bring psychiatry into the world of the humanities in a sense.

Coles: I've tried to do that and, of course, the teaching I do is all tied up with the humanities. I teach a course at Harvard College called "The Literature of Social Reflection," and I ask the students to think about social and cultural issues, racial issues, class issues, not through social science but through the writings of Williams Carlos Williams and Tillie Olsen and Flannery O'Connor and Walker Percy and James Agee and George Orwell and Raymond Carver. The culmination of the course are those three Victorian novelists: Dickens, Hardy, and George Eliot. In the medical school, in the same vein I use Chekhov and Tolstoy and, again, Raymond Carver and Tillie Olsen and, of course, Williams, and Walker Percy. I taught a course at Harvard Law School called "Dickens and the Law," using the novels of Dickens in which lawyers figure. I've taught a course at Harvard Business School that is very popular with the students. We read F. Scott Fitzgerald's *The Great Gatsby* and we read a lot of Cheever.

Cheney: You said once that even though *Gatsby* is about ambition, that it's not just business students who are interested in him—that these things translate.

Coles: They translate into all realms, so to speak. I could take *Gatsby,* or we also use *The Last Tycoon*—I could take *The Last Tycoon* to any part of the university and discuss with the students the whole question of ambition and the relationship between ambition and one's personal life and the kind of loneliness that can sometimes settle in on people who are so consumed by ambition that they get detached from other people in important ways. And the same thing goes for some of the other books we read in that business school course. We read *The Moviegoer;* we read Saul Bellow's *Seize the Day,* with the central figure that of a stockbroker; and we read William Carlos Williams' trilogy. The novels are *White Mule, In the Money,* and *The Build-Up.* They convey the whole story of the rise of working people in America as they work their way up the social and economic ladder. It's a fascinating trilogy, and it works very well in the business school with the students.

Cheney: A lot of the novels that you mention have characters in them that people come to regard almost as real. I was thinking of

Binx Bolling when you were talking about Walker Percy. Percy delivered our Jefferson Lecture and he decided to talk on semiotics. It was very enlightening, but there were a lot of people who were really disappointed that he didn't talk about Binx Bolling because to many people he's just intensely real.

Coles: I'll send you something I wrote on my friendship with him. It's called "Shadowing Binx." I first met Binx Bolling when I was living in New Orleans and in analysis in New Orleans, and when I myself was a bit of a moviegoer. The reality of Binx for me was so profound that it really shook me up and led to a lot of discussions with my analyst. Even as I did that work in New Orleans, the school desegregation study, I kept on looking for Percy's writing because he'd written essays as well as *The Moviegoer.* Years later I did a profile of him for *The New Yorker,* which eventually became a book called *Walker Percy: An American Search.* Getting to know him, I told him how much his writing had meant to me personally. And I'll never forget, he looked down and he said, "Well, it's hard for me to even talk about this because so much of it drew on my own personal search." I was never able to easily understand his writing on semiotics. I told him once, "Walker, it's just too complicated for me. I'll just stick with those stories of yours."

Cheney: When I look at the things you've criticized, you've criticized the new literary approaches, you've criticized the social sciences, but generally what you criticize is people trying to arrive at abstract and generalized theories about how people work and how the world works.

Coles: That's it. I have a real bone to pick with too much theory, whether it be too much psychoanalytic theory or too much literary theory.

The great genius of Freud was that he himself was a storyteller. He listened, he took his own dreams very seriously, and he wrote highly literate prose accounts of what took place in his own mind and in the minds of his patients. The best writing that he gave us are those stories about his patients, which really are the foundation of contemporary psychoanalysis; I wish that some of us would remember that.

And also remember that the two greatest followers of Freud, namely, his own daughter Anna and Erik H. Erikson—who also, by the way, gave a Jefferson Lecture—those two psychoanalysts are marvelously literate and very sensitive to the humanities, each of them. I knew both of them and worked with both of them and learned from both of them the importance that fiction and poetry can have for any of us who want to figure out human nature in all of its complexity. If you read *Middlemarch*, you will see, by the way, an important part of psychoanalysis anticipated by a generation or two. In *Middlemarch*, George Eliot understands the workings of the unconscious; she understands what we call the defense mechanisms of the ego. It's a marvelous novel not only as a great narrative telling of a story, but it's a wise novel filled with psychological insights. I tell my medical students and psychiatric residents that they could do no better than just sitting down with that novel and learning from it, learning from its psychology and its sociology, because it's really an analysis of a changing England in the nineteenth century done with great wisdom and sensitivity.

Cheney: The student that we spoke about at the beginning— Gordon—after talking about how people like Jude Fawley and Binx Bolling and Jack Burden are real for him, said something like, "Why don't college professors teach that way?" I've thought about that a lot because it would be regarded in some quarters now as very naive to teach that way. It's almost as though it's too easy and it makes literature too accessible.

Coles: God forbid that literature should be too accessible (laughter).

Cheney: It's a real concern to me because I see the number of young people who are looking for a vocation when they go to college and are seldom given reason to understand that there might be other cause for study, other rewards to be gained from study.

Coles: It's sad, I think, that presumably well-intentioned people who take these novels seriously and become critics and professors can have that relationship to students—a relationship of being instruments of disenchantment or distancing. The books, after all, were written by novelists who wanted to reach out to others, namely readers. Williams, I know, and Percy hungered for the response of readers. They weren't writing books that they wanted to see so analyzed that there was no longer a message, a story, a communication, a form of companionship left after that kind of analysis.

Cheney: I have another person that I quote along with Gordon. This other person is a professor of English who talks about how he used to regard Jane Austen as a great moral teacher, but now he understands that his proper role is to suspect her and to try to understand the corner that she's painting him into. He describes the "distancing" you're talking about. What is important is no longer a direct and immediate relationship, but a distant and adversarial one. That may be a point you have to arrive at in scholarship, but it's too bad when it dominates the classroom.

Coles: And it's too bad when at the very minimum there can't be some complexity and ambiguity to all of this, enough of it to allow for both approaches, so that if one is going to be suspicious, one can also be welcoming and grateful. I suppose suspicion is one human emotion that we all have and struggle with, but lord knows there's more to be gotten from Jane Austen than suspicion or self-suspicion.

Cheney: Someone—I think maybe a man named Paul Ricoeur— has this wonderful phrase about new approaches to literature. He calls them part of a "hermeneutics of suspicion"—which, on my more pessimistic days, I think is a pretty accurate description.

Coles: My students sometimes come to me, the ones who are majoring in English and have to contend with some of this. They come to me somewhat plaintively and say, "Well, you can get away with this, but we can't," and that is very painful to hear. We're all readers and we're all human beings in the sense that we're sojourners or pilgrims, and these novels that Dickens gave us, or Hardy or Tolstoy, are meant to help us along on that journey. It's a pity if the only reason I can get away with my approach to these novels has to do with the fact that I happen to have training in psychiatry and psychoanalysis and therefore can't too readily be dismissed as naive.

Remember, Dickens never went to college or even high school, nor did Hardy for that matter. They were self-educated, and they sat down and wrote these incredible stories. We have a right, without the intervention of college professors or critics, to respond to Dickens or respond to Hardy or respond to Tolstoy in *Anna Karenina* or in stories like "The Death of Ivan Ilyich" without feeling that we are in some way lacking in insight, let alone humanity.

Cheney: The Williams phrase that I keep thinking of when you talk about how these moral questions, these questions of character, come through specific stories is the famous "no ideas but in things." Is that phrase about generalizations not being true?

Coles: It's about the importance of particularity and it's about the importance of the instance—the importance of each and every one of us in all of our distinctiveness. Yes, I think he had a great suspicion of lofty abstractions that were untethered to individual life, to social reality, to cultural reality. I think there was a concreteness that he wanted to acknowledge and celebrate and explore through image and stories—a rendering of a language that's been heard by someone like him or by any of us. You know, in *Paterson,* where "no ideas but in things" is a clarion call that keeps coming up, he was exploring a certain tension, at a minimum, between art on the one hand and conduct on the other. He once said to me, "I can craft a poem and not necessarily be a good person." It was courageous of him to pick up on that polarity and to work it into *Paterson.*

There's a scene in *Paterson* where he moves from poetry to prose in order to get into the prosaic. In a confessional moment, he has himself picking away in his medical office at the label on a mayonnaise jar instead of paying attention to his patients. What he's basically saying is, "Okay, here's the poetry, but let me connect you with your life and mine, the way sometimes we fail." We fail, we tune out, we become insensitive, and this is part of what an artist-writer has to acknowledge with respect to himself or herself and with respect to all of us, namely, our capacity to come up with great ideas and yet not live up to them or not even take them into consideration in our daily life. He was haunted, of course, by his friend Ezra Pound and the fact that here was a great poet who also could become, as Williams called him, a damn fool with respect to his political ideas and his whole sense of the way the world worked. That was a lesson that Williams never forgot and took very seriously.

Cheney: It's not just a dichotomy between art and conduct that concerns you and that we all need to be aware of. You've talked also about intellect and conduct. A good education, vast knowledge, does not necessarily make a good person.

Coles: This, of course, is very unnerving for those of us who've tried to acquire knowledge and whose job it is to impart that knowledge to others as students. It's a rather horrifying reminder for people like me that psychiatrists have been an important part of the gulag in the Soviet Union, helping to run it, and that doctors worked for the Nazis in those concentration camps, and that indeed Hitler and the Nazis were able to gather around them important segments of the intellectual community. Some very well-known intellectuals embraced Nazism all too early on. Percy has a good moment in his novel, *The Second Coming,* when he describes a character as one of those people who got all A's and flunked ordinary living. I'm afraid this is something that we're all vulnerable to, that possibility.

Cheney: You have a story that makes this point, a story about Ruby, the little girl you first saw in the middle of a mob.

Coles: Well, Ruby is one of my great teachers—she was a six-year-old teacher of mine. I saw her in New Orleans in 1960 going through a mob to get into a totally boycotted school where she attended the first grade all by herself. This is a little girl whose parents were illiterate, who didn't know how to read or write, and who came from an extremely poor black family. I spent weeks and weeks getting to know her, months indeed, several years in fact.

One day I found out that the schoolteacher had watched her coming into the school building and had seen her talking to the people in the street. This infuriated them and they surged toward her, but she was accompanied by federal marshals, so they couldn't hurt her. The schoolteacher asked her why she had stopped that day to talk to the people, and Ruby said she hadn't talked to the people. So then the teacher became worried. She thought that Ruby was beginning to crack under the strain of this lonely, fearful life.

I knew Ruby then, and that evening I asked her why she had stopped and talked to those people and got them so worked up. She said that she hadn't talked to them at all. So I said, "Well, Ruby, your teacher saw your lips move. She was watching you from inside the school building." And Ruby said that she hadn't talked to the people, she had said a prayer, and that the reason she said the prayer that particular morning in front of the mob was that she forgot to say the prayer where she usually had said it, namely, two blocks before she got to the school. Then I learned from this little girl that she had an arrangement with the federal marshals to stop and say a prayer every morning a couple of blocks before the school, and after school she said a prayer again, and then in the evening she prayed also. And I found out that she'd been praying for these very people who wanted to kill her and swore at her so obscenely. I asked her that evening why she prayed for those people, and she looked at me and she said, "Well, don't you think they need praying for?"

Cheney: That is a marvelous story.

Coles: And then I said, "Well, Ruby, I can understand why they need praying for, perhaps, but I wonder why you should be the one who prays for them, given all that they do to you, all the threats and all the insults." And she looked at me again and she said, "Well, I'm the one who hears what they say, so I'm the one who should be praying for them." Then I asked her what she said in these prayers, and she said, "I always say the same thing," and then she told me what she said. She said, "I always say, 'Please, God, try to forgive those people because they don't know what they're doing.'"

Cheney: Some echoes there . . .

Coles: And when I heard that, I just said to myself, "Wow, I've heard this someplace before. Someone said this before in the history of the world."

Cheney: Yes, exactly.

Coles: Later my wife said to me, "What would you do if you had to go into the Harvard Faculty Club and there was a mob waiting for you every time you came there?" That was such a shrewd question on her part. We figured out that what I would do is call the police, which Ruby couldn't do because the police weren't protecting her. That's why the President had sent federal marshals there. The next thing I'd do is get a lawyer, and Ruby didn't have a lawyer to help her out. The third thing I'd do would be to mobilize the language of the social scientists and call these people all sorts of fancy words like disturbed and psychotic. And the last thing I would do probably would be to write an article about what I'd gone through. But Ruby didn't have social science language, and she was just learning how to read and write, and she was as vulnerable as could be, and yet she had those prayers available.

The other thing I learned about her and her parents is that they had memorized whole passages from both the Old and the New Testament by heart. They knew about the Hebrew prophets; they knew how Jesus lived his life and what he stood for. It was a remarkable kind of education that I gave them no credit for.

Cheney: That story is powerful testimony to the force that stories have.

Coles: Powerful indeed. And when I read social scientists and their descriptions of moral development in children, which is supposed to start at a very low level and slowly work up as you get more educated, I realized what they're talking about is moral reasoning, but not necessarily at all conduct. So you can learn a lot and take courses in moral reasoning—and some of my students do and get A's in those courses—and yet not necessarily live in your everyday conduct a decent and moral life, and that's the big tension. And that's what Tolstoy knew and Williams and Hardy and all the great writers.

Cheney: And Percy.

Coles: Percy, of course, and Raymond Carver in his wonderful way, especially toward the end of his life with those great stories of his, such as "Cathedral" and "A Small, Good Thing."

Cheney: I have really enjoyed this conversation. I read once that you referred to yourself as a psychoanalyzed liberal, and I thought, well, as an unpsychoanalyzed conservative, I'm not sure that you and I will find a great deal in common, but I think there's a lot of ground that we share.

Coles: Well, I was using a bit of irony with that self-description.

Cheney: I, too. I hope that's clear. We'll both hope that our audience understands that.

Robert Coles on His Work
Jay Woodruff/1991

From an interview conducted in Concord, Massachusetts, March 1991.

J: When you're ready to begin writing, how do you usually get started?

R: I work always in the morning. I can only write in the morning, early. I don't pace, I just stare out of the window. I have a large window and I can see a field and some woods and a fence, a stone fence, and I stare. I also stare at pictures I have of Walker Percy and William Carlos Williams, because both of these physician-writers have meant so much to me. I've been privileged to know both of them. I look at their pictures and remember them, and think to myself, frankly, how lucky, lucky, lucky I've been to know those two people and to be able to call them friends, and to be able to—to use the word "call" again—to call upon them, literally, on the phone, or in visits, and call upon them in my mind.

I'll tell you very frankly how I start a piece. Before I write I think in my head what the first sentence will be. I think to myself, what are you going to say and how are you going to begin this, and then I speak to myself and I have that sentence. I write it down and then I continue, you know, the conversation or the talk or whatever. It's done through my head listening to itself and coming up with a sentence, and that's the beginning. It's a bit of a ritual, but I always start out with that paragraph sign. That means to me that now I should think of a beginning. And then my eyes leave the page and I'll look out of the window and I'll speak to myself and say, well now what are you going to say, how are you going to begin this?

J: One of the most striking things about your writing is the combination of colloquialisms and old-fashioned words: "figure out" and "whither" side-by-side. I've heard you talk before about your parents' influences, and I wondered if some of that is the English idiom?

225

R: You're absolutely right. The whither comes right from my
father, from Yorkshire and from his somewhat formal way of talking.
Both my mother and father had somewhat idiosyncratic ways of
speaking. My mother always used words such as "edifying" and my
father would use words such as "whither." Sometimes he'd joke with
my brother and me and say, "Whither thou goest?" meaning,
"Where the hell are you going?" But it was his way of being funny
with language and I think I retain some of these words and use them
because they were so commonly used when I was growing up.
Another favorite of my father, which I don't use often because it's
such a noticeable word, is "rambunctious." He'd always say to us,
"Don't be so rambunctious." I have memories of these words. They
kind of haunt my mind. Some of them I use and some of them I
don't.

The colloquialisms, though, I deliberately try to use to distance
myself as much as I can from formal social science modes of
presentation. For many years I have cultivated just ordinary language
when I write about psychological, psychiatric, and psychoanalytic
matters. Some of this was helped along by the way Anna Freud
wrote, which I very much admired and tried to imitate, namely her
use of colloquialisms and ordinary figures of speech as she talks
about children. And some of it is a response, I think, to my great
friend and hero William Carlos Williams, who always pushed me
toward ordinary language when I talked about children. When I first
started my work in the South with black and white children going
through school desegregation, he was very much alive, although ill,
and was someone constantly pushing me to write about those
children in ordinary language and to present their stories to ordinary
readers, rather than to segregate, if I might use the word, their stories.
Segregate them from ordinary readers through writing about them
for psychiatric or psychoanalytic journals.

J: Is that the main reason that you choose ordinary language? Or
are there additional reasons that you'd choose ordinary language
over technical language?

R: I just don't like technical language. I find it unattractive. I don't
think in technical language. My mind has never absorbed that as part
of its life, even during the training period when I was learning the
language and learning to be a psychiatrist and an analyst. I don't

think in those terms, and I don't much like the sound of the words. I just come up with what my mind comes up with, which is the ordinary colloquialisms, the way I talk and write.

J: Have you taken heat for that from social scientists or psychiatrists?

R: A good deal of heat in the early years. I remember comments from colleagues, in some psychiatric articles, at a couple of American Academy *Daedalus* meetings, when people asked me why I so avoided sociological and psychological language, and why I constantly referred to that language as jargon. The animus behind it they were getting at. And I think they were right. There is a certain animus that I feel toward it. That animus came out in the very first article I wrote. ["A Young Psychiatrist Looks at His Profession," *The Atlantic Monthly,* July 1961.]

Language was important to me long before I became a writer because of my parents strong interest in literature. I've mentioned in *The Call of Stories* how they read to one another from Dickens and Tolstoy, and George Eliot especially, and it's no accident, I think, that I'm interested in literature and a teacher, and that my brother is a professor of English and American literature at the University of Michigan. This has been a family tradition of sorts. My father came from England. He used to be a great reader of novels. And my mother, I think, was reading Tolstoy in her adolescence in Iowa when she was growing up, so these writers were handed down to my brother and me more or less the way Walker Percy talks about our handing one another along at the end of *The Moviegoer.* Novelists were handed along to my brother and me while we were growing up, and I think they're in my mind, and their way of thinking and writing and using language is the only way I ever felt comfortable with. And then I came under the spell, so to speak, of William Carlos Williams, with that blunt, earthy language of his, and that impatience with hifalutin talk. It would be very hard, believe me, after all this, to start calling upon the social sciences to talk about human beings and the way they think and feel and love and hate and struggle.

J: I wonder whether you see technical jargon as representing in part an attempt to establish a sort of condescending relationship between the speaker and listener, or between the writer and reader.

R: It's a distinct possibility. At a minimum—if I may ironically be

perhaps a bit psychologically condescending myself—I think it's
evidence of nervousness and insecurity when we start distancing
ourselves this way and talking in this tongue.

J: I've heard you refer to some forms of jargon as sophisticated
name-calling.

R: There's plenty of that in the way we use psychological and
sociological words to put other people down. This is the worst of it. I
hear it all the time still at meetings. Clever innuendos, *ad hominem*
and *ad feminam,* innuendos directed at people, put-downs couched
in psychiatric or psychoanalytic terminology. It's very—as my father
would say, again— disedifying. My mother would use that word,
"disedify," too.

J: You write often in the first person. Some of my very favorite
essays of yours—"Shadowing Binx," and "The End of the Affair,"
and "Don't Worry, Dad"—seem almost in the confessional tradition
of Augustine or Tolstoy. Are you most comfortable writing in the first
person?

R: I don't think I initially was, because I was brought up to regard
talking about oneself as not bad taste, but sinful. My mother had a
very strong sense about the sin of pride and its manifestations. We
were rather reticent about ourselves and when I first began writing, it
was hard for me to write about what now comes much easier to me,
namely about my own reactions and feelings. I tried to distance
myself from both myself and from even the children I was writing
about, as I had learned to do when I was writing those early
psychiatric articles. But my wife, who was an English teacher, and
Williams, and even my parents also encouraged me to be open about
what I was experiencing. They encouraged me to write first about the
children and then to write abut my responses to the children, so I was
caught in a bind. On the one hand, you have a voice telling you to
keep away from yourself, so to speak, and on the other hand, you
have another voice telling you to draw upon yourself, which of course
is what I do as a psychiatrist anyway. You learn from your own
reactions to the patient's reactions and the patient's reactions to you.
On and on those questions of so-called transference and counter-
transference go! But I think there must have been some voice
struggling to find itself from the very beginning, because as I look
back, that first article I wrote for *The Atlantic* draws upon that

personal response of mine to this profession I'd just entered.
Although I should tell you that when I first wrote that article it wasn't
nearly as personal as it was when it was published. The man who
asked me to write it and then edited it, namely Whitney Ellsworth,
who was then working for *The Atlantic,* was the one who drew out of
me my personal reactions and pushed me toward the personal way
of narrating that article. He had to struggle to do it. But having done
that, I think I found it easier down the line to do this again. When I
got to know Erik Erikson in the middle sixties and left the South to go
back to Boston, he encouraged me to write personally about what I
had seen in the South. To use the first person singular more than I
was comfortable doing.

J: That *Atlantic* article was quite a bold statement for a thirty-year-
old not long out of training.

R: Well, I got plenty of negative response from some of my
supervisors, from people with whom I'd trained who felt that I was
perhaps too critical of the profession, and they wanted to know what
right I had to write about this profession anyway since I'd just
finished my training in it. So I said, well I'm telling you right off that
I'm a young psychiatrist writing about it and these are ruminations
from someone who's just beginning. But they felt that perhaps
someone who is just beginning shouldn't be ruminating so before the
public.

J: At that point did you have any urge or ambition to do any
further writing?

R: No, I didn't think of myself, immediately after that, as doing any
more writing. I thought this was a one-shot deal. It was a painful
process, writing that essay. It took a lot of work and a lot of Whitney
Ellsworth's help to write that in a reasonably coherent, forceful
manner. I think I was scared about such a vigorous critique even
though I wanted to express it. Remember, my whole career was
ahead of me, and I also think I was not a natural-born writer. It was
just hard for me to write a fluid, accessible essay, and if it did become
one, I think it's due to Whitney's prodding and pushing, and my
wife's prodding and pushing. Once having done it, however, I think I
did learn a little bit about how to write a reasonably coherent essay.

J: How did you get hooked up with Whitney Ellsworth?

R: His wife, Sallie Bingham, and my wife were college roommates and close friends. My wife was in their wedding. *The Atlantic* was putting together an issue on psychiatry and American life, and it was Whitney's idea to get me to write from the point of view of a young doctor who'd just finished his residency and was in the midst of psychoanalytic training. He thought this would be an idea that would be of some use. I said, well, okay, but what would I say? And then he reminded me of a lot of the things I'd already said.

J: To him?

R: To him and to Sallie and to others: the criticisms, and the doubts, and misgivings, and at times the real anger at some of what I thought was the arrogance and condescension we were prey to in this field, part of it egged on by a gullible public, and by what Philip Reiff has called "the therapeutic culture," that responds to psychiatry as a secular religion. That's what I was getting at in that article. Whitney had everything to gain I think by pushing me into an increasingly truculent posture. I'm not so sure I was as cautious as I perhaps should have been, were I to have stayed in the field in a conventional way. But of course, I didn't stay in the field, and the article never hurt me because I wasn't there to be hurt, so to speak. This is important, what I'm saying now. It never hurt me because I wasn't there to be hurt. I left the field, at least the conventional field.

J: Went *out* into the field.

R: Went *out* into the field, right. Left the field to go out *into* the field.

J: You weren't averse to taking risks at that point. I mean, you went down South. This was already after you were dragging around in the sports car.

R: Well, that was a risk. I was getting a lot of tickets for going too fast. I got to know some of the Louisiana highway patrol and Mississippi highway patrol people, but because I often drove in my captain's uniform, they were very generous, they didn't ticket me. In the South there's a strong military tradition, strong tradition of respect for the military. Of course it was the Air Force that took me to the South, and I was reluctant initially. Now, of course, I realize my whole life was changed by it, but I think once I started doing the work with school desegregation and started working with the civil rights movement, there were plenty of risks to go around for all of us for a few years.

J: I've heard you describe being chased by a truckful of people who were shooting at you.

R: That was during the Mississippi Summer Project in 1964. I was in a freedom house in McComb that was dynamited. Arrested a few times, thrown in jail, and threatened, no question, during those years '61, '62, '63, '64. Those were wonderful years of learning and association with extraordinary people, children and adults both, both black and white, but they were years of some risk. But I never minded that as much as I minded sitting in some of those psychiatric conferences hearing people torn apart with a language that I thought was really outrageous and insulting, not only to the people the language was meant to describe, but to the people who were using the language. And I don't think this was just me being finicky and snotty in my own way, I think it's a whole way that we have of thinking about the world, a way that is dangerous for us: to talk and think like that. This is where I think I connect with what Percy has reminded us about, the importance of language and how it influences—its significance to us and its possibilities to us, but also the dangers in it. In our choice of words and in the way it gives shape to meaning for us.

J: Assuming that you're a person who has taken a lot of risks and, assuming that you're a person who likes to continue to take risks, I wonder what kinds of risks you feel that you've taken in your writing?

R: Well, I think that the way I've tried to give voice to people out of what I've heard from them, mobilize what I have believed and felt to be the highest eloquence they're capable of, I think that hasn't always been easy and it hasn't always been easy to find those moments. It's difficult work, being with other people and learning from them and listening to them and getting to those moments. And it's also hard to capture them and do justice to them when you're presenting them to others, when you're an intermediary. I had to abandon essentially a psychiatric reductionism for a kind of story-telling narrator's role. Or so I decided that I had to.

J: Why?

R: I felt that this is the way to do this work, to present the stories of the individuals that I was meeting rather than to try to analyze their psychiatric status.

J: Don't a lot of people come to your work and say that you absolutely shouldn't abandon the psychiatric reductionism?

R: They wouldn't call it reductionism. And, yes, there are those people who want more, and more and more of that and don't get it and are frustrated and critical. Then there are those who are quite willing to read about the people I've met and learn about their lives, which is what I regard myself as doing, as a sort of an intermediary. And the same thing with Walker Percy, or William Carlos Williams, Flannery O'Connor, Simone Weil, or Dorothy Day. Anna Freud. I tell their stories as I've known them. I've met these people, or in the case of Simone Weil or James Agee, I've lived with them through their writing. I write about them, telling each story as I am responding to it, what in their writing has meant so much to me.

Walker Percy, especially, was so linked up to my life in Louisiana and Mississippi, and my life as a young psychiatrist seeing the president of the New Orleans Psychoanalytic Institute as an analysand, and as someone who lived on Maple Street in New Orleans, near Tulane, who knew that city, and knew the Gulf Coast, and also, I might add incidentally, knew some of the religious and spiritual and literary tradition that informs Percy's work. Certainly not as well as he knew it, but knew it well enough to appreciate it and respond to it. So, if I may be so bold as to say so, I think what you see in an essay such as "Shadowing Binx" is a young, aspiring soul encountering another soul of great depth and distinction and deciding yet again, yet again as I did with Williams, that this is someone well worth getting to know, in this case through his writing. I never thought I would meet Percy as I'd been lucky enough to meet Williams.

J: How did you meet Percy?

R: I met Percy years after I had first met him through *The Moviegoer.* I became the doctor who did the work I did in the South and wrote articles, and then a book titled *Children of Crisis: A Study of Courage and Fear,* and then further volumes of *Children of Crisis,* and other books. By the late 1960s I had written for a number of magazines, and I think it was in 1969 that I was approached by Mr. Shawn of *The New Yorker.* He asked me whether I would write a profile of Erik Erikson because he knew I had worked with Erikson, had taught in his course. After I wrote that profile and they published it, Mr. Shawn asked me if I would do book reviews and in general become a writer for the magazine. So I did fairly regular book reviews for a number of years for the magazine, and I did, for instance, a profile called "Una Anciana," which was basically a story of one of the elderly Spanish-speaking women I had met in New Mexico. We were doing a lot of moving around then. We moved from the South and went back to New England, where I worked with Erikson. Then we went out to New Mexico in 1972. I wrote that profile of an ordinary, Spanish-speaking woman who lived north of Santa Fe near Truchas. Then Mr. Shawn asked me if there were any other profiles that I was interested in doing, and I immediately said Walker Percy. He wasn't all that enthusiastic. I don't think he had read any of Percy's writing, and I had to indicate a certain enthusiasm, eagerness, and God bless him, he responded and said yes. So I found out Percy's address through one of those lists of writers' addresses, or Who's Who maybe, and I wrote him a letter. He called me up and he said he'd be delighted to talk with me. He reminded me that he had read my *Children of Crisis* book, and he didn't need to remind me that he'd done a review of it for *The New York Times*.

J: Of the first volume.

R: Yes. Which I'll tell you was the biggest thrill of the whole of my entire writing career up to that moment. Much more of a thrill than even writing the book was getting that review from him. That had meant so much to me, that review. After he wrote the review and I read it, I wrote him a letter—that had been in '67—and then he had written back telling me how much he enjoyed learning about those children in New Orleans, which everyone who lived in New Orleans knew about from the daily newspapers, the struggle for school desegregation there. And that was the end of our correspondence and I thought the end of any encounter I'd have with him. Until this, five years later. And this time I would get to meet him. So I went down there. I went there and began a friendship. He allowed me to stay at their home, and I stayed there for several days and got to know him, and we talked. We walked and ate or drank. Did a good deal of drinking. He was no stranger to drinking. We drank lots of bourbon together.

J: So between the time that you first approached Mr. Shawn and the time that the profile appeared in the magazine, how much time elapsed?

R: That's a good span of time because of scheduling problems in

The New Yorker. I was beginning to learn by then—I'd learned it
when I'd written the profile on Erik Erikson—that *The New Yorker*
was always slow to publish profiles unless they came out as a book,
in which case they *quickly* published them. And I had never intended
to write a book on Erik Erikson, I simply was responding to a request
by Mr. Shawn that I do a profile, and he himself said to me once,
now when is this going to appear as a book? I said, well Mr. Shawn, I
hadn't thought of it as a book. And I remember there was a pause
and he said, well, some people would think of it as a book. And I
guess I decided, well I should start thinking of it as a book. So I gave
it to Peter Davison, who decided to publish it, and when there was a
publication date for the book *The New Yorker* promptly published
the profile. I went through the same thing with the profile on Percy,
which I think came out around 1978.

J: How long did it take you to write that profile? How much time
did you spend on it? It seems like such a massive project.

R: Oh, this was a huge effort, because I had to immerse myself in
Kierkegaard, whom I had studied when I was in college at the behest
of Perry Miller. I took a course that he gave called The Classics of the
Christian Tradition, and he introduced us to Kierkegaard. This was
right after the Second World War. So twenty years later I had to go
back to that and do more reading of Kierkegaard. I had to become
familiar with Camus and Sartre, who were major influences on
Percy's writing, and remind myself about Dostoevski and Tolstoy too,
who were also major influences on Percy's writing, because he nods
to Dostoevski, for instance, in *The Moviegoer,* and that Alyosha scene
from *The Brothers Karamazov,* and I think, frankly, *The Last
Gentlemen* is modeled on *The Idiot.* So I had to renew that and
expand that aspect of the literary acquaintanceship and I had to learn
a substantial amount of philosophy of the existentialist kind, and I
had to go through his nonfiction, and I had to think about the life of
a very interesting and important American family, namely William
Alexander Percy and the significance, politically and socially and
culturally, of this distinguished family, and how all of this came to
bear on this man's writing. His fiction, primarily. It took me a couple
of years of immersion: interviews, thinking, reading, and then finally
writing a long piece that *The New Yorker* had to split up into two
segments when they published it.

Now, if Mr. Shawn liked something he called you up; if he didn't like it, you didn't hear from him. But he called me up and he said he very much liked the profile and wanted to use it, but it was very long and it was going to be a real problem for the magazine. And so it went along for a couple of years. Every year he would send me a little note, as he did to all the writers, renewing their contracts, and for a couple of years he'd mention that he hoped to publish the Percy profile soon, and after about two or three years of this I began to wonder what the word "soon" meant. So I finally took it to Peter Davison and asked if he'd want to publish it. As soon as Little, Brown set a publication date, Mr. Shawn immediately published the profile.

I think Walker was pleased with the profile. He told me so and wrote me so. That gave me enormous pleasure because I really wanted to please him. I very much admired him and loved him and respected him and looked up to him. As with the people I was working with and have worked with, young and old, black and white, rich and poor, rural and urban, I regarded myself as an intermediary between him and readers. That's my way of looking at a lot of my writing, that I'm an intermediary. We "hand one another along" in that sense—that's the imagery Percy uses at the end of *The Moviegoer,* and I think that's what I felt I was doing when I was working on that profile. At that time he was not quite as well-known by any means as he is now, has been in recent years. It was really the middle point of his career as a novelist, and I think—I know from the letters I got—that a lot of people met him through that profile, and that was just great.

J: He dedicated his last novel to you, didn't he?

R: A big moment in my life. He wrote me a very sweet letter telling me not precisely what he was going to do, but saying to me, "Dear Bob, I'm planning to take your name in vain and I hope you don't mind," and I didn't know what he was talking about. The next thing I knew, a friend of mine who worked at one of the magazines and had seen the galleys called me up to tell me this in great excitement, which was more than matched by my own excitement.

J: You later wrote another essay on Percy, a very personally revealing one—"Shadowing Binx." Was it easier by then to write about Percy?

R: I think that took a little longer than you might think. It was so important to me that I couldn't just sit there and tell the obvious story of how I stumbled into the novel and the significance it had for me personally, and the story of how I got to know the novelist. I think I did more staring out of the window because what I was really telling about is the irony of a given life, and the fatefulness of a life as I regarded that fatefulness, because it was my life that I was thinking about. And not just the story of my life because in a way there's a large circularity to all this, stumbling into a novel. The sympathy that I felt with the protagonist of the novel, or as it's put these days, the "vibes" I felt connecting me to not only the novel, but to the novelist, whose essays I'd already begun to become familiar with: that to me is a story of a big hunk of my life as an adult and as a writer. It's been very important for me to write about Percy, and it's been very important for me to write about William Carlos Williams, and especially important to collect those stories that he wrote about his medical life in that book called *The Doctor Stories,* and to persuade his son, the one and only time he's ever done it, to write about his father—the son who became a doctor himself, William Eric Williams. These are very important steps in my life. Nothing has been more important in my writing life than those kinds of connections I made with those two friends of mine.

J: You often talk about books as being friends and companions, and you've written about this in *The Call Of Stories* and elsewhere. My sense of your teaching is that you're very much dedicated to trying to give students the opportunity to develop friendships with these novels and these characters, too. Is that accurate?

R: I think that's quite fair. That's the way I do regard the books. I keep them near me. I keep, also, the pictures of some novelists near me. I read those books not just once or even twice, but I call upon certain passages in the course of my life as I think about matters and struggle with matters. So I regard these writers—Agee, Orwell, George Eliot, Hardy, Tolstoy, Walker Percy, Flannery O'Connor, William Carlos Williams, Raymond Carver, Ralph Ellison, Tillie Olson—sometimes I regard them as a jury. Sometimes I regard them as companions, and revered companions, and as mentors, a word you hear used a lot today, but I prefer ultimately the word "friend," as good friends.

J: It seems a little unusual, these days, to encourage such a traditional response from students. In that sense, you're teaching seems to involve a good deal of risk-taking—to encourage students to respond to these books in such a basic way. These days so many professors of literature are into post-structural and audience-oriented criticism and hermeneutics and what not. To be encouraging college students to respond to literature this way, when the academy is full of literary theorists and people who don't approach books as potential friends, don't approach characters as—

R: As *real,* in a very important sense of the word "real."

J: Rather these sort of inert objects that one approaches and performs various forms of calisthenics on.

R: Texts. Tests to be analyzed and abstracted. Well, I'm loyal to my parents who taught my brother and me to regard these books as friends. That's what my mother called *War And Peace.* She said, "This is a good friend for you to have this summer," when she gave it to me when I was seventeen years old, and a very troublesome young seventeen I was. She said, "Take this book and read it and let it give you some knowledge, maybe even wisdom and comfort, and some insight about life." See, my parents were not ready to send us to psychotherapists. They were ready to send us to Tolstoy. He was going to be the one who would heal us. My mother's judgment I still respect in that regard, exclamation point. But they took those writers very seriously and I do too.

What is writing? It's the mind pouring forth what it is trying hard to find within itself as the best possible communication to offer others. And I think it ought to be taken that way, not as something to be torn apart and analyzed only, but as something to be understood and taken to heart as well as thought about. That old expression "taken to heart." That's what I used to hear from my parents, take these books to heart. And I try to tell students to take them to heart. I try to take them to heart myself. They're on my desk, they're right nearby, and right over there is Walker Percy, and Dorothy Day, and Simone Weil, and all the others. I've tried hard to live with these people and I hope that some of what they stand for informs my life, but of course we all fail every day. But they're good friends. They're good people, I think. They're good people in the sense they have a lot to teach us and a lot to offer us as we try to figure out what this life is about.

J: It seems sort of ironic that you're a man of significant scientific

training, a physician, a psychiatrist, and yet your approach to
teaching literature is not post-modern. It's more traditional, whereas
most of the people who are teaching literature in the universities are
not trained scientists yet seem so eager to adopt this sort of objective,
almost *clinical* approach to the books.

R: That is an irony, and I think maybe they're trying too hard to be
clinical in a way that is misinformed. At the risk of being a little
condescending, I'm not sure they understand what it means to be
clinical. What we were taught in medical school, and what I was
taught when I was learning first to be a pediatrician and then a
psychiatrist, was to open up our hearts as well as our minds to the
patients, to feel with them, to empathize and understand what they're
going through and to respond out of whatever fullness of being we
could mobilize to respond to them. Not only with our interpretations
of what was wrong—that is, our diagnoses. And not only with the
medicines we had to offer, but with our human responses. How can
you work with children who have polio or are suffering from brain
tumors or terrible infectious diseases that threaten their lives, such as
fulminating pneumonia or various congenital disease that some
young children struggle with—how can you work with them and not
respond to them emotionally and with your whole being? And how
can you not become friendly with them and interested in them and
feel drawn to them? That's part of what clinical work is, and ought to
be. I think it is a bit ironic that some people in the literary criticism
line of work try to take these books and treat them in that kind of
cold analytic way that maybe some of us were taught as a posture—
some of us were taught to adopt for ourselves when we were learning
psychoanalysis in the fifties, but which, believe me, one wants to get
rid of in practicing psychoanalysis. Certainly, why take it up in
reading? They're trying to be more analytic almost than we are—in
the way they analyze these texts. I think they're trying to establish a
relationship to these texts similar to that which they imagine
psychiatrists take toward their patients. But I think they're wrong
about the attitude that a lot of us psychiatrists take toward our
patients. If we do take such an attitude, then I think we're wrong as
psychiatrists. This becomes like the blind leading the blind at times. A
lot of us feel quite comfortable in being warmly responsive to our

patients and learning from our patients. And why can't we be
warmly to responsive to and learn from our books as well?

I think a lot of literary critics also overestimate the contributions
that psychoanalysis and psychiatry can offer literature, and maybe
overestimate the contributions that the analytic mind can offer
literature, since I think literature is among other things a communication. It is a human activity, namely an offering of mind, heart, and
soul presumably meant for another. And in that existentialist sense, I
think it's incumbent upon some of us to respond similarly with our
own being, not only with our constructs.

J: You seem, if not comfortable, than at least resigned to the idea
that some things aren't easily explained or even explainable and that
some things you just don't understand. It seems to me that a lot of
literary theorists seek to explain what the authors themselves—

R: Don't.

J: Yes. What a lot of authors are willing to rise up and scratch their
heads about. Tobias Wolff talks about these moments in his stories
that just occur to him, as if out of nowhere. And then the literary
theorists sit down and explain it all very neatly, or try to.

R: Well, I would bow to the mystery that Tobias Wolff feels and
celebrate that mystery rather than try to explain it away. Remember
what Flannery O'Connor said: "The task of the novelist is to deepen
mystery." I think I've got that approximately right. And then she
added, "Mystery is a great embarrassment to the modern mind." I'll
tell you, I may say this with a perhaps sinful pride, but mystery is not
an embarrassment to me; it's a great joy. Now, I'm not trying to be
deliberately murky or perplexed. I simply feel that we'll never—and
even Freud at his most ambitious came to know this when he wrote
about Dostoevski—we'll never really understand the workings of
talent and genius. We can only celebrate and honor such workings
and be grateful for such workings as they are offered to us in stories,
poems, novels, plays, art, music. This is what we are: the creature
who can come forth with this, and God gave it to us, and bless us for
it. I respect the right of the analytic mind to try and pour over all of
this—the mind and its nature—and come up with things, and such
an effort can have its own beauty. But it can also be overdone, and
we can con ourselves with words and not get much further into the

penetration of these mysteries. I guess I'm ready just to have a drink
or two and enjoy the experience.

J: This discussion about literary analysis or theory and psychiatry
reminds me that I wanted to ask you about the relation of your
psychiatric training to your work as a writer and your approach to
what you write, but listening to you talk makes me wonder whether
you've been less influenced by the theory that you studied than by
the clinical experience you've had of working with children who were
suffering, and adults who were in pain.

R: True. I've never been a theorist, nor wanted to be. I may
indirectly for a second draw on Shakespeare's way of putting it: I was
not nor was meant to be. Once I got into the third year of medical
school, I really enjoyed not only learning about medicine, but
learning how to meet people and learn from them, and this was a
great joy to me, in medical school during my internship years and
residency years, and I think that's the heart of what my work has
been like. I've continued that work in homes and in schools rather
than in offices and hospitals, and I think I know how to do it with
some competence, and I think my writing career has been essentially
an effort to convey what I've learned, and since what I think I've
learned has to do with the directness and simplicity, almost, of
human encounters with children, I think the writing may have taken
on some of that directness and simplicity, because children can be
quite direct, as we know, and very vigorously pared down in the way
they confront one another and the adult world. They speak with
candor and often with great energy and sometimes with a kind of
stark force that can knock one over, and maybe some of that has
challenged me in my writing to try and simply—and not so simply of
course—use words in such a way that I do justice to those experiences I have had with children, and continue to have with children. I
have in my head the voices of these people I've met, so many of
them, and I can call them up without the help of a tape recorder. The
mannerisms of speech that they use, the style, the language, the way
they choose to carve out verbal reality, so to speak, for themselves
and for others. That's part of what I think I'm drawing on when I'm
writing besides the actual stories that I've heard and the actual
experiences I've had, that supply of voices that live on in my head.
And maybe what those voices tell me about language—namely try to

listen to those voices, try to remember the way they've been offered to you. When I tell the Ruby story, which also took place in New Orleans—this little girl who went through mobs and prayed for those who wanted to kill her in order to desegregate a school totally abandoned by the white population—I am calling upon a kind of biblical directness that this girl offered me as she told me what she thought and felt and had to say. And I think that experience has affected not only what I know about her and how I present her, but it's affected my view of how one ought to think and respond to life.

J: How so?

R: Well, I think of Ruby and her prayerful forgiveness at certain moments when I'm going through my own stresses. Maybe not mobs, but there are mobs and mobs, so to speak. Harvard mobs or colleagues. Mobs at faculty meetings. Mobs of cars on the road from Concord to Cambridge. And I think of a certain attitude that she had, and the way that attitude was put into words, and I try to have those words in my head as I think about what I ought to do and how I ought to feel.

I think of Walker Percy's way. He was shy, he could be reticent. He had at times a mild, a very mild but noticeable, stammer, which would give way to a wonderfully familiar and friendly, but more often than not restrained, manner of conversation. But pithy and striking and at times quite unforgettable. That is, what he has to say and, yes, the way he said it. When I can hear those words, I can hear the voice, I can see him in my head. I summon him up here sitting at my chair and connect with him. Until he died, there could always be a telephone call to give new emphasis and energy to a connection, but the connection was there, it lives on in one's head. Maybe in the heart, too.

J: Do you think of yourself more as a physician or a writer?

R: I think of myself primarily as a physician who happens to write. I think of myself more as physician than I do even as a psychiatrist. I think it's the physician in me that does the work I do with children, with their families, and that's the heart of what my life has been. And then I've tried to be a chronicler of sorts in the sense I've written that work up, but I think of myself as a physician.

J: You have a neurological hammer on your writing desk.

R: That's true, I do have a neurological hammer on my desk. I've never let go of that. I still have my stethoscope, I even have my black bag from my original work when I was a young doctor, and I can't let go of those things. Because that's the work I do.

That hammer brings back memories. When I look at it I think of particular patients, and my examining them. I still remember a lot of the patients I worked with in the early years. I remember conversations I had with them, I remember them telling me about their lives, and I remember at that point in my life my increasing interest in these stories of lives that I was so lucky to be privy to. So in a way, I think I was learning even before I started something called, quote, research, unquote, to listen to people and get to know them and understand them as best I could. And then came the task later on in the sixties as to how to offer what I'd heard and seen to other people.

J: I've never heard you describe yourself as a writer without qualifying it.

R: Qualifying, right.

J: You don't seem willing to call yourself a writer. In fact, when I've mentioned other writers, I've heard you say, "Well, he's a *writer.*"

R: Or *"She's* a writer."

J: Right.

R: Well, I make a distinction between many people who are called writers and myself in the sense that I feel that my writing is based on the work I do as a physician. Now you would say how about with some of the biographies I've written. But I think those biographies have been my way of trying to understand particular lives and writing about them, and I don't regard them as biographies. I regard them as stories of others based on, again, my relationship with those others or, in the case of someone such as Simone Weil, long intimacy with her in writing. Most of the people I've written about I've known. Dorothy Day, Percy, Williams, Anna Freud, Erik Erikson.

J: Flannery O'Connor.

R: And Flannery O'Connor. So, maybe I'm quibbling about language here. Maybe it's just a shyness or feeling of inadequacy manifesting itself in this kind of quibbling, but I regard myself as an observer of other people, as a doctor, as a field worker, whatever, who happens to write a lot.

In any case the doctor in me matters a lot to me. I've seen patients through thick and thin, and I still see patients. I still see a few patients. I've always had a few patients. They're necessary, I think, for my own—how does the expression go?—mental health, exclamation mark. I love talking with people and trying to be of some help, and understanding what's happened to them, and through them what's happening to myself. It goes back and forth, this work.

Index

A

Abernathy, Ralph, 173
Adams House, 168
Addison-Wesley Press, 113
Agee, James, 5, 7, 18, 21, 24, 32, 56, 73, 92, 93, 110, 113, 117, 119, 166, 170, 174, 179, 183, 211, 217, 232, 236; *Let Us Now Praise Famous Men,* 11, 57, 106, 110, 113
AIDS, 193
Air Force, 92, 97, 99, 115, 202, 215, 230
Albuquerque, New Mexico, 119–20
Allen, Woody, 69, 121
American Psychiatric Association, 41, 184
Appalachia, 7, 10, 26, 29
Appalachian Volunteers, 21, 259
Atlantic Monthly Press, 108, 180
Atlantic Monthly, 118, 173, 180, 227–29
Atlantic-Little, Brown, 65

B

B'nai B'rith, 41
Barth, Karl, 205
Beach, Kenneth, 73, 173
Bellow, Saul, 217
Bernanos, Georges, 5, 17, 21, 32, 77, 84, 93, 106, 110, 116, 117, 170, 174, 178
Berrigan, Daniel, 12, 13, 17, 22, 29, 32, 34, 75, 80
Bible, 15–16, 20, 21, 123, 189, 191, 195, 196, 199, 223
Bingham, Sallie, 229
Boardman Parents Group, 5
Bond, Julian, 75, 173
Bonhoeffer, Dietrich, 17, 32, 183
Boston City Hospital, 3, 173
Boston Globe, 31
Boston Latin High School, 54, 71, 172
Bowen, Elizabeth, 92, 195
Bresson, Robert, 106

Bridges, Ruby, 55, 56, 66, 74, 115, 121, 146, 176, 186, 203, 222–23, 241
Burroughs, William, 106

C

Cambridge City Hospital, 43
Camus, Albert, 17, 84, 234
Carter, Rosalynn, 68
Carver, Raymond, 164, 165, 170, 172, 179–80, 213, 217, 224, 236
Catholic Church, The, 25
Catholic Worker, The, 22, 78
Catholic Workers Movement, The, 21, 106, 110, 113, 146, 179
Caudill, Harry, 5, 37
Céline, 106, 107
Chavez, Cesar, 43
Chekhov, Anton, 99
Child Association, The, 41
Children's Hospital, Boston, 39, 92, 97, 189, 202, 205, 215
Clark, Kenneth, 64, 67
Coles, Daniel Agee, 39, 78, 115, 141, 174, 179
Coles, Jane Hallowell, 39, 56, 65, 74, 78, 79, 92, 115–16, 123, 141, 144, 145, 174, 179, 185, 228–30
Coles, Michael Hallowell, 39, 78, 115, 141, 174, 179
Coles, Phillip, 71, 98, 116, 172, 185, 208, 226, 227, 228
Coles, Robert Emmet, 39, 78, 115, 141, 174, 179
Coles, Robert: *A Study of Courage and Fear,* 10, 18, 31, 32, 41, 115, 176, 232; America's youth, 46, 142, 143; being Christian, 153–54, 200–01; busing crisis, 31–34, 169; *Chicanos, Indians, and Eskimos,* 42, 65, 176; child rearing, 52, 79, 114; *Children of Crisis,* 18, 31, 32, 37, 54, 56,

245

NG